HISTORICAL
ALMANAC
OF THE
UNITED STATES
SENATE

United States Senator Bob Dole
Photo by Brad Markel

HISTORICAL ALMANAC
OF THE
UNITED STATES
SENATE

A Series of "Bicentennial Minutes"
Presented to the Senate During the One Hundredth Congress

BOB DOLE
United States Senator

With a foreword by
Senator Robert C. Byrd

Edited by
Wendy Wolff
and
Richard A. Baker
U.S. Senate Historical Office

U.S. Government Printing Office
Washington

100th Congress, 2d Session
S. Con. Res. 146
A U.S. Senate Bicentennial Publication

Senate Document 100–35
U.S. Government Printing Office
Washington: 1989

Supt. of Docs. No.: 052–071–00857–8

COPYRIGHTED MATERIALS

Library of Congress Cataloging-in-Publication Data

Dole, Robert J., 1923–
    Historical almanac of the United States Senate: a series of "Bicentennial minutes" presented to the Senate during the One Hundredth Congress/Bob Dole: with a foreword by Robert C. Byrd: edited by Wendy Wolff and Richard A. Baker.
        p. cm.—(A U.S. Senate bicentennial publication) (Senate document: 100–35)
    Supt. of Docs. no.: 052–071–008578
    30.00 (est.)
        1. United States. Congress. Senate—History.   I. Wolff, Wendy.
    II. Baker, Richard A.   III. Title.   IV. Series.   V. Series: Senate document (United States. Congress. Senate); No. 100–35.
JK1158.D65 1989
328.73'071'09—dc20   89–600234
                                                                                                CIP

To My Mother and Father
Bina and Doran Dole

Contents

Foreword

Each day that the Senate was in session during the One Hundredth Congress, Senator Bob Dole took the floor to remind us of some individual or event connected with that date in the Senate's two-hundred-year history. His series of "Bicentennial Minutes" contained anecdotes and delightful vignettes about the origins of certain Senate practices, and dramatic occurrences in our past. Taken together, these brief essays outlined two centuries of development of the United States Senate and the role that this premier legislative body has played in our nation's history.

Believing that Senator Dole's "Minutes" deserved a wider audience than those who heard him deliver them, or read them in the *Congressional Record*, the Commission on the Bicentennial of the United States Senate sought congressional authorization to collect and publish his remarks in book form. This was accomplished through a special concurrent resolution, adopted in the closing days of the One Hundredth Congress.

Reorganized in chronological format, Senator Dole's "Minutes" have become the *Historical Almanac of the United States Senate*. Here, we learn not only about such famous senators as Henry Clay, Daniel Webster, and John C. Calhoun, but also about such lesser known, but still important, figures as Hiram Revels, the first black senator, and James Shields, who served, at various times, as a senator from three different states. We find useful information about such powerful senators of the past century as Iowa's William B. Allison and Maryland's Arthur Pue Gorman. We enjoy profiles of Senate doorkeepers, sergeants at arms, pages, and the ever-watchful inhabitants of the Senate press galleries.

I commend Senator Dole for his lively panorama of the Senate's history. It was a superb undertaking on behalf of the Senate's bicentennial, one worthy of the attention of all senators and citizens.

Robert C. Byrd

Preface

On January 6, 1987, the first day of the One Hundredth Congress, I announced on the floor of the United States Senate that, over the coming two years, I intended to deliver a series of short statements to be known as "Senate Bicentennial Minutes." I explained that these historical vignettes would focus on significant people, unusual customs, and memorable events associated with the development of the Senate during its first two centuries.

The convening of the One Hundredth Congress served to remind us of the long history of this great institution. Most senators are aware that they are members of a continuous body that began in 1789; that they sit in the chamber at desks once used by Henry Clay, Daniel Webster, and John C. Calhoun; that they occupy offices in the Senate Office Building once used by Robert Taft, Harry Truman, and Everett Dirksen; and that they serve on committees that were created in the early nineteenth century.

During 1987 and 1988, I delivered nearly three hundred "Bicentennial Minutes," usually at the beginning of the Senate's daily session. Each of these commemorated an event that had occurred on that date, during one of the previous two hundred years. They include the obvious as well as the unusual, the serious and the whimsical. Events were selected, researched, and described by the staff of the Senate Historical Office and my own Senate staff.

At the conclusion of the One Hundredth Congress, both houses of Congress authorized separate publication of these "Minutes" as part of the 1989 congressional bicentennial commemoration. In this book edition, they have been rearranged to appear in chronological order.

I am particularly grateful to other senators, who have encouraged me in this project. None deserves more credit for support and inspiration than my colleague and fellow floor leader during the One Hundredth Congress—Senator Robert C. Byrd. His monumental, multi-volume history of the Senate inspired this work; and the two seek to stimulate wide interest in the Senate's history and traditions.

But, the two works are entirely different in scope, organization, and format. It is my hope that senators and the general public will benefit from both of these bicentennial publications for decades to come.

I wish to acknowledge the assistance of the Senate Historical Office. The office's director, Dr. Richard A. Baker, developed the "Bicentennial Minute" concept and selected the specific topics. The text was drafted by Dr. Baker and his colleagues, Dr. Donald A. Ritchie and Dr. Kathryn Allamong Jacob. They received invaluable research and writing assistance from Susan Gerson, James Hope, Jonathan Marcus, Stephanie Marcus, Mary Anne Moore, Dorothy Rosenbaum and Jonathan Warmflash. Kathryne Bomberger, the book's photo editor, tirelessly searched countless sources to assemble its nearly two hundred illustrations. Wendy Wolff, a supremely gifted editor, skillfully converted this work from its *Congressional Record* version. Also, my press secretary, Walt Riker, faithfully edited and prepared my actual Senate floor remarks each and every day for two years. Marilyn Sayler also assisted as an invaluable liaison between my Leader's Office and the Historical Office. Senate Photohistorian John Hamilton produced the book's layout and design. Finally, Tom McGlinn of the Senate's Office of Printing Services and Larry Boarman and others at the Government Printing Office provided skilled assistance in preparing the manuscript for production through an automated typesetting system.

Bob Dole

Facing page, Independence Hall, where the Constitutional Convention met in 1787

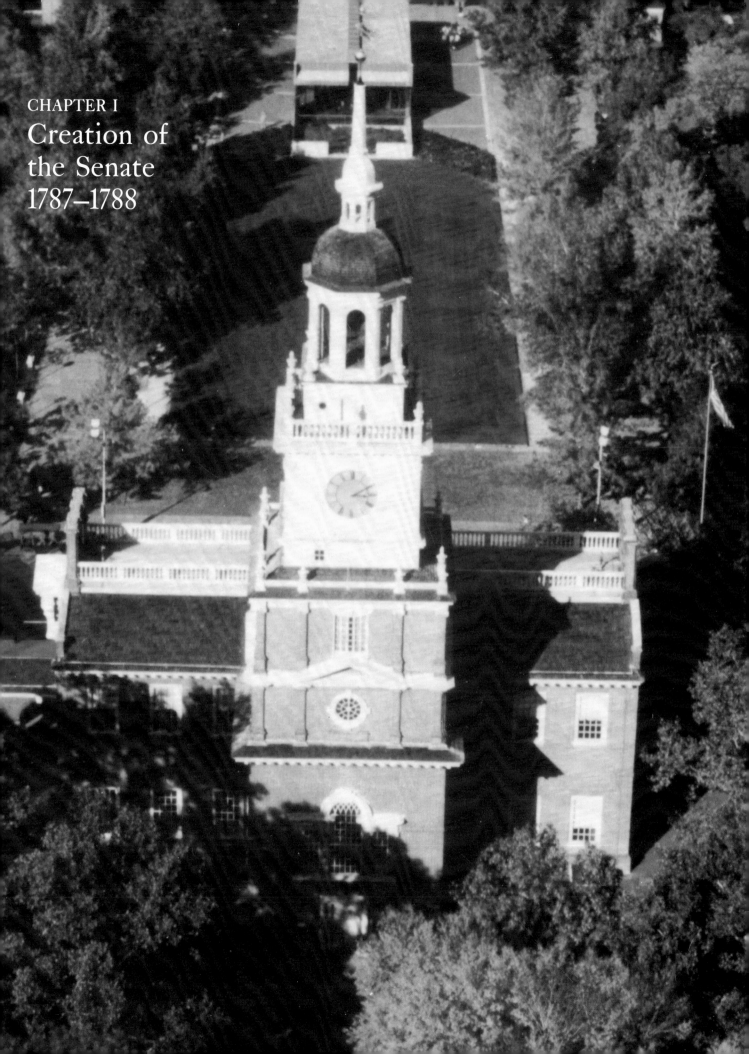

CHAPTER I
Creation of
the Senate
1787–1788

1787
JUNE 7

Method of Senatorial Election Decided

On June 7, 1787, the Constitutional Convention reached agreement as to who, within the new governmental system, would elect senators. The "Virginia plan," the first working draft of the Constitution, had proposed that the House select senators from candidates nominated by individual state legislatures. A few delegates advanced alternative methods, such as selection by the president, or by direct popular vote. Most believed, however, that involvement by the House, or the president, would deprive the Senate of its necessary independence.

On June 7, Delaware's John Dickinson moved that the Senate be chosen by state legislatures. He believed that state legislative elections would produce senators who were more sympathetic to the interests of the nation's moneyed classes, and that the Senate would thus appropriately resemble Great Britain's House of Lords. This would also provide balance to the earlier agreement that House members would be popularly elected. Connecticut's Roger Sherman agreed, observing that this method would closely bind the individual states, which were ever suspicious of centralized power, to the national government.

Although the convention unanimously accepted this plan on June 7, 1787, its delegates remained undecided on the crucial related question of how many senators each state legislature would be allowed to select. Virginia's James Madison worried about the Senate becoming too large. He assumed that senators would be selected in proportion to the population of the individual states. He reasoned that for each of the smallest states to have one senator, the entire membership of the Senate would swell to as many as eighty. This, he believed, would destroy the Senate's principal role of "proceeding with more coolness, with more system, and with more wisdom" than the House. The delegates wisely decided to leave this decision to another day.

1787
JUNE 9

Equal or Proportional Representation in the Senate?

On June 9, 1787, the framers of the Constitution turned to the difficult issue of how the states were to be represented in Congress. The outcome of that debate was to have a great impact on the Senate's eventual organization and structure.

Delegates from the smaller states generally favored the arrangement then prevailing under the Articles of Confederation. States in that body's single-chambered Congress each had a single vote. This system guaranteed that small states would have an equal voice with such large states as New York, Pennsylvania, and Virginia.

On the other side of the issue, delegates from the larger states sought a system of congressional representation that would be based either on state population or wealth, as outlined in the working draft of the Constitution known as the Virginia plan. This fundamental question proved to be one of the most difficult that the framers had to face.

3

Several delegates from small states offered proposals to reduce the "crushing inequity" they foresaw in a proportional plan. New Jersey's David Brearley suggested that "a map of the United States be spread out, that all the existing boundaries be erased, and that a new partition of the whole be made in 13 equal parts."

Against assertions that small states would never agree to proportional representation, Pennsylvania's James Wilson ominously brought the June 9 proceedings to a close by declaring, "If no State will part with any of its sovereignty, it is in vain to talk of a national government."

Two days later, Roger Sherman of Connecticut would offer a proposal from which the convention ultimately fashioned a solution. He moved that each state be represented in the House in proportion to its free population, and in the Senate on an equal basis, with each state having just one vote.

1787
JUNE 18

Alexander Hamilton Proposes Lifetime Senate Terms

Alexander Hamilton, at five feet seven inches, was one of the towering figures of this nation's early history. On June 18, 1787, the thirty-two-year-old Hamilton, a New York delegate to the Constitutional Convention, unveiled his own plan for the Constitution. In a lengthy address during one of the season's hottest days, he proposed a structure in which the president and senators would be elected for life terms. House members would serve three-year terms.

Focusing on the proposed Senate, Hamilton set as his model the British House of Lords. He said:

To the proper adjustment of the power of government between the few and the many, the British owe the excellence of their Constitution. Their House of Lords is a most noble institution. Having nothing to hope for by a change, and a sufficient interest, because of their property, in being faithful to the national interest, they form a permanent barrier against every pernicious innovation, whether attempted on the part of the Crown or the Commons.

He continued, "No temporary Senate would have firmness enough to answer the purpose."

Hamilton believed that a seven-year term for senators, the one then under consideration, would not likely "induce the sacrifices of private affairs which an acceptance of public trust would require, so as to ensure the services of the best citizens."

Of Hamilton's speech, a Connecticut delegate observed, "A gentleman from New York, with boldness and decision proposed a system totally different from both [the preliminary drafts]; and though he has been praised by everybody, he has been supported by none."

For the rest of his life, Hamilton paid a price for this speech. His enemies, of whom there were many, called him a "monarchist." He countered that his remarks had been made "without due reflection." Several days after Hamilton's notable remarks, the convention settled on a six-year term for senators.

Alexander Hamilton, *above,* and *right,* Hamilton's outline of his proposals to the Constitutional Convention, June 18, 1787

pg 71.

[1787, June 18]

I   The Supreme Legislative Power of the United States of America to be vested in two distinct bodies of men — the one to be called the *Assembly* the other the Senate; who together shall form the Legislature of the United States, with power to pass all laws whatsoever, subject to the *negative* hereafter mentioned.

II   The Assembly to consist of persons elected by the People to serve for three years.

III   The Senate to consist of persons elected to serve during good behaviour. Their election to be made by *Electors* chosen for that purpose by the People. In order to this the States to be divided into election districts. On the death removal or resignation of any Senator his place to be filled out of the district from which he came.

IV   The Supreme Executive authority of the United States to be vested in a *governor* to be elected to serve during *good behaviour*. His election to be made by *Electors* chosen by *electors* chosen by the people in the election districts aforesaid. The Governor to have a *negative* upon all laws about to be passed — and to have the execution of all laws passed — to be the Commander in Chief of the land and naval forces and of the Militia of the United States — to have the direction of war when authorised or begun — to have with the *advice and approbation* of the Senate the power of making all treaties — to have the appointment of the heads or chief officers of the departments of finance war and foreign affairs — to have the *nomination* of all other officers (ambassadors to foreign nations included) subject to the *approbation or rejection* of the Senate — to have the power of pardonning all offences but treason; which he shall not pardon without the approbation of the Senate.

5

A recent rendition of the signing of the Constitution, by artist Louis S. Glanzman

1787
JUNE 26

Constitutional Convention Decides on Senate Term and Pay

On June 26, 1787, the Constitutional Convention arrived at two major decisions about the structure of the proposed Senate.

By a vote of seven states to four, the delegates agreed to Gorham of Massachusetts' recommendation that senators serve six-year terms. South Carolina's Pinckney had urged a four-year term, fearing that senators would become too detached from the interests of their states if they were away at the national seat of government for a longer period. Read of Delaware, to the contrary, preferred an unlimited term of service "during good behavior." As he knew there was no support for this, he settled on the longest term then being considered—nine years. James Madison agreed, saying: "In framing a system which we wish to last for ages, we should not lose sight of the changes which ages will produce. An increase of population, will of necessity increase the proportion of those who will labor under the hardships of life, and secretly sigh for a more equal distribution of its blessings." Madison feared that, without a stable Senate, power could slide into the hands of the numerous poor rather than the few rich. Despite Madison's wishes, the convention defeated the nine-year term in favor of six.

South Carolina's Pinckney then moved that senators should receive no salary. As the Senate was to represent the wealth of the nation, its membership should be composed of persons of wealth. Ben Franklin agreed. He hoped that many of the convention's delegates would become senators. If those positions were well paid, the public might charge the delegates with carving out comfortable positions for themselves. When this was defeated by a vote of 5 to 6, the delegates then rejected a motion that senators be paid by their respective states. Ultimately, the convention left the touchy issue of the amount of salaries to the First Congress.

1787
JULY 16

The Great Compromise

On July 16, 1787, the Constitutional Convention, meeting at Independence Hall in Philadelphia, adopted what we now call the Great Compromise, which established the basis of representation in the Senate and House of Representatives.

A dispute over representation between large and small states almost caused the convention to collapse at its midpoint. James Madison's original Virginia plan had called for Congress to be apportioned according to population. But the smaller states feared they would be swallowed up under such an arrangement. William Paterson introduced the "New Jersey plan," which provided simply for strengthening the Articles of Confederation, where all states had equal representation in a single-chambered Congress. James Wilson of Pennsylvania responded heatedly: "Can we forget for whom we are forming a government? Is it for *men*, or for imaginary beings called *states*?"

The Committee to whom were referred the "eighth Resolution reported from the Committee of the whole House, and so much of the seventh as hath not been decided on," submit the following Report.

That the subsequent propositions be recommended to the Convention, on condition that both shall be generally adopted.

1st That in the first Branch of the Legislature each of the States, now in the Union, be allowed one Member for every forty thousand Inhabitants, of the description reported in the seventh Resolution of the Committee of the whole House. — That each State not containing that number shall be allowed one Member. — That all Bills for raising or appropriating Money, and for fixing the Salaries of the Officers of the Government of the united States, shall originate in the first Branch of the Legislature, and shall not be altered or amended by the second Branch: and that no Money shall be drawn from the Public Treasury ~~of the United States~~ but in pursuance of appropriations to be originated by the first Branch.

2dly That in the second Branch of the Legislature, each State shall have an equal vote.

Agreed
6 Ay. 3 no.
2 divided.

40

The two positions seemed so diametrically opposed that the convention became stalemated, and George Washington privately feared that the entire effort would surely fail. Benjamin Franklin suggested that each session should be opened with a prayer, in order to "implore the assistance of heaven" in reaching a compromise.

Before the delegates recessed to celebrate the Fourth of July, they appointed a committee of eleven to try to resolve their differences. Working in Philadelphia's sweltering summer heat, this committee devised the Great Compromise. On July 5, Elbridge Gerry read the committee's report to the convention. They had melded the Virginia and New Jersey plans to create a House with proportional representation, and a Senate where states would be equally represented. After some debate on July 16, the convention adopted the plan by a narrow one-vote margin, thus making possible the Constitution of the United States and creating the United States Senate.

1787
SEPTEMBER 15

Elbridge Gerry Opposes the Senate

On September 15, 1787, delegates from nine of the twelve states represented at the Constitutional Convention in Philadelphia unanimously agreed to approve the newly drafted Constitution. Although outnumbered in the Massachusetts delegation, Elbridge Gerry, a signer of the Declaration of Independence and the Articles of Confederation, refused to sign the Constitution. In particular, he objected to the document's specific provisions for a Senate in which members would serve six-year terms and be eligible for reelection. During the subsequent ratification campaign, Gerry wrote: "A Senate chosen for 6 years will, in most instances, be an appointment for life,

Elbridge Gerry of Massachusetts

10

as the influence of such a body over the minds of the people will be coequal to the extensive powers with which they are vested, and they will not only forget, but be forgotten by their constituents. A branch of the Supreme Legislature thus set beyond all responsibility is totally repugnant to every principle of a free government."

Elbridge Gerry, described as a "man of sense, but a Grumbletonian," also objected to the unlimited power of Congress over its members' own salaries. He feared the role of the vice president as the Senate's presiding officer would destroy the Senate's independence. He was particularly bothered by "the general power of the Legislature to make what laws they may please to call necessary and proper" and Congress' ability "to raise armies and money without limit." The Massachusetts delegate concluded that the best thing the convention could do would be "to provide for a second general convention."

Despite his misgivings, Gerry reported to the Massachusetts legislature that in many respects the Constitution had great merit. He believed it could be improved by the addition of a few amendments, including a bill of rights. Such was the spirit among the Constitution's framers, that even its opponents were willing to see it given a chance.

1787
SEPTEMBER 17

United States Senate Created

On September 17, 1787, thirty-nine delegates to the Constitutional Convention signed the Constitution of the United States. Among the many significant consequences of their action was the creation of the United States Senate.

Benjamin Franklin was one of the few convention delegates to oppose a two-house legislature. It is fitting, then, to read from his final statement to the convention:

> I confess that there are several parts of this constitution which I do not at present approve, but I am not sure I shall never approve them: For having lived long, I have experienced many instances of being obliged by better information, or fuller consideration, to change opinions even on important subjects, which I once thought right, but found to be otherwise. It is therefore that the older I grow, the more apt I am to doubt my own judgment, and to pay more respect to the judgment of others. . . .
>
> In these sentiments, Sir, I agree to this Constitution with all its faults, if they are such; because I think a general Government necessary for us, . . . I doubt too whether any other Convention we can obtain, may be able to make a better Constitution. For when you assemble a number of men to have the advantage of their joint wisdom, you inevitably assemble with those men, all their prejudices, their passions, their errors of opinion, their local interests, and their selfish views. From such an assembly can a perfect production be expected? It therefore astonishes me, Sir, to find this system approaching so near to perfection as it does; and I think it will astonish our enemies, who are waiting with confidence to hear that our councils are confounded . . .

Franklin concluded, "Thus I consent, Sir, to this Constitution because I expect no better, and because I am not sure, that it is not the best."

1787
SEPTEMBER 28

Congress Sends the Constitution to the States

On September 28, 1787, the Congress of the Confederation agreed to transmit the newly adopted Constitution to the individual states for ratification. In the thirteen state ratifying conventions, provisions for the Senate received sharp scrutiny. Supporters characterized the Senate as a bulwark against tyranny and a source of stability, legislative wisdom, and the states' ultimate guarantee of sovereignty. Behind the convention's closed doors, the Constitution's defenders had argued that the Senate's great strength would be in its independence from dictation by outside forces. In public, these supporters altered their tune, assuring the states that senators would serve as their "ambassadors," subject to state legislative instruction.

Despite these assurances, critics feared that the Senate might evolve into an unreachable aristocracy because of its longer terms, greater powers, and smaller numbers. One amendment that frequently surfaced in the various state conventions would have permitted state legislatures to remove senators from office. Critics also focused on the six-year term and the Senate's treaty powers. To prevent the creation of a senatorial aristocracy, opponents sought to restrict senators to one six-year term in any twelve-year period.

The Constitution's defenders dismissed these fears, explaining that limitations of terms would drive away the best men. They noted that biennial elections of one-third of the body's members would be sufficient to check abuses of power. They also observed that the Senate was hardly an independent entity. Its actions would be subject to restraint by state legislatures, which selected senators; by the House, which shared the Senate's approval power; and by the president, who alone had the power to nominate key officials and to negotiate treaties. Ultimately, the framers' initial provisions for the Senate remained unchanged until the direct election amendment of 1913.

"The Federal Edifice," July 26, 1788, commemorated New York's ratification of the Constitution.

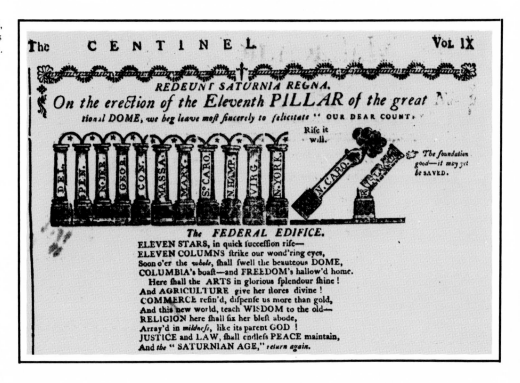

1787
OCTOBER 27

First Federalist Paper Published

On October 27, 1787, the first letter signed "Publius" appeared in the New York *Independent Journal*. Actually written by Alexander Hamilton, the letter was part of a campaign to win ratification of the Constitution in New York. Collectively using the pseudonym "Publius," Hamilton, James Madison and John Jay published eighty-five letters, which were then collected and printed as the Federalist papers.

This remarkable piece of scholarship and public relations has been called one of the three most important documents in American history, ranking only after the Constitution and the Declaration of Independence. The courts have frequently cited the Federalist papers as evidence of what the framers intended, and serious students of American government still draw insights into the workings of our political system from its pages.

Two of the letters, numbers 62 and 63, written by James Madison, deal specifically with the United States Senate. The Congress that existed under the Articles of Confederation consisted of only one chamber. Madison argued that a Senate was needed, noting "the propensity of all single and numerous assemblies to yield to the impulse of sudden and violent passions, and to be seduced by factious leaders, into intemperate and pernicious resolutions." Madison anticipated that the Senate, with its longer term of service, would "possess great firmness" and resist such pressures.

Although the Constitution provided at that time that senators were to be elected by state legislatures, Madison concluded that, balanced by the popularly elected House, the Senate could never become "an independent and aristocratic body." Instead, he believed that it could exert its influence only by "a display of enlightened policy, and attachment to the public good."

A copy of the first Federalist
paper published

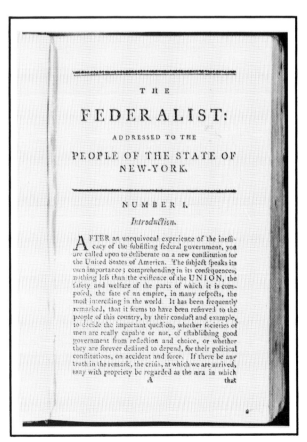

13

1788
APRIL 1

Alexander Hamilton on the Senate's Confirmation Power

On April 1, 1788, Alexander Hamilton prepared, as one of the Federalist papers, a major statement explaining the respective roles of the Senate and the president in appointing key federal officers under the newly signed Constitution.

Hamilton reasoned that "one man of discernment is better fitted to analyze and estimate the peculiar qualities adapted to particular offices, than a body of men of equal, or perhaps even superior discernment." He argued that "a single well directed man, by a single understanding, cannot be distracted or warped by that diversity of views, feelings and interests, which frequently distract and warp the resolutions of a collective body."

Hamilton explained the wisdom of dividing the appointment powers. Each party to the process would have to consider the powers of the other. In need of Senate approval, the president would consider his own reputation and political future before proposing "candidates who had no other merit, than that of coming from [the president's own] State, or of being in some way or other personally allied to him." If the Senate rejected a presidential nominee, it would realize that the president would still be able to select another candidate of his choice. The Senate "could not even be certain that a future nomination would present a candidate in any degree more acceptable to them," Hamilton continued, "and as their dissent might cast a kind of stigma upon the individual rejected; and might have the appearance of a reflection upon the judgment of the chief magistrate; it is not likely that their [approval] would often be [withheld]."

Alexander Hamilton placed great confidence in the Senate's ability to resist undue pressure from the president. Although a president "might occasionally influence some individuals in the Senate," he remained confident that no president could "purchase the integrity of the whole body."

1788
SEPTEMBER 30

First Senators Elected

On September 30, 1788, the first two members of the United States Senate were elected. The Pennsylvania state assembly, under the provisions of the newly ratified U.S. Constitution, chose Robert Morris and William Maclay.

Planning for Senate elections had begun in earnest after June 21, 1788, when New Hampshire's ratification of the Constitution provided the necessary margin to put that charter into effect. When New York ratified the following month, the existing Congress under the Articles of Confederation set to work on an election ordinance, which it issued in mid-September. The ordinance provided that states that had ratified the Constitution could begin electing senators immediately and that presidential electors would be chosen, within such states, on the first Wednesday in January 1789. The electors would convene in their respective states on the first Wednesday in February to cast their ballots for president and vice president. Finally, the new Congress would meet to count the electoral ballots on the first Wednesday in March—March 4, 1789.

A half-dozen prominent Pennsylvanians were mentioned as candidates for the two Senate seats in the six months preceding the legislature's action. On September 29, a large contingent of assembly members adjourned to a nearby tavern and agreed to support Morris and Maclay, whom the assembly elected the following day. The unsuccessful contenders then shifted their attention to the forthcoming popular elections for Pennsylvania's eight seats in the House of Representatives.

Both Morris and Maclay had worked actively for the adoption of the Constitution. A Philadelphia merchant and signer of the Declaration of Independence, Morris had served as the nation's superintendent of finance from 1781 to 1784. Well regarded within the state, Maclay provided a western and agrarian balance to Morris, who identified clearly with Philadelphia's eastern and commercial orientation. Maclay and Morris thus became the first of the 1,792 persons chosen to serve in the United States Senate during its first two centuries.

William Maclay of Pennsylvania

Robert Morris of Pennsylvania

15

Facing page, Archibald Robertson's 1798 view
of Federal Hall, where the First Congress met

CHAPTER II
The First Senate
1789–1791

1789
MARCH 3

Demise of the Confederation Congress

On March 3, 1789, the old Confederation Congress ceased to exist. Created in 1781 under the Articles of Confederation, that legislative body had replaced the Second Continental Congress, which had been established in 1775. As we commemorate the Constitution of 1787 and the Senate that came into existence on March 4, 1789, it is appropriate that we take a brief look at the national legislature the Constitution's framers sought to replace.

The structure of the Confederation Congress resembled that of the earlier Continental Congress. The framers of the Articles of Confederation, affected by the continuing war for independence from Great Britain, were understandably suspicious of centralized power. As members of a confederation, each of the thirteen states gave up very little power to the Congress. This was made clear in the second article, which provided that "each State retains its sovereignty, freedom and independence, and every power, jurisdiction and right, which is not expressly delegated to the United States in Congress assembled."

In this Confederation Congress, which was the sole organ of the government, each state had one vote. Delegates, as the members were called, served one-year terms. No member could remain in office for more than three years in any six-year period. As a further guarantee of control, states paid members' salaries and reserved the right to recall them at any time and for any reason. State legislatures also determined the qualifications and the method of electing their individual delegates.

The Confederation Congress met in Philadelphia until June 1783. During the latter half of 1783 and in 1784, it met successively at Princeton, New Jersey; Annapolis, Maryland; and Trenton, New Jersey. In 1785, the Congress settled in New York City, where it remained until its demise.

1789
MARCH 4

Absence of a Quorum on the First Day

Late in 1788, the dying Congress under the Articles of Confederation determined that March 4, 1789, would be the day the newly ratified Constitution would take effect.

Because the new government desperately needed revenue, all agreed that, despite the difficult late winter travel conditions, the new Congress should convene as quickly as possible. This would allow the Senate and House the opportunity to pass a tariff law in time to apply it to the spring imports.

In an effort to convince Congress to select New York City as the permanent seat of government, local merchants and others underwrote a handsome restoration of the old city hall. The Senate chamber, located on the second floor, occupied a richly carpeted space forty feet long and thirty feet wide. The chamber's most striking features were its high arched ceiling, tall windows curtained in crimson damask, fireplace mantels in handsomely polished marble, and a presiding officer's chair elevated three feet from the floor and placed under a crimson canopy. The ceiling was adorned in the center with a sun and—expressing optimism that Rhode Island and North Carolina would soon join the Union—thirteen stars.

Delays in selecting senators and terrible travel conditions frustrated the scheduled opening of the Senate. On March 4, 1789, only eight of the twenty senators already elected answered to the first quorum call. New York had not yet elected its senators, due to a deadlock in the state legislature. Finally, on April 6, the necessary twelve of the eligible twenty-two had arrived, and the Senate got down to business. March 4 in odd-numbered years remained the starting date for new congressional terms until 1934 when the Twentieth Amendment changed the date to January 3.

1789
APRIL 6

First Senators Present Election Credentials

On April 6, 1789, the arrival of Virginia's Richard Henry Lee brought the number of senators present to twelve, the quorum necessary to conduct business. When they presented their election credentials at the Senate chamber in New York City's Federal Hall, the first Senate began operation. The process of selecting these senators, most of whom strongly supported the newly ratified Constitution, proved crucial to the success of the embryonic government.

Unlike elections for president and House members, Senate elections in 1788 stimulated little popular interest because the public had no direct role in the process. As provided in the Constitution, senators were to be elected by state legislatures. That document's framers had left the details of the selection process to the individual states. Most legislatures decided that senators should be elected in joint sessions of both houses—a practice then common for selecting key state officials. Only New Hampshire, Massachusetts, and New York believed that the selection of senators should be han-

Richard Henry Lee of Virginia

dled by proceeding concurrently, as with any other legislative act. This latter method gave equal weight to the state senates, unlike the joint voting arrangement in which these bodies were overwhelmed by the larger lower houses. The drawback with the concurrent method, as future deadlocks would demonstrate, was that both houses had to agree independently on the same candidate.

In choosing their senators, many states openly recognized existing economic and geographical divisions. Some elected one senator from candidates favorable to the more aristocratically inclined upper houses and the other suitable to the popularly elected lower chambers. The Maryland assembly divided its Senate representation according to geography, stipulating that one senator was to be chosen from the state's Eastern Shore, and the other from the larger region west of the Chesapeake Bay. New York, Pennsylvania, and Georgia followed similar regional divisions.

1789
APRIL 7

Senate Doorkeeper Elected

On April 7, 1789, the Senate created its first staff position—the post of Senate doorkeeper. An official doorkeeper was considered essential in a body that intended to conduct all its meetings behind closed doors. From a field of three applicants, the Senate selected James Mathers, an Irish immigrant who earlier had distinguished himself in the Revolutionary War. Following the war, Mathers had served as doorkeeper for the old Congress under the Articles of Confederation.

As the First Congress was preparing to adjourn on March 3, 1791, the Senate expanded Mathers' job responsibilities, authorizing him "to take care of the rooms appropriated for the use of the Senate, until the next session of Congress, and also to make the necessary provision of fire wood for the next session." Additional changes occurred in December 1795, when the Senate first regularly opened its doors to the public for routine legislative sessions. Mathers oversaw the operation of the Senate's first gallery in its Philadelphia chamber and responded to the presiding officer's direction to clear the gallery and lock the doors whenever the Senate took up business relating to executive nominations and treaties.

Early in 1798, James Mathers acquired an additional title. As the Senate was preparing to conduct an impeachment trial, it resolved that "the Doorkeeper of the Senate be, and he is hereby, invested with the authority of Sergeant at Arms, whose duty it shall be to execute the commands of the Senate." Until then, the Senate had no officer vested with the police powers necessary to compel attendance of absent members as provided under the Constitution. In establishing this position, the Senate followed the English Parliament, which had employed a sergeant at arms since the sixteenth century, and the House of Representatives, which created the post in 1789. James Mathers served the Senate for twenty-two years until his death in 1811.

1789
APRIL 7

Senate Appoints First Committees

On April 7, 1789, just one day after the Senate established its first quorum and began work, it appointed two committees. Eight members were selected to "bring in a bill for organizing the Judiciary of the United States." Five senators were appointed "to be a committee to prepare a system of rules to govern the two Houses in cases of conference, and to take under consideration the manner of electing Chaplains." The latter committee was also authorized "to prepare a system of rules for conducting business of the Senate."

This was in the days before the Senate operated through standing committees. Instead, these first two committees were ad hoc committees, designed to go out of existence when they had completed their specific assignments.

The first committee produced the most important legislation of the First Congress, the Judiciary Act of 1789. This act set up the federal court system that still operates today. It provided for the organization of a six-member Supreme Court, thirteen district and three circuit courts, and established the office of attorney general.

The second committee created the first rules of the Senate. A reading of these first twenty rules shows them to be remarkably similar to the rules under which the Senate continues to operate.

Today, I think it is safe to say that U.S. senators spend more time in committee work than in any other legislative activity. There, more than on the Senate floor, legislation is shaped, compromises are forged, and consensus is reached. Only through committees could the Senate handle a workload that has grown so phenomenally over the past two hundred years.

1789
APRIL 7

Oliver Ellsworth Appointed to Two Committees

Although little known today, except to constitutional scholars and political historians, Oliver Ellsworth must rank as one of the most productive and influential persons ever to serve in the United States Senate. Born in Windsor, Connecticut, in 1745, Ellsworth served in the Continental Congress, and as a Connecticut delegate to the 1787 Constitutional Convention. There, he was instrumental in forging the so-called "Connecticut compromise." He promoted the idea that states should be equally represented in the proposed Senate, as they were in the existing unicameral Congress under the Articles of Confederation. The resulting compromise included his plan for the Senate, while basing representation in the House on the size of a state's population. Ellsworth was elected as one of Connecticut's first two senators, and he served in this body until 1796, when President Washington nominated him as chief justice of the United States.

Ellsworth brought to the Senate of the First Congress great organizational and administrative skills. On April 7, 1789, the day after the Senate achieved its first quorum, he was named to serve on the first two committees. One was established to prepare a set of rules of procedure and the other was to provide for the appointment of chaplains. Ellsworth's reputation for brilliance and hard work elevated him to the chairmanship of many committees during his seven years in the Senate. He guided legislation proposing the first twelve amendments to the Constitution; he reported a bill providing for the administration of U.S. territories south of the Ohio River; he drafted a measure regulating the U.S. consular service; and he vigorously supported plans for funding the national debt and establishing a bank of the United States. His most notable contribution was as a member of the committee that drafted the Judiciary Act of 1789, which provided for the organization of the federal judiciary.

Aaron Burr, who served with Ellsworth in the Senate—referring more to the Connecticut senator's influence and tenacity than to the Senate's efficiency—once declared that "if Ellsworth had happened to spell the name of the Deity with two d's, it would have taken the Senate three weeks to expunge the superfluous letter." Oliver Ellsworth died in 1807 at the age of sixty-two.

Oliver Ellsworth of Connecticut

Samuel A. Otis, first secretary of the Senate, by Gilbert Stuart

1789
APRIL 8

The First Secretary of the Senate

On April 8, 1789, the Senate elected its first secretary, Samuel Otis of Massachusetts. It was in New York, on the third day of Senate business, that Otis began twenty-five years of faithful service as secretary. During that time he never missed a single day that the Senate was in session.

Otis came well qualified. Harvard educated, he had been an ardent supporter of the revolutionary cause, serving as a member of the Massachusetts Board of War in 1776 and collector of clothing for the Continental army in 1777. He had been speaker of the Massachusetts house of representatives from 1784 to 1787 and a member of the Confederation Congress in 1787 and 1788.

Otis was responsible for keeping the Senate's legislative journal—recording each session's minutes by hand—and for purchasing ink, quills, parchment, and other supplies. He disbursed salaries and travel allowances to the senators, carried Senate legislation to the House of Representatives, and received and transmitted all presidential messages and vetoes. It was Otis who held the Bible during George Washington's 1789 inaugural ceremony.

Samuel Otis, who served through both Federalist and Jeffersonian majorities in the Senate, died on April 22, 1814 in Washington, where the capital had moved in 1800. The Senate was so preoccupied with other matters that it had not elected a successor at the time the British launched an assault on Washington in August 1814 and was without a secretary until October 12, 1814. To show their respect for Secretary Otis, upon his death, senators went into mourning for a month, each wearing a black crepe armband in memory of Otis' long and effective service.

From Otis' day down to our own, twenty-five persons have served as secretary of the Senate.

1789
APRIL 16

First Senate Rules Adopted

On April 16, 1789, the Senate adopted its first set of standing rules.

The framers of the Constitution in 1787 set down only a handful of rules to govern Congress' internal procedures. Among them were provisions that the vice president of the United States serve as the Senate's presiding officer; that the Senate could choose its own officers, including a president pro tempore to preside in the absence of the vice president; that Congress was to assemble at least once a year; that a minority of members could compel the attendance necessary to achieve a quorum; that each house would judge the eligibility of its own members; and that a two-thirds vote was required to expel a member, to override a presidential veto, to approve treaties, and to convict in impeachment trials. Otherwise, the Senate was free to determine its own rules of procedure.

After achieving its first quorum on April 6, the Senate created a temporary committee of five members to devise its rules. All five were lawyers and all had extensive legislative experience either in state assemblies, in the

Congress under the Articles of Confederation, or in the Constitutional Convention. All were well acquainted with British parliamentary practice.

In six days the special Senate committee drafted nineteen rules. Many of them were drawn from the rules that governed the previous Continental and Confederation congresses. Committee members were particularly concerned with establishing rules that would preserve decorum and promote faithful attendance. In the years since 1789 the Senate has accomplished a general revision of its rules on only seven occasions, the most recent being in 1979. The forty-one standing rules that govern Senate deliberations today, in both substance and spirit, bear a direct resemblance to those first rules of 1789.

John Adams

1789
APRIL 21

John Adams Delivers Inaugural Address

On April 21, 1789, in New York City, John Adams delivered his inaugural address as the first vice president of the United States. Senators Ralph Izard and Caleb Strong conducted Adams into the Senate chamber that day in the remodeled city hall at the corner of Wall and Nassau Streets. There, the Senate's first president pro tempore, John Langdon, addressed Adams, saying, "I have it in charge from the Senate, to introduce you to the Chair of this House, and also to congratulate you on your appointment to the office of Vice President of the United States of America." Then Langdon escorted Adams to the rostrum.

Adams gave a short prepared speech in which he identified the greatest problem that his new role as president of the Senate would pose for him: "Not wholly without experience in public assemblies, I have been more accustomed to take a share in their debates, than to preside in their deliberations." The job as the Senate's presiding officer required that Adams behave counter to his every instinct and passion. Time after time, he rushed into action, only to be forced to check himself. Time after time, he tried in vain to hold his tongue. As the first Senate labored to establish precedents of protocol and conduct, Adams was vociferous as he campaigned endlessly for elaborate titles and ceremonies.

For the next eight years, Adams chafed at a job for which, as never before in his life, he felt truly unsuited. He had, however, the satisfaction of often exercising one of his only constitutionally mandated powers—breaking tie votes. During his service as vice president, John Adams cast twenty-nine tie-breaking votes, more than any of his forty-two successors in that position.

1789
APRIL 23

Protocol for Presenting a Bill

Visitors in the galleries, and those watching congressional proceedings on television, often express curiosity over the formal behavior of the Senate and House clerks who officially present the bills and messages from the other chamber. From time to time, even some of the clerks who have performed this function have wondered why they were required to bow entering and leaving the chamber. The fact is that the protocol for presenting a bill was set during the First Congress. On April 23, 1789, the Senate approved a committee report establishing the following procedures: when a Senate bill was sent to the House of Representatives it would be carried by the secretary of the Senate, who was instructed to "make one obeisance"— that is, to bow—to the chair when entering the House chamber, bow again when delivering it at the front desk, and bow again when leaving the chamber.

The Senate then provided that, when the House sent bills to the Senate, they should be carried by two members of the House, who would similarly bow to the president of the Senate. Of course, the House would hear nothing of such inequality and instead assigned the clerk of the House to carry messages to the Senate.

Today, bill clerks representing the secretary of the Senate and clerk of the House perform this ritual in the manner prescribed by the first Congress. The only alteration has been to eliminate the middle bow, for the papers are presented inside the door. Otherwise, the courtly manners of the eighteenth century still survive and flourish in the twentieth-century Senate.

1789
APRIL 25

John Adams on the Vice Presidency

On April 25, 1789, John Adams, the first vice president of the United States, rose from his seat as presiding officer of the Senate and delivered a speech in which he cataloged his distress with the job that he had held for only four days. His lament was prompted by the business of the hour: the consideration of the report of the committee appointed to propose a time, place, and procedure by which Congress would administer the oath to the first president of the United States.

Among those in Adams' audience that day was the irascible Senator William Maclay of Pennsylvania, who each night poured out into his diary his displeasure with his colleagues and his impatience with the new government. Maclay regarded Adams as a pompous Federalist and saved some of his harshest words for the vice president. Although he mocked Adams, Maclay faithfully recorded his words on April 25. Bemoaning the uncertainties of his position, Adams complained:

Gentlemen, I do not know whether the framers of the Constitution had in view the two kings of Sparta or the two consuls of Rome when they formed it; one to have all the power while he held it, and the other to be nothing. Gentlemen, I feel great difficulty how to act. I am possessed of the two separated powers. I am Vice President. In this I am nothing, but I may be everything. But I am president also of the Senate. When the President comes into the Senate, what shall I be? I cannot be [president] then. No, gentlemen, I cannot, I cannot. I wish gentlemen to think what I shall be.

Adams' listeners, some sympathetic, some derisive, could offer little solace. Maclay recorded his own reaction. He wrote, "God forgive me, for it was involuntary, but the profane muscles of my face, were in Tune for laughter, in spite of my indisposition."

The Senate's First Chaplain

On April 27, 1789, the Senate opened its session with a prayer by the Reverend Samuel Provoost, the Episcopal Bishop of New York. Then, as Bishop Provoost looked on, the Senate took up two matters that were of direct interest to him.

First, the Senate agreed to a resolution providing that, following the administration of President Washington's oath on April 30, both houses would proceed to nearby St. Paul's Chapel for a worship service. That service was to be conducted by Bishop Provoost. The Senate's action in this instance has, in the intervening two centuries, served as a foundation for religious involvement with presidential inaugurations.

Also on April 27, 1789, the Senate formally received a letter from Bishop Provoost accepting an appointment as the Senate's official chaplain. Earlier, on April 15, a special Senate committee had recommended a system for the appointment of chaplains. That plan, which both houses accepted, provided that the Senate first select a chaplain and report that action to the House. The House would then select its chaplain, with the requirement that he be from a different religious denomination. The resolution also provided that the chaplains would "commence their services in the Houses which appoint them, but shall interchange weekly." On May 1, the House appointed William Linn, a Presbyterian minister. He and Bishop Provoost alternately served the Senate and the House for two years, until Congress moved from New York City to Philadelphia.

From Bishop Provoost in 1789 to the Reverend Richard C. Halverson today, the Senate has had sixty official chaplains. Among the denominations represented have been Episcopalians (19), Methodists (17), Presbyterians (13), Baptists (6), Unitarians (2), as well as a Congregationalist, a Lutheran, and a Roman Catholic.

The Reverend Samuel Provoost, first chaplain of the Senate

George Washington

Facing page:
George Washington's first Inaugural
Address, in his handwriting

1789
APRIL 30

First Presidential Inauguration

On April 30, 1789, nearly two months after the date set for the new government's first meeting, the Senate and the House were finally able to carry out their arrangements for George Washington's first inauguration in New York City.

Washington arrived at Federal Hall dressed in a dark brown coat with metal buttons embossed with eagles, knee breeches, white stockings, and a steel-hilted sword. His hair was powdered and drawn back. Escorted by a committee made up of Senators Tristram Dalton, Ralph Izard, and Richard Henry Lee, Washington entered the Senate chamber and advanced between the senators and representatives, bowing to each. Vice President John Adams led him to the chair. The Senate and Adams, its president, were arrayed on Washington's right, the House and its speaker on his left. Washington then stepped out onto a balcony and acknowledged the shouts from the crowd below with a bow. He laid his hand upon the Bible, solemnly repeated the oath administered by the chancellor of the state of New York, Robert Livingston, and bending reverently, kissed the book. Livingston stepped forward and raising his hand, cried, "Long live George Washington, President of the United States!" On that note, cannons pounded, bells rang, and three cheers erupted from the crowd.

Washington returned to the Senate chamber and read his inaugural address to a standing Congress. Afterwards there was a grand walking procession to St. Paul's Chapel for prayers. The Senate resumed business after the service, appointed a committee to draft a reply to Washington's address, and adjourned. That night New York was illuminated with bonfires, marking the end of an auspicious, exciting day.

Fellow Citizens of the Senate
and
of the House of Representatives.

Among the vicissitudes
incident to life, no event could have
filled me with greater anxieties than
that of which the notification was
transmitted by your order, and received on the fourteenth day of the
present month: ——— On the one hand,
I was summoned by my Country, whose
voice I can never hear but with venera-
tion and love, from a retreat which
I had chosen with the fondest prede-
lection, and, in my flattering hopes,
with an immutable decision, as the
asylum of my declining years: a retreat which was rendered every day
more necessary as well as more dear
to me, by the addition of habit to in-
clination, and of frequent interrup-
tions in my health to the gradual waste
committed on it by time. ——— On the
other hand, the magnitude and difficulty of the trust to which the voice
of my Country called me, being sufficient to awaken in the wisest and most
experienced of her citizens, a distrust-
ful

ment must depend. —

G: Washington

1789
MAY 5

Senate Passes Bill for Administering Oaths

On May 5, 1789, the Senate passed its first bill. That measure provided for the administering of oaths in support of the Constitution. When President George Washington signed the act on June 1, it became the first statute of the First Congress.

Article VI of the Constitution requires that all members of Congress, state legislators, and all federal and state executive and judicial officers take such an oath. Accordingly, legislators in the spring of 1789 forged an act spelling out the wording of that oath and provisions for its administration. The oath they devised was short, stating simply, "I do solemnly swear or affirm that I will support the Constitution of the United States."

The Senate's consideration of this first bill triggered debate on matters of form and substance that went far beyond the specifics of a seemingly routine piece of legislation. Some members questioned whether Congress could pass legislation applying to state officials. Others, arguing that the dignity and preeminence of the Senate was at stake, debated the proper terminology for the bill's enacting clause. For the original version, which read "Be it enacted by the Congress of the United States," they substituted "Be it enacted by the Senate and Representatives of the United States of America in Congress assembled." The House reluctantly agreed to this change.

On June 4, 1789, the Senate president pro tempore administered the oath to Vice President John Adams. The vice president, in turn, administered it to all members of the Senate. The oath was revised in 1862, during the Civil War, requiring members to swear that they had never borne arms against the United States. It was again modified in 1868 to provide that members "support and defend the Constitution of the United States against all enemies, foreign and domestic."

1789
MAY 15

Senators' Classifications Determined

On May 15, 1789, senators of the First Congress, all of whom began service together, drew lots to determine the length of the term that each would serve, either two, four, or six years. Article I of the Constitution had expressly provided that there would be three classes of members.

On May 14, the Senate divided its members into three classes in such a way that each class would contain no more than one member per state, with members drawn from all sections of the country. As recorded in the *Senate Journal*, the resolution declared, "that three papers of an equal size, numbered 1, 2, and 3, be by the Secretary rolled up and put into a box, and drawn by Mr. Langdon, Mr. Wingate, and Mr. Dalton, in behalf of the respective classes in which each of them are placed; and that the classes shall vacate their seats in the Senate according to the order of numbers drawn for them, beginning with number one." And, "that when Senators shall take their seats from States that have not yet appointed Senators, they shall be placed by lot in the foregoing classes, but in such manner as shall keep the classes as nearly equal as may be in numbers."

On May 15, Senators John Langdon, Paine Wingate, and Tristram Dalton drew the lots that would determine each senator's length of term. Lot one, drawn by Dalton, contained the names of senators who would serve two-year terms; lot two, drawn by Wingate, those whose seats would be vacated after four years; and lot three, drawn by Langdon, those who would serve for a full six years.

Those classes continue today. For example, the Class 3 term drawn by Senator Samuel Pomeroy, one of the first two senators to represent the new state of Kansas in 1861, is the seat I hold today.

1789
MAY 18

The Senate Replies to Washington's Inaugural Address

On May 18, 1789, the Senate began the relatively short-lived tradition of responding formally to the president's inaugural addresses and annual messages. At a quarter to eleven that Monday morning, the full Senate arrived by carriage at President George Washington's house. With Vice President John Adams leading, the senators bowed to the president as they entered an elegant, long dining hall that had been emptied of furniture. Washington, clad in a black velvet suit with black silk stockings and silver buckles, carried a sword with a shining steel hilt and a white leather sheath. Standing before the fireplace while greeting the procession, he held a hat with cockade and plume in his yellow-gloved hands. His hair was powdered white and drawn back by a silk bag.

On behalf of the Senate, Adams proceeded to deliver the address that did little more than pledge the Senate's full cooperation with the president. According to the journal kept by Antifederalist Senator William Maclay, Adams was trembling and confused, reading the beginning of the reply awkwardly, but assuming a smoother delivery for the remainder. Washington then tucked his hat under his arm, put on his spectacles, and read his reply of gratitude. Upon concluding his speech, the president handed his reply to Adams, bowed to the Senate, and asked all to be seated. Refusing to sit, Adams made a low bow and retired from the room. The senators then rose, bowed, and walked to the door to await their carriages back to Federal Hall.

This formal ceremony of reply was discontinued in 1801, when President Thomas Jefferson began the practice of sending his annual messages in writing. He believed the president's address and the formal congressional reply resembled too closely the ceremonies of the British monarchy.

William Short

1789
JUNE 16

First Nomination Sent to the Senate

On June 16, 1789, the United States Senate received its first nomination for confirmation. This was not a cabinet post, or a military or judicial position, as we might expect, but a diplomatic nomination.

Having chosen Thomas Jefferson to be his secretary of state, President George Washington submitted the name of William Short to take charge of American affairs at the French court of Versailles. Some members of the Senate were disappointed that Washington had chosen to make this nomination in writing rather than in person. They had expected the Senate to act as an advisory council to the president and wished to give the chief executive their advice as well as their consent. But, while Washington was initially willing to present treaties in person, he feared—correctly, as it turned out—that there would be too many nominations for such personal service.

All the Senate could do was request that acting Secretary of State John Jay (Jefferson being still in France) submit any papers relating to Short's nomination for their consideration. The following day, Jay appeared in the Senate chamber with the requested papers, and, as the Senate's *Executive Journal* recorded, the Senate "proceeded to consider the nomination of William Short, Esquire." That is about all we know of the debate, since no transcripts of Senate proceedings were taken in those days.

The Senate continued its debate on Short's nomination the following day and then voted. Negative votes were recorded by blank ballots while affirmative votes were recorded by the word "aye."

It is worth noting that the Senate took only three days to confirm Short, which was the average length of a confirmation during the First Congress.

1789
JUNE 18

Senate Establishes Voting Method for Executive Business

On June 18, 1789, the Senate established a rule governing the manner in which it would vote on executive business, such as treaties and nominations.

Like so many of those first decisions, this one was reached only after much wrangling. President Washington had asked the Senate's advice and consent in appointing a minister to France. The question seemed only to require a simple yea or nay vote, but a controversy arose as to whether the decision should be made by voice vote or by secret written ballot. Vice President John Adams supported a voice vote, claiming that written ballots encouraged intrigue and bargaining. Senator Oliver Ellsworth of Connecticut agreed, observing that voting by secret ballot might suit bashful men, a category he thought fit few of his colleagues, and that it favored unprincipled men, who would not have to account for their actions.

Senator William Maclay, the prickly Pennsylvanian, vehemently objected. Secret ballot voting, he argued, was in fact the antidote to cabals: men made bargains for sure things, but it was in vain to bargain for a vote one could not verify. Maclay was also concerned about other ramifications of a voice vote: a senator who openly voted against the chief executive might lose the president's favor or, conversely, he might vote against his conscience to win the president's nod.

Maclay's arguments triumphed on June 18, 1789, and, by secret written ballot, the Senate declared its advice and consent to the minister's nomination. Maclay's victory, however, was short lived. Two weeks later, when the Senate adopted rules concerning communications with the president, members reversed themselves and included a clause providing for a voice vote on nominations.

1789
JUNE 27

First Conference Committee

On June 27, 1789, members of the Senate and House conducted their first conference committee meeting.

Conference committees had not been needed in the single-body legislature that had met under the Articles of Confederation. But when the Constitution created two houses of Congress, conferences became necessary to resolve the differences in the bills passed by each chamber.

Four weeks earlier, the Senate had received from the House a "tonnage act," which would impose duties on imported goods. The Senate then proceeded to enact some forty amendments to the House bill, changing duties on a variety of items ranging from tea and playing cards to shoes and gunpowder. On June 15, the House responded by accepting half of the Senate's amendments. The Senate debated again, this time agreeing to drop most of the disputed items, but insisting that eight of its amendments be retained. The House was willing to accept two more of the Senate's amendments but requested a conference to settle their differences on the other six.

Thus, on June 25, three senators, Robert Morris, Richard Henry Lee, and Oliver Ellsworth, were appointed to represent the Senate in the first congressional conference committee. On June 27, the conferees reported back to the Senate a series of compromises. The House was willing to recede from its disagreements on most of the disputed items, and the Senate agreed to a few changes. It took three additional days to settle the last of their differences and send the tonnage bill to President George Washington, who signed it on July 20, 1789. Thus ended the first of the countless conferences that have resolved legislative disputes over the past two centuries.

1789
JULY 17

Senate Passes Judiciary Act

On July 17, 1789, the first Senate passed the Judiciary Act of 1789, which established the federal judicial system. Although the House initiated most of the substantive legislation during the First Congress, a Senate committee originated the judiciary bill.

The Senate placed a high priority on establishment of a federal court system. Consequently, the day after it achieved its first quorum, the Senate created a special committee to consider such legislation. The committee consisted of eight members, the most active of whom were Oliver Ellsworth of Connecticut, William Paterson of New Jersey, and Caleb Strong of Massachusetts. Because of his extensive legal and political experience, Ellsworth led in drafting the judiciary bill, but not all the other members approved of the first draft. Virginia's Richard Henry Lee and Pennsylvania's William Maclay, the only Antifederalists on the committee, attempted to amend the measure. Lee's motion to limit district courts' jurisdiction to admiralty and maritime issues failed, but Maclay succeeded in persuading the committee to significantly decrease federal chancery powers from what was originally proposed. After lengthy debate, the Senate adopted the legislation on July 17, the House passed the measure on September 17, and President George Washington signed it into law on September 24, 1789.

The Judiciary Act of 1789 is a landmark in Senate history, which set in motion the federal court system as we know it today. It created a delicately balanced mechanism, including a Supreme Court with a chief justice and five associate justices, thirteen federal district courts, and three traveling circuit courts. The original 1789 system has remained essentially intact, with the addition in 1891 of a separate level of appellate circuit courts.

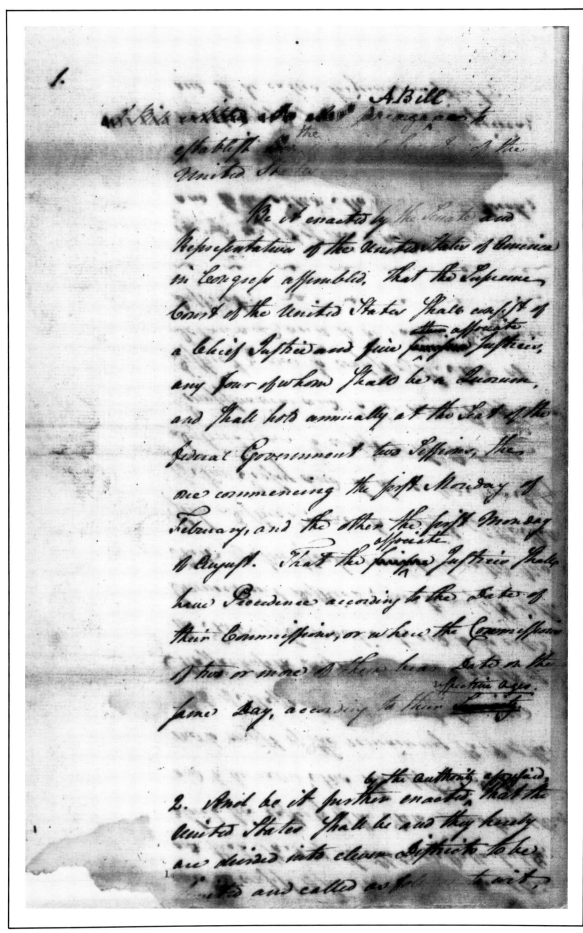

1.

A Bill

to establish the ~~Judicial~~ the ~~Courts~~ of the
United States

Be it enacted by the Senate and
Representatives of the United States of America
in Congress assembled, That the Supreme
Court of the United States shall consist of
a Chief Justice and five ~~foreign~~ *then associate* Justices,
any four of whom shall be a Quorum,
and shall hold annually at the Seat of the
federal Government two Sessions, the
one commencing the first Monday of
February, and the other the first Monday
of August. That the ~~foreign~~ *associate* Justices shall
have Precedence according to the Date of
their Commissions, or where the Commissions
of two or more of them bear Date on the
same Day, according to their ~~____~~ *respective ages.*

2. And be it further enacted, *by the Authority aforesaid* that the
United States shall be and they hereby
are divided into eleven districts to be
limited and called as follows to wit,

The Judiciary Act of 1789

1789
AUGUST 4

Establishment of the Department of War

On August 4, 1789, the Senate approved legislation to establish the third of the three original executive branch agencies, the Department of War. Under the Articles of Confederation, the seeds of the future War Department had been planted and cultivated by Henry Knox, a distinguished Revolutionary War commander. In September 1789, the Senate confirmed Knox as the first secretary of war.

With a personal staff of only two clerks, Knox supervised the nation's two armories, in Springfield, Massachusetts, and Harper's Ferry, Virginia. The armed forces consisted of a small regular army of 560 men, supported by a well-regulated militia. The War Department's administrative structure included a quartermaster's section, a fortifications branch, a paymaster, an inspector general, and an Indian office. By 1800, as the federal government moved to its new capital in Washington, the department's original tiny staff had expanded to eighty people to handle the growing task of governing the military affairs of the entire nation.

The young War Department was plagued by mismanagement, failure, and incompetence. Following a 1791 Indian victory over federal forces, a congressional investigating committee blamed improper organization, and a lack of troop training and discipline, for the embarrassing defeat. In 1794, Secretary Knox resigned, having been undercut by President Washington, who considered military affairs to be his own personal area of expertise.

During the following century and a half, the War Department was headed by such notable national figures as James Monroe, John C. Calhoun, Jefferson Davis, and William Howard Taft. Under the 1947 National Security Act, the War Department was merged with the Navy Department to create the new Department of Defense.

1789
AUGUST 6

Establishment of Senate-House Joint Rules

On August 6, 1789, the Senate agreed to establish a set of joint rules with the House of Representatives. This action came in response to questions of procedure that confronted both houses from the first day of their existence.

A special Senate committee took the lead in proposing many of the joint rules that were subsequently adopted, among them:

That while bills are on their passage between the two Houses, they shall be on paper, and under the signature of the Secretary or Clerk of each House respectively.

When [enacted] bills are enroled, they shall be examined by a joint Committee of one from the Senate, and two from the House of Representatives, . . . who shall carefully compare the enrolment with the engrossed bills, as passed in the two Houses, and correcting any errors that may be discovered in the enroled bills, make their report forthwith to the respective Houses.

That when the Senate and House of Representatives shall judge it proper to make a joint address to the President, it shall be presented to him in his audience Chamber by the President of the Senate, in the presence of the Speaker and both Houses.

Over the following years, the joint rules were updated from time to time. In 1876, after questions arose concerning their legitimacy, the Senate agreed to a resolution adopting all former joint rules as Senate rules. The last major revision occurred in 1884. Since 1889, there have been no further efforts to revise the joint code, and it has been replaced by statute law, by individual orders pertaining to the operation of each body, and by custom.

1789
AUGUST 7

President Washington Scolds the Senate

On August 7, 1789, the Senate received a bitter message from President George Washington. Only four months into the first session of the First Congress, the president and the Senate clashed over what would become a perennial question: should senatorial confirmation be based only on the competence of the nominee, or should political ideology also be a factor?

President Washington appointed Benjamin Fishbourn to the position of naval officer of the Port of Savannah. In the first instance of what would later be called "senatorial courtesy," the Senate rejected that nomination because the two Georgia senators, William Few and James Gunn, favored another candidate, Lachlan McIntosh, a member of their own faction in Georgia politics.

Yielding to the Senate's wishes, Washington nominated McIntosh to the office but added these polite, but scolding, words to the upper house: "Whatever may have been the reasons which induced your dissent, I am persuaded they were such as you deemed sufficient. Permit me to submit to your consideration whether on occasions where the propriety of nominations appear questionable to you, it would not be expedient to communicate that circumstance to me, and thereby avail yourselves of the information which led me to make them, and which I would with pleasure lay before you."

After expounding upon Fishbourn's military and political qualifications for the post, Washington concluded his message abruptly: "It appeared therefore to me, that Mr. Fishbourn must have enjoyed the *confidence* of the Militia Officers, in order to have been elevated to a Military Rank; the *confidence* of the Freemen, to have been elected to the Assembly; the *confidence* of the Assembly, to have been selected for the Council; and the *confidence* of the Council, to have been appointed Collector of the Port of Savannah."

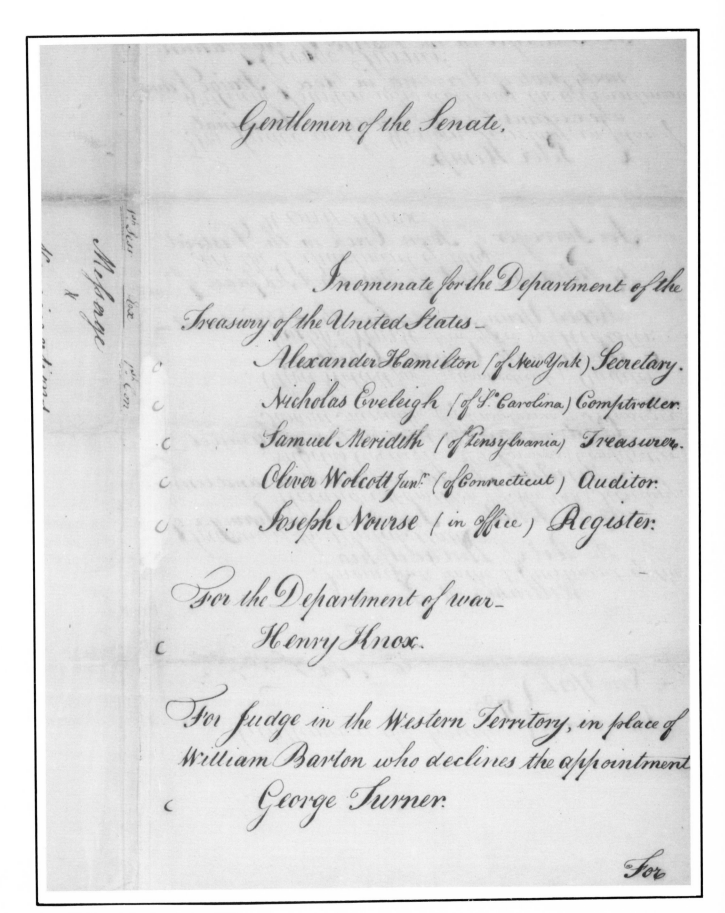

Gentlemen of the Senate,

I nominate for the Department of the Treasury of the United States—

Alexander Hamilton (of New York) Secretary.

Nicholas Eveleigh (of S.ᵗ Carolina) Comptroller.

Samuel Meridith (of Pensylvania) Treasurer.

Oliver Wolcott Jun.ʳ (of Connecticut) Auditor:

Joseph Nourse (in office) Register:

For the Department of war—

Henry Knox.

For Judge in the Western Territory, in place of William Barton who declines the appointment

George Turner.

For

George Washington's list of nominations, 1789

1789
SEPTEMBER 11

Senate Receives and Confirms First Cabinet Nomination

On September 11, 1789, President George Washington sent his first cabinet nomination to the Senate, appointing Alexander Hamilton secretary of the treasury. Moving quickly, the Senate confirmed his nomination later that day.

The congressional statute creating the Treasury Department contained greater detail than those establishing the other two cabinet-level agencies, the departments of State and War. Treasury was the largest of the three agencies and, during the early years of the new government's existence, it grew at a faster rate than the others. Congress singled it out for special attention by requiring the treasury secretary specifically to "digest and prepare plans for the improvement and management of the revenue, and for the support of the public credit." He was also directed to "make report, and give information to either branch of the legislature, in person or in writing . . . respecting all matters referred to him by the Senate or House of Representatives, or which shall appertain to his office."

Six days after the Senate agreed to Hamilton's nomination, the House abolished its Committee on Ways and Means. This action suggests that the House intended the secretary to take the initiative in shaping financial policy. The combination of Hamilton's leadership and the Treasury Department's vital function in raising revenue made that agency preeminent.

Alexander Hamilton had actively campaigned for the position well in advance of his appointment. While many friends urged him to avoid the Treasury—with the nation's finances in a "deep, dark, and dreary chaos"— and run for the Senate, or seek nomination as chief justice of the United States, Hamilton correctly believed that he was one of the few men available who possessed the training and experience to handle this difficult assignment.

1789
SEPTEMBER 25

Senate Passes Bill of Rights

On September 25, 1789, the Senate of the First Congress approved a package of twelve amendments to the Constitution. Ten of these amendments were approved by the states, and we honor them today as our Bill of Rights.

The framers of the Constitution had not considered it necessary to guarantee specifically the rights of citizens, believing that state bills of rights would be sufficient. When the Constitution reached the state ratifying conventions, however, much of the opposition centered on the lack of a bill of rights. James Madison's pledge to introduce such a bill as a first order of business in the new Congress helped win the Constitution's approval. As a leader in the House of Representatives, Madison, therefore, felt obligated to lead the fight for a bill of rights.

On August 25, the Senate received seventeen House-passed amendments. By combining separate amendments, the Senate consolidated these to twelve. For instance, they combined the idea of freedom of religion, free-

The Conventions of a Number of the States having, at the Time of their adopting the Constitution, expressed a Desire, in Order to prevent misconstruction or abuse of its Powers, that further declaratory and restrictive Clauses should be added : And as extending the Ground of public Confidence in the Government, will best insure the beneficent ends of its Institution—

RESOLVED, BY THE SENATE AND HOUSE OF REPRESENTATIVES OF THE UNITED STATES OF AMERICA IN CONGRESS ASSEMBLED, two thirds of both Houses concurring, That the following articles be proposed to the Legislatures of the several States, as amendments to the Constitution of the United States, all or any of which articles, when ratified by three fourths of the said Legislatures, to be valid to all intents and purposes, as part of the said Constitution—Viz.

ARTICLES in addition to, and amendment of, the Constitution of the United States of America, proposed by Congress, and ratified by the Legislatures of the several States, pursuant to the fifth Article of the original Constitution.

ARTICLE THE FIRST.

After the first enumeration, required by the first article of the Constitution, there shall be one Representative for every thirty thousand, until the number shall amount to one hundred; to which number one Representative shall be added for every subsequent increase of forty thousand, until the Representatives shall amount to two hundred, to which number one Representative shall be added for every ... thousand persons.

ARTICLE THE SECOND.

No law, varying the compensation for the services of the Senators and Representatives, shall take effect, until an election of Representatives shall have intervened.

ARTICLE THE THIRD.

Congress shall make no law establishing articles of faith, or a mode of worship, or prohibiting the free exercise of religion, or abridging the freedom of speech, or of the press, or the right of the people peaceably to assemble, and to petition to the government for a redress of grievances.

ARTICLE THE FOURTH.

A well regulated militia, being necessary to the security of a free State, the right of the people to keep and bear arms, shall not be infringed.

ARTICLE THE FIFTH.

No soldier shall, in time of peace, be quartered in any house, without the consent of the owner, nor in time of war, but in a manner to be prescribed by law.

ARTICLE THE SIXTH.

The right of the people to be secure in their persons, houses, papers, and effects, against unreasonable searches and seizures, shall not be violated, and no warrants shall issue, but upon probable cause, supported by oath or affirmation, and particularly describing the place to be searched, and the persons or things to be seized.

Amendments to Constitution U.S.

[2]

ARTICLE THE SEVENTH.

No person shall be held to answer for a capital, or otherwise infamous crime, unless on a presentment or indictment of a Grand Jury, except in cases arising in the land or naval forces, or in the militia, when in actual service in time of war or public danger; nor shall any person be subject for the same offence to be twice put in jeopardy of life or limb; nor shall be compelled in any criminal case, to be a witness against himself, nor be deprived of life, liberty or property, without due process of law; nor shall private property be taken for public use without just compensation.

ARTICLE THE EIGHTH.

In all criminal prosecutions, the accused shall enjoy the right to a speedy and public trial, to be informed of the nature and cause of the accusation, to be confronted with the witnesses against him, to have compulsory process for obtaining witnesses in his favour, and to have the assistance of counsel for his defence.

ARTICLE THE NINTH.

In suits at common law, where the value in controversy shall exceed twenty dollars, the right of trial by Jury shall be preserved, and no fact, tried by a Jury, shall be otherwise re-examined in any court of the United States, than according to the rules of the common law.

ARTICLE THE TENTH.

Excessive bail shall not be required, nor excessive fines imposed, nor cruel and unusual punishments inflicted.

ARTICLE THE ELEVENTH.

... shall not be construed to deny or disparage others retained by the people;

ARTICLE THE TWELFTH.

The powers not delegated to the United States by the Constitution, nor prohibited by it to the States, are reserved to the States respectively, or to the people.

[NEW-YORK, PRINTED BY THOMAS GREENLEAF.]

dom of speech, and freedom of the press into a single amendment, which we now honor as the First Amendment. After the Senate returned the amendments with changes, the House called for a conference committee and appointed James Madison, Roger Sherman, and John Vining as its conferees. The Senate appointed Oliver Ellsworth, Charles Carroll, and William Paterson; thus, four of the six conferees had been delegates to the Constitutional Convention. The Senate conferees reported back on September 24, and the following day the Senate voted to send the twelve amendments to the states. The states adopted ten of these; the two which were rejected would have fixed the size of the House of Representatives and prevented any congressional salary increase from taking place during the Congress in which it was passed.

1789
SEPTEMBER 29

Final Day of the Senate's First Session

September 29, 1789, was the final day of the first session of the First Congress.

Then, as now, the last day's agenda was long and crowded, with appropriations bills being the most pressing item of business. Even though we do not have a verbatim record of that session at Federal Hall in New York City, the minutes make clear that it was a hectic time. On several occasions during the day, the clerk of the House, John Beckley, appeared with announcements that the House had passed an appropriations bill, a pension bill, or trade legislation. Similarly, President Washington's personal secretary, Tobias Lear, was in and out of the Senate chamber carrying messages from the president. The committee on enrolled bills announced a series of end-of-the session bills that were ready to be sent to the president for his signature.

We read that the clerk of the House returned to announce that the House had passed the military bill but that it disagreed with one of the Senate's amendments. The Senate deliberated and held firm on its position. At last, word came that the House would accept the amendment. Private pensions also required attention, and the Senate appears to have spent a good deal of time debating a bill for payment of an army captain.

At last, the agenda was completed. The Senate gave orders to its doorkeeper to take charge of the chamber during its adjournment, "that he lay in a sufficiency of Fuel, and have Stoves so placed to give warmth to the Room" when they returned in January. Then Vice President John Adams gaveled the session closed. After five months, the first session of the Senate had finished its work.

1790
AUGUST 12

Senate Conducts Final Session in New York

On August 12, 1790, the Senate met for the last time at Federal Hall in New York City. The next day, clerks began packing up the Senate's records for the move to Philadelphia, where Congress would meet for the next ten years while the new federal capital in the District of Columbia was made ready.

Federal Hall was the Senate's first home. It was there in its ornate second-floor chamber that the Senate achieved its first quorum on April 6, 1789, established its first rules of conduct, elected its first officers, and tried out its various constitutional powers. In these quarters, the Senate took the major initiative in shaping the vitally significant Judiciary Act of 1789 that gave shape to the third branch of government. With the House, it crafted legislation putting the executive branch into operation with the creation of three cabinet agencies, the departments of State, War, and Treasury.

Crusty senator William Maclay, a major figure in all of these early debates, anticipated the move to Philadelphia with loathing. Though a senator from Pennsylvania, he had no great love for its principal city. New York's "allurements," he grumbled:

are more than ten to two compared with Philadelphia. To tell the truth I know no so unsocial a city as Philadelphia. The gloomy severity of the Quakers has proscribed all fashionable dress and amusement. . . . While at the same time there are not in the world more scornful nor insolent characters than the wealthy among them.

Maclay was in the minority. Most senators looked forward to the move to Philadelphia, many remembering fondly the handsome city where they had met as members of the Continental Congress and the Constitutional Convention. On August 12, after thanking the city of New York for the "elegant and convenient accommodations," the senators set off to their homes prepared to reassemble in December at the Senate's new Philadelphia quarters.

1790
NOVEMBER 9

James Monroe is Sworn In

On November 9, 1790, James Monroe was sworn in as senator from Virginia. While Monroe is best remembered as our fifth president and author of the Monroe Doctrine, he devoted his entire life to serving the young nation he helped mold.

Born in Westmoreland County, Virginia, in 1758, Monroe entered the College of William and Mary in 1774, only to leave two years later to enlist in the Continental army at the start of the American Revolution. After the war, Monroe studied law with Thomas Jefferson, then governor of Virginia. In the years that followed, Monroe was elected to the Virginia legislature, the Continental Congress, and the Virginia ratifying convention. In 1789, he was defeated by James Madison for a seat in the First Congress, but the

Cartoon of Congress' move from New York to Philadelphia

next year, when a Virginia senator died in office, Monroe won a Senate seat—becoming the first of fifteen future presidents to serve in this body. Leaving the Senate in 1797, Monroe served as minister to France and England. After defeating Monroe for the presidency in 1808, James Madison named him secretary of state in 1811. Monroe held this position until 1817 when he himself became president.

As president, James Monroe blossomed. In his early years, he had been strongly sectional, narrowly partisan, and exceedingly ambitious. His diplomatic achievements were less than brilliant. While Jefferson said of him, "he is a man whose soul might be turned wrong side outwards without discovering a blemish to the world," many contemporaries disagreed. In the presidency, however, Monroe exhibited a capacity for administration and for accurate interpretation of the mood of the nation that commanded great respect. Less intellectual than either Jefferson or Madison, Monroe surpassed them both as an administrator.

When James Monroe died on the Fourth of July 1831, at the age of seventy-three, his public service spanned more than five decades, from youthful Continental soldier to president of the United States.

Facing page, William Birch's engraving of Congress Hall
in Philadelphia, where the Senate met from 1790-1800

CHAPTER III
The Formative
Years
1792–1820

Roger Sherman of Connecticut

1793
JULY 23

Death of Roger Sherman

On July 23, 1793, Senator Roger Sherman of Connecticut died in office. Although he served in the First and Second congresses, Sherman was better known for his achievements in the Continental Congress and the Constitutional Convention. Born in Massachusetts in 1721, Sherman moved to Connecticut at the age of twenty-two. He began his political career two years later as surveyor for New Haven County. Sherman also served for many years in the Connecticut general assembly.

In 1774, Sherman became a member of the First Continental Congress. By serving eight years in the Continental congresses, he held office in those bodies longer than any other member. He served on both the committee to draft the Declaration of Independence and the committee to draft the Articles of Confederation. At the Constitutional Convention, on June 11, 1787, Sherman introduced the famous Connecticut Compromise, which established the basis of representation between the Senate and House and ended a deadlock that threatened to destroy the convention. When he inscribed his name on the Constitution he helped craft, Sherman earned the distinction of being the only person to sign the Constitution, the Articles of Confederation, the Declaration of Independence, and the Articles of Association of 1774. John Adams referred to Sherman as "an old Puritan, as honest as an angel and as firm in the cause of American independence as Mount Atlas."

In 1789, Sherman was elected to the House of Representatives of the First Congress. Two years later, the Connecticut legislature elected him to the Senate, where he began his service on June 13, 1791. When Sherman died in office just over two years later, the country lost a leading statesman who had helped to frame our system of government.

1793
SEPTEMBER 18

George Washington Places Capitol Cornerstone

On September 18, 1793, a large and boisterous crowd jostled around President George Washington as he placed the cornerstone of the Capitol Building. When Pierre Charles L'Enfant designed the new federal city, he had saved the choice rise of land known locally as Jenkins' Hill expressly for the Congress' home. It stood, he declared, "as a pedestal waiting for a monument." Choosing the right "monument" to crown this pedestal, however, proved difficult. None of the first designs was satisfactory, and some were downright ludicrous. Then, at the last minute, William Thornton, a physician and amateur architect, asked permission to submit a design. When it arrived, another amateur architect, Secretary of State Thomas Jefferson, reported with relief, "it captivated the eyes and judgment of all."

Work on the new Capitol began immediately. By September 18, 1793, all was in readiness for the cornerstone to be laid. Festivities began with a grand parade. With drums beating and flags flying, brightly uniformed members of the Alexandria Volunteer Artillery and local Masonic lodges escorted President Washington across the Potomac, into the District, and up to the top of Capitol Hill. Masonic rituals, dating from the middle ages when stonemasons and the Masonic Order were closely associated, dominated the ceremonies. President Washington laid the cornerstone wearing a Masonic apron, reportedly made by the wife of General Lafayette. Using a silver trowel and a marble-headed gavel to set the stone in place, he then attached to it a silver plate proclaiming the date to be the thirteenth year after American independence, the first year of his second term, and the year 5793 of Masonry.

After fifteen salutes from the artillery, the Alexandria *Gazette* reported that "the whole company retired to an extensive booth, where an ox of 500 pounds' weight was barbequed, of which the company generally partook."

Artist Allyn Cox's portrayal of the Capitol cornerstone ceremony of 1793

1794
FEBRUARY 20

First Public Session of the Senate

On February 20, 1794, the Senate held its first public session. The Constitution's framers had assumed that the Senate would follow their own practice of meeting in secret. The remarkable feature of the newly created Congress was not that Senate meetings would be secret, but that House meetings would be open.

In the first few years of the Senate's existence, defenders of secrecy looked with disdain on the House, where members were tempted to perform for the gallery, and occupants routinely cheered and hissed as issues were debated. Nonetheless, from the very beginning, some senators advocated an open-door policy. In particular, minority party members believed public scrutiny would expose various schemes of those in the majority. Also, state legislators realized that they had no way to keep tabs on the behavior of the senators they elected.

Eventually, the Senate's Federalist majority recognized that their views could more easily win popular support if aired publicly rather than concealed. The spreading notion of the Senate as a "lurking hole" in which conspiracies were hatched against the public interest had to be put to rest. Additionally, press coverage of the House helped popularize that body's role, and the public began to use the words "House" and "Congress" interchangeably. The Senate was in danger of becoming the forgotten chamber.

A dispute early in 1794 over whether to accept the credentials of a newly elected Pennsylvania senator provided the shove that opened the Senate's doors. At that time, the capital was located in Philadelphia. Senators recognized the delicacy of moving, behind closed doors, to reject a man just selected by the Pennsylvania legislature. Consequently, the Federalist majority agreed to open the doors just for that occasion. Shortly afterwards, the Senate decided to make the change permanent.

1795
JUNE 24

Senate Approves the Jay Treaty

On June 24, 1795, the United States Senate consented to the ratification of the most important and controversial treaty that had yet come before it. This was John Jay's treaty with Great Britain.

Although the United States had signed a peace treaty with Britain in 1783, disputes remained between the two countries. Britain had not evacuated its forts in the old Northwest Territory, on the grounds that the Americans had not compensated British merchants and former loyalists for debts and property seized during the Revolutionary War. The United States also accused Britain of interfering with its neutral shipping.

To negotiate a settlement of these matters, President Washington chose John Jay, a New York lawyer who had headed the Department of Foreign Affairs under the Confederation before becoming the first chief justice of the United States. Jay achieved a treaty under which the British would withdraw from their forts on American soil, American ships were allowed into British ports on the same terms that British ships were permitted in American ports, a limited trade with the West Indies was opened to American ships, and a joint commission was created to resolve any debt questions.

The terms of Jay's treaty brought strong opposition from those who for various reasons considered it too weak and too favorable toward the British. Newspapers denounced Jay as a traitor, copies of his treaty were burned, and effigies of Jay were publicly hanged, burned, and guillotined. Despite such public pressure, the Senate recognized the advantages of the Jay treaty and, after a lengthy debate, approved the treaty by exactly a two-thirds vote of 20 to 10.

1795
JULY 1

John Rutledge Appointed Chief Justice

On July 1, 1795, President George Washington appointed John Rutledge to be chief justice of the United States. Rutledge received only a temporary commission, however, for he was appointed during a congressional recess, and the Senate had to consent to his nomination before he could attain permanent status.

Born to a wealthy South Carolina family, Rutledge served as a delegate to the Continental and Confederation congresses, as governor of South Carolina, and as a delegate to the 1787 Constitutional Convention. In 1789, President Washington nominated him as senior associate justice of the newly formed United States Supreme Court. Although Rutledge accepted this post, he failed to attend any of the Court meetings and resigned in 1791 to become chief justice of the South Carolina Court of Common Pleas.

In 1795, anticipating that Chief Justice John Jay would accept the governorship of New York, Rutledge wrote to the president to offer himself as a replacement. Washington responded enthusiastically and gave him a recess appointment on July 1. Two weeks later, on July 16, 1795, Rutledge delivered a speech in which he intemperately attacked the highly controversial Jay Treaty, which the president and the Senate's Federalist majority supported. This treaty settled numerous points of contention between the United States and Great Britain, but many viewed it as a surrender to the British. It is unclear whether Rutledge knew that Washington had just appointed him chief justice when he delivered his offensive speech. Aware of it or not, his imprudence cost him dearly.

When the Senate reconvened in December 1795, it rejected Rutledge by a vote of 10 to 14, its first such refusal of a Supreme Court justice. While the whole story is not clear, Rutledge's untimely and harsh speech, as well as rumors that he was prone to bouts of insanity, severely damaged his cause.

John Rutledge of South Carolina

1797
JUNE 29

A Senator Reports to His Constituents

On June 29, 1797, Senator William Cocke sent a circular letter to his Tennessee constituents. Most such letters were addressed individually and sent at politically opportune moments to both potential and active supporters. To gain wider circulation, these communications were posted in local post offices for public viewing and were reprinted in local newspapers. Though personal and partisan, the letters generally provided informative reports for an educated audience. Although their distribution was predominantly a practice of House members, a handful of senators used circular letters to keep their constituents abreast of the latest Senate activities and other issues of national concern.

Following the form of other congressional letters sent at the end of the eighteenth century, Cocke in his June 1797 letter first discussed issues of home state concerns. He proudly reported that, thanks to his efforts, "there appears a considerable change of sentiment in a number of respectable members of the Senate of the United States favorable to the State of Tennessee, and friendly to the extinguishment of the claims injurious to our rights." He then summarized recently passed acts of Congress. Cocke concluded with a survey of developments related to foreign affairs, including the ratification of a peace treaty with Tunis and Tripoli, and his worried assessment of the tenuous relations between the United States and France.

Although they might seem trivial to some today, these letters were of great importance. President John Adams once said, "I would give all that I am worth for a complete collection of those circular letters." Precursors of today's congressional newsletters, such letters provide us with a valuable glimpse of how our government functioned in its formative years.

William Blount
of Tennessee

1797
JULY 8

The Expulsion of William Blount

On July 8, 1797, the Senate expelled Senator William Blount of Tennessee. In two hundred years, only fifteen of the Senate's approximately eighteen hundred members have been expelled. Blount was the first; the remaining expulsions occurred during the Civil War.

William Blount was a signer of the Declaration of Independence, a former North Carolina Federalist turned Tennessee Republican, and an unscrupulous, chronically overextended land speculator. On July 3, 1797, President John Adams, a staunch Federalist, transmitted to the Senate a letter from Senator Blount to James Carey, an interpreter for the Cherokee Nation. In the letter, undeniably written by Blount, the senator imprudently spelled out plans to launch an attack by Cherokee and Creek Indians and frontiersmen, aided by the British fleet, in order to wrest Louisiana and Florida away from the Spanish and turn them over to England. From this blatant conspiracy with the British, Blount stood to profit handsomely.

Blount's highly incriminating letter was referred to a select Senate committee. The evidence against him was conclusive, and the committee recommended his expulsion for "a high misdemeanor, entirely inconsistent with his public trust and duty as a Senator." Blount's grandiose plotting was so distasteful to his fellow senators that they expelled him on July 8, 1797, by a nearly unanimous vote of 25 to 1.

Blount's expulsion did him little harm in Tennessee, where he was promptly elected speaker of the state senate. His problems with the federal Congress, however, were far from over. In 1798, Federalist leaders in the House, not content with his expulsion, adopted five articles of impeachment against Blount. His impeachment trial in the Senate in January 1799 was the first ever held. Blount's lawyers argued vehemently that the Senate had no jurisdiction over their client, since he was a private citizen. By a vote of 14 to 11, his former colleagues agreed, refusing jurisdiction in the case.

1800
MARCH 18

Senate Cites Newspaper Editor for Contempt

On March 18, 1800, the Senate, meeting in Philadelphia, issued its first contempt of Congress citation. The citation went to a Philadelphia newspaper editor, William Duane, for failing to appear before Congress to explain how he had obtained the text of a bill that had been debated in secret.

The secret bill was a scheme by the Federalist majority in the Senate to change the method of settling disputes over presidential electors. Supporters of Thomas Jefferson, leader of the Democratic-Republican party, feared that this move was designed to deny Jefferson the presidency in the forthcoming election. Jefferson's allies in the Senate leaked a copy of the bill to William Duane, who published the story in his paper, the Philadelphia *Aurora*. Offended Federalists demanded an investigation of Duane and his illicit sources.

At that time, Thomas Jefferson presided over the Senate as vice president. The Federalists called Duane into the Senate chamber and directed the vice president to read him a list of prepared questions about who had given him the bill. Duane, who had been carefully coached by the Democratic-Republicans, asked that he be given additional time to seek counsel, and Jefferson gladly ruled in favor of the request.

That was the last the Senate saw of William Duane. When he failed to reappear, the Senate issued a contempt citation in his name, but Duane hid out through the remainder of the congressional session. Not only did Duane escape prosecution, but that fall Thomas Jefferson was elected president and the Democratic-Republicans took the majority in both houses of Congress. Needless to say, the new Senate majority had no intention of pursuing charges of contempt against William Duane.

Free Postage for Martha Washington

On April 3, 1800, the Congress sent to the president a bill granting franking privileges to Martha Washington, widow of our first president. It was a simple resolution of one sentence, stating, "*Resolved,* That all papers and packets sent to Mrs. Martha Washington, relict of the late General George Washington, shall be received and conveyed by post, free from postage, for and during her life."

Free postage was one of the few services that the government could offer a distinguished citizen in those days. The frank was extended to members of Congress, the president, cabinet secretaries, and other executive branch officers. It also went to certain private citizens. For instance, every newspaper printer could send one paper, postage free, to every other newspaper printer in the country, to encourage the exchange of news.

When George Washington died in December 1799, the nation mourned the leader of its Revolutionary War army and its first president. It was natural that Congress would seek ways of aiding his widow at Mount Vernon, and, in March 1800, Representative Henry Lee of Virginia introduced a resolution granting Mrs. Washington franking privileges. A veteran of the Revolution himself, Lee had delivered the eulogy for George Washington before both houses of Congress, characterizing Washington with those now famous words, "first in war, first in peace, and first in the hearts of his countrymen."

The House quickly passed the measure and sent it to the Senate on March 31. The next day, the Senate adopted it unanimously, and on April 3 the bill went to President John Adams. The act began a tradition that we continue today of providing assistance to the widows of our former presidents.

The Senate Meets for the Last Time in Philadelphia

May 14, 1800, was the last day of the first session of the Sixth Congress. More importantly, it was the last day on which the Senate met in Philadelphia. The chamber on the second floor of Congress Hall had been the Senate's home since December 1790. In that year the government had moved from New York to Philadelphia under the terms of the bargain struck during the First Congress that created a new capital city to the south and provided that Congress would meet in Philadelphia for a decade while its new home was readied.

By 1798, many members had come to regret that bargain. They faced the grim prospect of abandoning bustling, cosmopolitan Philadelphia, with its sophisticated social life and handsome houses, for the wilds of the Potomac River's shores. Rumors that the new capital was still a swampy morass of half-finished federal buildings hardly lifted their spirits. Vice President Thomas Jefferson, who had supported the move, charged that John Adams and the Federalists in Congress, who opposed the transfer, were toying with the idea of merely going through the formality of moving the government to Washington in order to comply with the law—and then moving right out again. While they did not disavow Jefferson's charges, the Senate's Federalist majority passed, and Adams signed, the construction bill for the new capital. That measure included an authorization of $9,000 to furnish the new Senate and House chambers and move the records of Congress to the new site.

Within days of the May 14 adjournment, sloops carrying the Senate's records sailed out of Philadelphia harbor. In late May, they docked at Lear's wharf on the Potomac and the task of unpacking began. When the Senate reconvened in November, it met in the unfinished north wing—the only wing—of the Capitol Building, perched in lonely isolation atop Jenkins' Hill. Its travels were over.

1800
NOVEMBER 21

Senate Meets in Washington for the First Time

On November 21, 1800, the Senate met for the first time in Washington, DC, in the unfinished Capitol Building. This important event was actually to have taken place on November 17, but when that day dawned, only fifteen of thirty-two senators had arrived in the new capital city. Members had to wait for four more days until a quorum could be raised to bring the Senate to life in its new home.

Although federal officials had had a decade to carve out a town along the Potomac for the government's permanent home, it was a sorry sight that greeted those first arrivals. As he tried to find decent accommodations, New York Senator Gouverneur Morris caustically observed that the new seat of government needed only "houses, cellars, kitchens, well informed men, amiable women, and other little trifles of this kind to make our city perfect." Aware of grumblings like Morris', town boosters planned a huge parade to welcome the Sixth Congress. But nothing went as intended. First, a heavy snow blanketed the area on November 16, and then, when quarrels broke out over who should be grand-marshal, the procession was abandoned entirely. When so few members actually showed up for opening day, everyone was disheartened. In view of the difficulty of getting to the new capital, it was remarkable that a quorum was mustered so soon. Even under the best of conditions, which seldom prevailed, the stage journey from Philadelphia to Washington took a minimum of thirty-three hours.

Finally, on November 21, the Senate notified President John Adams that a quorum was present. The president himself appeared before the assembled Congress in the Senate chamber the next day. While members still complained about conditions that one called "both melancholy and ludicrous," Adams congratulated them "on the prospect of a residence not to be changed." As we all know, Washington indeed became the government's home, and, as Adams predicted that day, conditions have improved a great deal.

William Birch's watercolor of the
north wing of the Capitol in 1800

1803
OCTOBER 20

Senate Approves Louisiana Purchase

On October 20, 1803, the Senate consented to the ratification of the Louisiana Purchase treaty.

Soon after becoming president in 1801, Thomas Jefferson learned of the secret agreement in which Spain had returned the Louisiana territory to France. Napoleon intended to use the province as the base for a French colonial empire in North America. Jefferson correctly feared that this would pose a great threat to the nation's security.

Early in 1803, Napoleon changed his plans and decided to sell the Louisiana territory. American negotiators successfully offered nearly $15 million for the 828,000 square miles lying between the Mississippi River and the Rocky Mountains. This extraordinary transaction more than doubled the land area of the United States, giving the country more tillable land than any other nation.

Jefferson called Congress into session before its regular December convening date to present the treaty to the Senate and to obtain necessary funding. The Senate acted immediately. Fearing that the French might change their minds, senators voted 24 to 7 to approve the treaty. Only New England's Federalist senators opposed the pact, arguing that the president lacked the power under the Constitution. New Hampshire's Senator William Plumer complained that "the Senate have taken less time to deliberate on this important treaty than they allowed themselves on the most trivial Indian contract."

As Secretary of the Senate Samuel A. Otis carried the approved treaty to the White House, he passed John Quincy Adams, who had just arrived in Washington to take his oath as a newly elected senator. Adams later observed that he was sorry he had not arrived at the Senate in time to vote for the treaty, for he "regarded it as one of the happiest events which had occurred since the adoption of the Constitution."

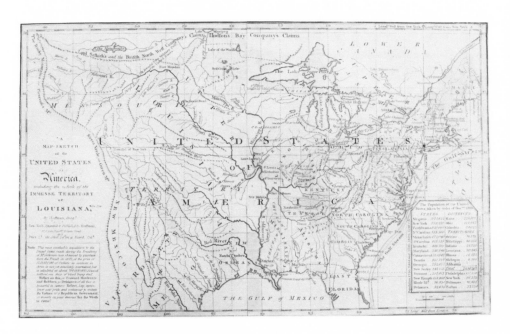

An 1819 map reflecting the newly acquired territory of Louisiana

1804
FEBRUARY 25

The "Grand Caucus" of Republicans

On February 25, 1804, a "grand Caucus of the Republican Members of Congress" drew 108 senators and representatives together in the Senate chamber. These were not Republicans in the modern sense, but Jeffersonian Republicans, and the caucus was not a legislative conference in the modern sense, but in fact an early version of our national conventions to nominate presidential candidates.

Professor Noble Cunningham, a Jeffersonian specialist, has pointed out that this caucus was "the key party mechanism in the national organization of the Republican party and gave the Republican members of Congress control over the selection of the party's candidates for President and Vice-President." He adds that, while the caucus played no role in the legislative process—at a time when there were no formal party offices in either house—"it was indicative of the importance of party in Congress and demonstrated the ability of congressional Republicans to make major party decisions."

The caucus that met in 1804 agreed unanimously to renominate President Thomas Jefferson for a second term and chose New York Governor George Clinton for vice president to replace Aaron Burr. Jefferson and Clinton went on to win the election by an overwhelming margin over the decaying Federalist party.

One senator who attended reported that the caucus conducted its business "with remarkable decorum and harmony; and was dispatched at an early hour in the evening." Although this system worked well in 1804, it collapsed twenty years later. Supporters of Andrew Jackson complained vigorously against the influence of "King Caucus" in choosing the president. Jackson's election in 1828, and the development of national conventions, spelled the end of the congressional caucus as the means of nominating our presidential candidates.

1804
MARCH 12

The Senate Convicts a Federal Judge

On March 12, 1804, the Senate, for the first time in its history, exercised its constitutional power to remove a federal judge from office.

The bizarre and deeply partisan behavior of New Hampshire District Court Judge John Pickering brought him to the attention of President Thomas Jefferson in 1803. Failing to engineer the resignation of Pickering, who had a history of mental illness and alcoholism, the president asked the House to impeach him. Leaders of the newly ascendant Republican party in the House drew up articles of impeachment that carefully avoided mention of Pickering's madness. They believed the introduction of his insanity would make it impossible to find him guilty of "high crimes and misdemeanors." Accordingly, he was charged with violating a statute and with "being a man of loose morals and intemperate habits [who appeared on the bench] in a state of total intoxication [and who] in a most profane and indecent manner, invoke[d] the name of the Supreme Being, to the evil example of all good citizens."

There were ample substantive grounds for the House decision, on a 45 to 8 vote, to impeach Pickering, but the action also had clear political overtones. Federalists saw this as the first in a series of steps by Republicans, who dominated Congress and the presidency, toward a general housecleaning of the judiciary, which they dominated.

The Senate trial began in January 1804. Pickering complicated matters by refusing to attend and by challenging the president to a duel. In a bitter proceeding, Federalists argued that the Senate should wait until Pickering was sane enough to participate in his own defense. On March 12, however, with the entire House of Representatives crowded into the Senate chamber, the Senate voted 20 to 6 to remove Pickering. Federalists correctly feared that a sane Supreme Court justice might be the Republicans' next target.

1805
MARCH 1

Supreme Court Justice
Samuel Chase

The Senate Acquits a Supreme Court Justice

On March 1, 1805, the Senate, by a four-vote margin, failed to remove a U.S. Supreme Court justice from office.

A year earlier, on a strict party-line vote, the Senate, under the control of the Jeffersonian Republicans, had found Federalist U.S. District Court Judge John Pickering guilty of decisions contrary to law and of drunkenness and profanity on the bench. By all accounts, Judge Pickering was insane and the Senate's action was justified. On that same day in March 1804, the Republican-dominated House of Representatives—linking a questionable decision to an appropriate one—voted to impeach the eloquent and intemperate Supreme Court Justice Samuel Chase for biased conduct and an "anti-Republican" attitude.

The Chase trial began on February 4, 1805 in the Senate chamber, specially fitted out for the event with a ladies' gallery. Following four weeks of deliberation, the Senate voted to acquit Chase. The Senate's action was highly significant, for it effectively insulated the judiciary from further congressional attacks based on disapproval of judges' opinions. If the Republicans in the Senate had removed Chase, there is little doubt that their next target would have been Federalist Chief Justice John Marshall.

A few days later, Senator John Quincy Adams wrote to his father to express his surprised appreciation for the Senate's action in the face of fierce contrary desires by certain Republican members who wished to deliver a crippling blow to the already weakened Federalist opposition. He noted that "some of those whose weakness had yielded to the torrent of popular prejudice in the [removal of Judge Pickering] had the integrity to reflect, rallied all their energy to assist them, and took a stand which has arrested for a time that factious impetuosity that threatens to bury all our national institutions in one common ruin."

1805
MARCH 2

Aaron Burr's Farewell to the Senate

On March 2, 1805, the Senate witnessed a moment of extraordinary drama. In the final hours of the Eighth Congress, Vice President Aaron Burr delivered a farewell address that remains a classic in the Senate's history. Less than eight months earlier, he had killed former Treasury Secretary Alexander Hamilton in a duel at Weehawken, New Jersey. Following that tragic event, Burr fled southward to escape indictment.

In his address, the vice president apologized for any offense that his actions as the Senate's presiding officer might have given to senators. Burr asserted that during the past four years, he had followed his belief that error was preferable to indecision and that his errors, "whatever they might have been, were those of rule and principle, and not of caprice."

Burr concluded his address with the following stirring remarks about the nature of the Senate. He said:

This House is a sanctuary; a citadel of law, of order, and of liberty; and it is here—it is here, in this exalted refuge; here, if anywhere, [that] resistance [will] be made to the storms of political phrensy and the silent arts of corruption; and if the Constitution be destined ever to perish by the sacrilegious hands of the demagogue or the usurper, which God avert, its expiring agonies will be witnessed on this floor.

Senator Samuel Mitchill recorded what happened immediately following Burr's address:

When Mr. Burr had concluded he descended from the chair, and in a dignified manner walked to the door, which resounded as he with some force shut it after him. On this the firmness and resolution of many of the Senators gave way, and they burst into tears. There was a solemn and silent weeping for perhaps five minutes.

Aaron Burr of New York

Young John Quincy Adams
of Massachusetts

1805
MARCH 8

The End of a Hectic Congressional Session

On March 8, 1805, thirty-seven-year-old Senator John Quincy Adams wrote to his father, former President John Adams, to describe the hectic and portentous closing days of the Eighth Congress.

"From ten o'clock in the morning until seven in the evening," he recalled:

the Senate was constantly in session, with the interval of only half an hour each day for a slight collation, which the members took at the Capitol itself; and this, together with a walk of an hour to reach that place, and a walk of an hour to return to it, scarcely left me the hours of the night for repose. The scene has now closed. On Sunday evening last, [on March 3], at half past nine o'clock, the two Houses adjourned [sine die], and thus terminated a session which it was high time to bring to an end.

The session had concluded with the Senate voting to acquit Supreme Court Justice Samuel Chase of impeachment charges lodged by the House. This bitterly emotional partisan battle had raised a serious threat to the continuing independence of the federal judiciary. Adams reflected on the role of the Senate in maintaining that independence:

[The trial] has exhibited the Senate of the United States fulfilling the most important purpose of its institution by putting a check upon the impetuous violence of the House of Representatives. It has proved, that a sense of justice is yet strong enough to overpower the furies of faction; but it has, at the same time, shown the wisdom and necessity of that provision in the Constitution which requires the concurrence of two-thirds for conviction upon impeachments.

He concluded: "The essential characters which *ought* to belong to the Senate are *coolness* and *firmness*. I hope that when the occasion shall call they will be found to possess them; and it would be doing an injustice to the body and its members not to acknowledge that in this memorable instance these qualities have been eminently displayed."

1806
MARCH 12

The Value of Senate Oratory

Over the Senate's two hundred years of existence, only a few of its members have kept and published diaries. William Plumer of New Hampshire carefully recorded his involvement in Senate activities between 1803 and the end of his brief service in 1807. Here is a portion of his entry for the session that met on March 12, 1806:

I have for sometime been convinced that speeches in the Senate in most cases have very little influence upon the vote. I believe that in nineteen cases out of twenty, they do not change a single vote. For this inefficiency there are various causes. All our documents, communications, reports, bills and amendments are printed and laid on our tables and those of us who examine subjects for ourselves, and do not vote on the faith of others, read and examine and form opinions for ourselves. Having read and examined a subject, we converse with each other and freely exchange our sentiments. This not only confirms or changes the opinions of some, but fixes the vote of others who never give themselves the trouble of examination. Some senators are implicitly led by the administration. Others have their [faction] leader. When a senator is making a long speech, the chairs are most of them deserted and the vote is often settled in a conversation at the fireside. The conversation is there often so loud as to interrupt the senator who is speaking, for our vice president has not the talents requisite for a good presiding officer. Under these circumstances it is often difficult for a man who knows he is not [listened to], to deliver an able and eloquent argument. To this, add that we have no stenographer, and seldom any hearers in the galleries . . . I speak none, . . . and yet my influence on many subjects is not confined to my own vote.

Very little seems to have changed since that time. As I look around, the chamber is empty, even though this was not a long speech. Except that we now have stenographers and an efficient presiding officer, everything is the same.

1812
JUNE 17

Senate Votes for War with Great Britain

On June 17, 1812, the United States Senate voted to go to war with Great Britain.

The United States' relations with Britain, not particularly friendly since the American Revolution, had deteriorated further during the British war with France. Britain issued Orders in Council that forbade any neutral ship from trading in Europe unless it stopped first at a British port. Thereafter, Britain interfered with American shipping and impressed American seamen—that is, forced Americans to serve in the British navy. The Americans retaliated by passing embargo and nonintercourse acts to cut off trade with the warring countries.

President Madison and many Americans, particularly in the maritime states of the Northeast, hoped to mend relations between the two countries, but a vocal band of "warhawks" in Congress were eager for a clash. These hawks included such young and ambitious western and southern political leaders as Henry Clay and John C. Calhoun. Finally, on June 1, 1812, Madison sent a war message to Congress, charging the British with impressing sailors, inciting Indians on the frontier, establishing blockades of American trade, and rejecting American peace overtures. Congress was by no means unified on the issue, but on June 4 the House voted 79 to 49 for war, and on June 17 the Senate agreed by a vote of 19 to 13.

Six days after the Senate voted, the British government canceled its Orders in Council, due both to a bad harvest and to petitions from British manufacturers, who pleaded to reopen their American markets. Madison's policy of economic pressure had finally worked. Sadly, however, in those days of slow communications, the war message and the cancellation of the orders passed each other on the Atlantic. The course for war was irrevocably set.

The city of Washington taken by British forces, August 24, 1814

1814
SEPTEMBER 21

The Senate Meets After Capitol is Burned

September 21, 1814 marked the third day of the third session of the Fourteenth Congress. An examination of the *Annals of Congress* reveals that something unusual was afoot. On the twenty-first, for example, a resolution passed without opposition authorizing Senate Sergeant at Arms Mountjoy Bayly "to employ one assistant and two horses." Why, in the fall of 1814, did the Senate suddenly find itself in need of assistants and horses? The answer lies in the fact that the senators were not meeting in the Capitol Building, but in Blodgett's Hotel downtown.

The War of 1812 was still raging on American soil. Scarcely a month before, on August 24, the British had marched into Washington virtually unopposed and had set fire to the Capitol. Only a torrential rainstorm prevented them from burning it to the ground. As it was, the roofs of both wings lay in ashes. Smoke-stained walls, pierced by gaping holes where windows once had been, memorialized the nation's humiliation. The new assistants and horses, along with other special provisions passed in the early days of this 1814 special session, represented the Senate's efforts to get its affairs back in order.

For more than a year, the Senate met at Blodgett's, with assistants and horses making frequent trips between the blackened Capitol and the old hotel. Then, in December 1815, the Congress moved to new quarters on Capitol Hill. Washington businessmen, eager to keep the government in their city, built a large red brick structure specifically to house the displaced members, on the site now occupied by the Supreme Court Building. Congress met in the "Brick Capitol" for four years, until the Capitol across the street was refurbished in time for the opening of the Sixteenth Congress in December 1819.

1815
DECEMBER 4

Senate Convenes in Brick Capitol

On December 4, 1815, the Senate met as usual on Capitol Hill, but its meeting place was hardly regular, and the circumstances of its displacement were far from commonplace. The Senate was meeting for the first time just across the street from the Capitol in a new, red brick building, which would eventually become known as the old "Brick Capitol." In August 1814, the British had marched into Washington and burned the Capitol, leaving it a blackened mass of cracked sandstone.

An old hostelry that had stood at First and A Streets, N.E. since 1795 was pulled down in 1815 to clear space for a temporary meeting place for Congress, which had been meeting in Blodgett's Hotel since the British attack. Fearing that the Congress might move the capital to another city, local citizens had quickly raised $25,000 to erect the three-story, Federal-style building that would be the Congress' home until the Capitol was repaired. Congress met in the Brick Capitol for four years, with the Senate meeting on the first floor, the House on the second.

The Capitol was restored in time for the Congress to return in December 1819. Afterwards, the Brick Capitol was used as a private school, then as a boardinghouse for congressmen. Senator John C. Calhoun died in his apartment there in March 1850. During the Civil War, the building was used as a prison for political prisoners, the most notorious being the beautiful southern spies Belle Boyd and Rose O'Neal Greenhow. The Brick Capitol, scene of events both triumphant and tragic, finally disappeared from the cityscape in the early 1930s when it was demolished for the new Supreme Court Building.

1816
DECEMBER 10

Senate Creates Standing Committees

On December 10, 1816, the Senate first created standing committees. That day it established eleven committees: Foreign Relations, Judiciary, Ways and Means—which later became the Finance and Appropriations committees—Commerce, Military Affairs, Naval Affairs, the Militia, Public Lands, Claims, Post Office, and Pensions.

Prior to 1816, the Senate had done its work through a series of temporary committees, appointed to handle specific bills, treaties, or nominations. In any session of Congress, several hundred of these ad hoc committees would be created and disbanded as they performed their assignments. Obviously, there could be no seniority system as we know it, although some senators were repeatedly reappointed to certain types of committees according to their areas of expertise. Inequalities also prevailed, for a few senators drew a great number of committee appointments while others received none.

The Senate did already have three standing committees for housekeeping functions: for Enrolled bills, Engrossed bills, and Contingent Expenses. But in the aftermath of the War of 1812, with major social, economic, and diplomatic issues facing the United States, the Senate realized the need to create permanent committees that would provide continuity and stability for the legislative process.

In December 1816, the Senate received President James Madison's annual State of the Union message. Virginia Senator James Barbour proposed that instead of creating a host of special committees to address each provision of the message, standing committees be appointed. On December 10 the Senate adopted Barbour's proposal; within the week, the first permanent committee appointments were made, establishing a committee system that continues today.

Facing page, photograph of the U.S. Capitol, attributed to John Plumbe, Jr., taken about 1846

Henry Clay of Kentucky, *right*, and his nemesis,
John Randolph of Virginia, *left*

1826
APRIL 8

John Randolph and Henry Clay Fight a Duel

On April 8, 1826, Virginia Senator John Randolph fought a duel with Henry Clay, the secretary of state and future senator from Kentucky.

Easily one of the most eccentric men ever to serve in the United States Senate, John Randolph was famous for his terrible temper and vitriolic tongue. In 1826, he outdid himself in an attack on President John Quincy Adams and Secretary of State Henry Clay, accusing them of political and personal corruption, and calling the two a combination of "the Puritan with the black-leg." Wounded by this sarcasm, the secretary of state challenged the Virginia senator to a duel—a form of combat to which politicians in those days too often resorted.

Late in the afternoon on April 8, the two men met on a dueling field in the Virginia countryside. Henry Clay was determined to go through with the deed, while John Randolph had come to regret his harsh words and the necessity of a duel. He told his second that he might not return fire, unless he saw "the Devil in Clay's eye." At first, Randolph's pistol misfired, but Clay called for a replacement. Then both men fired. Randolph's shot hit a stump behind Clay, while Clay's bullet passed through Randolph's flowing cloak. Clay fired a second shot, again penetrating Randolph's garment. Now, however, Randolph fired into the air and announced, "I do not fire at you, Mr. Clay."

With this gesture, the secretary of state concluded that his honor had been satisfied and came forward to greet his antagonist. "I trust in God, my dear sir, you are untouched," inquired Henry Clay. "You owe me a coat, Mr. Clay," said John Randolph. "I am glad the debt is no greater," the secretary of state responded.

1828
MAY 13

Senate Passes "Tariff of Abominations"

On May 13, 1828, the Senate passed the "Tariff of Abominations," a high-protective tariff that inflamed sectional passions and triggered a major constitutional crisis.

Tariff rates were tricky business. Manufacturing interests generally favored a higher tariff to raise the cost of imports and promote American manufactured goods; agricultural interests favored a lower tariff to promote cheaper imports and encourage overseas sales of their produce. Those representing agrarian interests in Congress thought they had found an ingenious solution. They would vote for the highest possible tariff rates—exactly the opposite of what they wanted. They believed President John Quincy Adams, who was sympathetic to the manufacturers, would be forced to veto the high tariff. He would then carry that stigma in his election campaign against Andrew Jackson.

But the high tariff passed and Adams signed it. The South was outraged, and some southerners began to talk of secession. It was the "Tariff of Abominations," as they called it, that prompted Vice President John C. Calhoun to write an anonymous pamphlet denouncing the tariff as unconstitutional and unjust, and declaring that the state legislatures had the power to refuse to enforce—or nullify—a federal law. When South Carolina adopted Calhoun's proposal, President Jackson hotly denied the right of nullification and threatened to send troops to uphold the tariff. The crisis was at last averted when Senator Henry Clay devised the Compromise Tariff of 1833, which removed some duties immediately and gradually lowered the rest. But the sectional angers thus aroused never completely disappeared in those tense decades before the Civil War.

The moral to this story, I suppose, is that senators should be careful of what they vote for, because they might actually get it.

1829
DECEMBER 7

The First Senate Page

When the Senate of the Twenty-first Congress convened on December 7, 1829, there was a new, very young face in the chamber. The youngster was the first Senate page, nine-year-old Grafton Hanson, grandson of Senate Sergeant at Arms Mountjoy Bayly.

The Senate had had older messengers ever since 1789, but it was not until Senator Daniel Webster of Massachusetts appointed Hanson that the tradition of employing young pages began. Hanson grew up in the Senate, serving it in a variety of jobs and leaving only in the 1840s to fight in the Mexican War, in which he was decorated for bravery. Hanson's affection for this institution has been shared by many pages. The second page, appointed by Webster in 1831, was twelve-year-old Isaac Bassett, who served the Senate for the rest of his life. For sixty-four years, from 1831 to 1895, from Presidents Jackson to Cleveland, from page to assistant doorkeeper, Bassett seldom missed a day.

The pages who served the Senate in the nineteenth century were expected to keep the inkwells and sand shakers filled, to light the gas lamps, and to keep the chamber's wood stoves burning. When messages needed to be delivered downtown, a page was dispatched on horseback. Once a week all pages were given tickets entitling—and expecting—them to bathe in the big marble bathtubs down in the Capitol basement.

While their duties have changed since the days when they wore blue knickers and jackets with shiny brass buttons, pages' attachment to this institution has remained constant. It is not surprising that several pages have returned as senators, representatives, or Senate officers. Our colleagues Senators David Pryor of Arkansas and Christopher Dodd of Connecticut began their careers on Capitol Hill as pages, as did Joe Stewart, our current secretary of the Senate.

I commend all current pages for the good work they are doing, even though we no longer have horses.

The Pages as Mock-Senators.

Senate pages imitating senators

1830
JANUARY 26

Webster's Reply to Hayne

On January 26, 1830, Daniel Webster rose in the old Senate chamber to deliver one of the most famous speeches in Senate history, and one of the greatest defenses of the American Union. On the previous day, Senator Robert Y. Hayne of South Carolina had delivered a speech in which he denounced a pending tariff bill as unconstitutional and suggested the superiority of the states over the federal government.

The next day, Senator Webster, defender of the tariff and the Union, responded with these emotion-laden words:

> When my eyes shall be turned to behold for the last time the sun in heaven, may I not see him shining on the broken and dishonored fragments of a once glorious Union; on states dissevered, discordant, belligerent; on a land rent with civil feuds, or drenched, as it may be, in fraternal blood! Let their last feeble and lingering glance rather behold the gorgeous ensign of the republic . . . bearing for its motto . . . Liberty and Union, now and forever, one and inseparable!

In the galleries sat Robert Scott, a Kentucky lawyer, who jotted down his eyewitness description of the scene:

> January 26, 1830. This morning a dense crowd of the most respectable gentlemen and ladies assembled, crowding the floor and galleries. They listened for two hours and a half to Mr. Webster, [who spoke with] the grandest and most interesting parliamentary eloquence which it has ever been my good fortune to hear. [He attacked] his antagonist with the most [clever] satire and cutting sarcasm, refuting his facts and subverting his arguments. . . . Mr. Webster concluded his speech with the most convincing argument and forcible eloquence. . . . [He] closed in appropriate and eloquent terms, [calling for] union, happiness, and glory for our common country.

Detail from George P.A. Healy's painting
Webster's Reply to Hayne

Alexis de Tocqueville Visits Congress

During the week of January 16, 1832, French aristocrat and social observer Alexis de Tocqueville visited Washington, met with President Andrew Jackson, and attended sessions of Congress. Following his extended tour of the United States, de Tocqueville produced a highly influential survey of his impressions regarding the operation of this nation's democratic institutions. His *Democracy in America*, first published in 1835, remains a classic today. The work is routinely quoted in historical studies of Congress for its author's views on the differences between the Senate and the House. Addressing that subject, he wrote:

On entering the House of Representatives at Washington, one is struck by the vulgar demeanor of that great assembly. Often there is not a distinguished man in the whole number. Its members are almost all obscure individuals, whose names bring no associations to mind. They are mostly village lawyers, men in trade, or even persons belonging to the lower classes of society. In a country in which education is very general, it is said that the representatives of the people do not always know how to write correctly.

By contrast, de Tocqueville—whose aristocratic views could hardly be considered objective—saw the Senate in a decidedly more positive light. Impressed with senators because they were elected by state legislatures rather than by the people directly, he observed:

At a few yards' distance [from the House chamber] is the door of the Senate, which contains within a small space a large proportion of the celebrated men of America. Scarcely an individual is to be seen in it who has not had an active and illustrious career. The Senate is composed of eloquent advocates, distinguished generals, wise magistrates, and statesmen of note, whose arguments would do honor to the most remarkable parliamentary debates of Europe.

Thomas Hart Benton, a veteran of thirty years in the Senate, in 1854 dismissed this evaluation, arguing that the best senators of his day had earlier served in the House and thus owed their selection directly to the people.

Alexis de Tocqueville

The Senate Rejects a King's Decision

On June 23, 1832, the Senate rejected a decision by the king of the Netherlands, who had been asked to arbitrate a longstanding dispute between the United States and Great Britain over the boundary of Maine.

The Maine boundary dispute had grown out of ambiguities in the terms of the 1783 Treaty of Paris, which ended the Revolutionary War. In essence, England wanted a military road on British soil that would link the cities of Montreal and Quebec with St. John and Halifax. The trouble was that the road would cross seven million acres of land claimed by the United States. Diplomats had failed to settle the matter in 1815, during negotiation of the Treaty of Ghent which ended the War of 1812. Finally, in 1827,

Great Britain and the United States had agreed to submit the question to arbitration by the king of the Netherlands.

In 1831, the royal arbitrator decided on a compromise that evenly divided the disputed territory. Britain declared itself satisfied. President Andrew Jackson also was willing to accept the terms, but the citizens of Maine were not. Expecting to get much more than was awarded them, they protested vehemently. In June 1832, the Senate responded to the outcry from Maine, narrowly rejecting the king's decision by a vote of 20 to 21.

After the Senate's action, the matter of the Maine boundary festered for another decade. In the end, Maine would have gained more acreage had it accepted the king's solution. The terms of the Webster-Ashburton Treaty of 1842, which ultimately settled the matter, were less generous to the state of Maine than the king of the Netherlands had been.

William I, king of the Netherlands

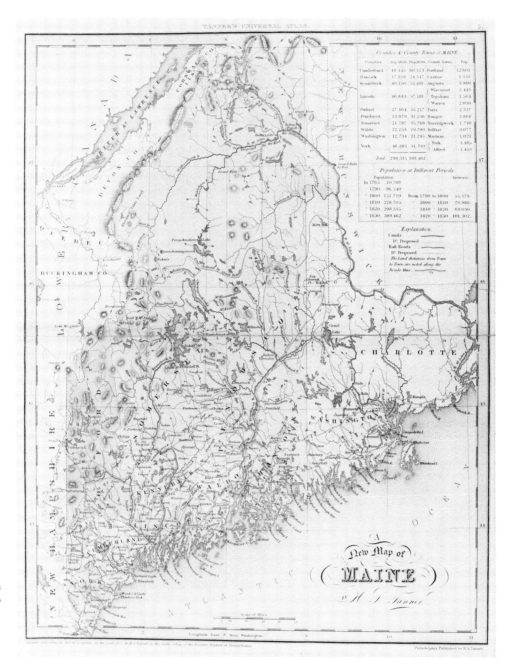

A map of the state of Maine
published in 1833

Charles Carroll Dies

On November 14, 1832, Charles Carroll, one of the first United States senators and a signer of the Declaration of Independence, died in Baltimore. Born in 1737, he was educated in Europe, and he returned to Maryland in 1765 to take over operation of a ten thousand-acre family estate. Banned from political activity in Maryland due to his Roman Catholic faith, Carroll nonetheless was drawn into the ranks of those defending American resistance to British taxation. His articulate writings in support of the colonial cause earned him a prominent place among the public figures of his day. In 1776 he and Benjamin Franklin were members of a delegation sent to convince Canada to enter the Revolutionary War on the American side. Following the failure of that mission, Carroll was elected to the Continental Congress on July 4, 1776. He arrived in Philadelphia just in time to sign the Declaration of Independence.

In 1777 Charles Carroll began a twenty-three-year career in the Maryland state senate. While there, he also served several one-year terms in the Continental Congress. Late in 1788, the Maryland legislature elected him as one of that state's first two U.S. senators.

For the next three and a half years, Carroll served simultaneously in the Maryland Senate and in the U.S. Senate. When the state legislature passed a law prohibiting such dual service, Carroll chose to resign from the U.S. Senate. His decision to serve at the state level reflected a common attitude among U.S. senators of his era, who found public service close to home a great deal more rewarding than that in the nation's capital (then located in New York and Philadelphia). During the Senate's first decade, members' average service amounted to less than five years.

At the time of his death in 1832, the ninety-five-year-old Carroll was the wealthiest man in America and the last surviving signer of the Declaration of Independence.

Charles Carroll of
Carrollton, Maryland

1833
DECEMBER 2

One Senate Seat—Two Duly Elected Claimants

On December 2, 1833, the Senate faced an extraordinary situation. For the first time in the Senate's nearly half-century of existence, two newly elected members arrived in the Senate chamber to claim the same seat. Asher Robbins and Elisha Potter each possessed properly validated credentials as a senator from Rhode Island.

In January 1833 the Rhode Island legislature had reelected Robbins to a second full term, and the governor issued him the appropriate election credentials for the Twenty-third Congress. Although the term of that Congress began on March 4, 1833, it was not actually scheduled to convene until December 2.

During 1833, political shifts in Rhode Island brought a new state legislature to power. In October that body declared Robbins' earlier election void and elected Elisha Potter in his place. When the Senate met on December 2, Robbins reached the chamber first, presented his credentials, and was administered the oath of office. When Potter appeared later in the day, the Senate referred the contest to a select committee.

After four months, the committee recommended that Robbins be declared the duly elected senator. The issue revolved around an interpretation of the Rhode Island constitution—a charter granted by King Charles II in 1663. Potter asserted that, under that instrument, the term of the legislature had expired by the time it elected Robbins. Robbins, for his part, argued that he was elected by a legitimate legislature, for the 170-year-old charter intended that the previous legislature remain in power until elections for its successor had been completed.

Debate dragged on until May 1834, when the Senate voted in favor of Robbins. In so doing, the Senate established a precedent that it would henceforth seat the first individual presenting valid credentials. Credentials of subsequent claimants would be referred to committee for study.

1833
DECEMBER 11

Fight Over Executive Privilege

On December 11, 1833, a great constitutional issue was brewing as the United States Senate challenged President Andrew Jackson over what we now call "executive privilege."

The Senate and the president were locked in combat over Jackson's refusal to recharter the Bank of the United States. Prominent Whigs like Henry Clay, Daniel Webster, and John C. Calhoun supported the bank but had been unable to override the president's veto. Nevertheless, when the Jackson administration began withdrawing federal funds from the bank, the Senate demanded to see the paper he had read to his cabinet on this issue. On December 11, 1833, the Senate voted 23 to 18 in favor of Senator Henry Clay's resolution that the president turn over this document.

The following day, the Senate received this message from President Jackson: "The Executive is a co-ordinate and independent branch of the Government equally with the Senate, and I have yet to learn under what constitutional authority that branch of the Legislature has a right to require of me an account of any communication, either verbally or in writing, made to the heads of departments acting as a cabinet council."

This marked the first time that a president had denied records that Congress requested. An outraged Senate then censured President Andrew Jackson, but they could not make the iron-willed chief executive back down. Jackson, of course, continued to provide Congress with information on other executive branch activities and initiatives and pledged his willingness to explain his policies to the American people. But the stand he took has enabled his successors to insist that their conversations with cabinet members are privileged.

1834
MAY 7

Senate Refuses to Print President's Message

On May 7, 1834, the Senate voted to reject a message from the president of the United States. That action occurred several weeks after the Whig-controlled body took the unprecedented step of censuring Democratic President Andrew Jackson for his refusal to support recharter of the Bank of the United States.

Jackson responded to his censure with a message to the Senate denying its power to take such an action. He wrote: "Without notice, unheard and untried, I thus find myself charged on the records of the Senate, and in a form hitherto unknown in our history, with the high crime of violating the laws and Constitution of my country." The president requested that the Senate accept his "solemn protest" against its censure proceedings.

The Senate, following heated discussions, agreed, by a party-line vote, to the following four motions:

1) *Resolved,* that the protest communicated to the Senate, . . . by the president of the United States asserts powers as belonging to the president which are inconsistent with the just authority of the two houses of Congress, and inconsistent with the Constitution of the United States. 2) That while the Senate is, and ever will be, ready to receive from the president all such messages and communications as the Constitution and laws, and the usual course of public business, authorize him to transmit to it, yet it cannot recognize any right in him to make a formal protest against votes and proceedings of the Senate, declaring such votes and proceedings to be illegal and unconstitutional, and requesting the Senate to enter such a protest on its journals. 3) The aforesaid protest is a breach of the privileges of the Senate, and it [will] not be entered on the journal. 4) That the president of the United States has no right to send a protest to the Senate against any of its proceedings.

1834
JUNE 24

Senate Rejects Roger Taney as Treasury Secretary

On June 24, 1834, the United States Senate for the first time rejected the nomination of a cabinet secretary. Since then, the full Senate has turned down only eight other cabinet nominees.

President Andrew Jackson, during his struggle with the Senate over the Bank of the United States, had nominated Roger B. Taney in September 1833 to be secretary of the treasury. The previous year, Jackson had vetoed a bill to renew the bank's charter. He was determined to remove all federal funds from what he considered an unconstitutional and aristocratic institution. When two treasury secretaries refused to withdraw funds from the bank, Jackson decided to give the job to his attorney general, Roger Taney.

Taney served nine months as a recess appointment, carrying out Jackson's wishes by removing government funds and depositing them in various state banks. When the Senate returned to session, a coalition of National Republicans and independents outnumbered the Jacksonian Democrats by a margin of 28 to 20. Senator Henry Clay, a leader of that opposition, introduced resolutions requiring federal funds to be restored to the bank and, in March, the Senate voted to censure Jackson for his bank policies. Under those circumstances, it was inevitable that the Senate would also reject Taney, as it did by a vote of 28 to 18 on June 24. Jackson reluctantly replaced Taney with former Senator Levi Woodbury.

Less than two years later, however, President Jackson had the satisfaction of seeing the Senate vote to confirm Roger B. Taney for another post. Restored to Democratic control, the Senate consented to Taney's appointment as chief justice of the United States. Taney served as chief justice until his death, twenty-eight years later.

Roger Taney as chief justice

Senator Accused in Plot to Assassinate President

On January 30, 1835, as President Andrew Jackson walked through the Rotunda of the Capitol, two pistols snapped in quick succession, but neither gun discharged. Bystanders quickly grabbed the gunman, Richard Lawrence, who was subsequently judged to be insane. This incident was the first attempt upon the life of a president, and it highlights the venomous partisan and personal hatreds engendered by the political struggles of the late 1820s and 1830s.

President Jackson's detractors immediately labeled the incident a publicity ploy staged to win sympathy for Old Hickory. His friends countered by circulating rumors of a conspiracy to kill the president. Jackson himself charged that a U.S. senator was involved in the plot. Jackson and Senator George Poindexter of Mississippi, both veterans of the War of 1812, had once been good friends. By 1830, however, a dispute over political patronage destroyed that friendship. Failing to get his man appointed, the outraged Poindexter broke with Jackson, and his hatred of the president became palpable.

Once considered a genius, Poindexter had degenerated into a profligate. He denied paternity of his children and plunged into a life of reckless dissipation. Nevertheless, Poindexter was clearly innocent of plotting against the president. He asked the Senate to appoint a special committee to investigate the rumors linking him with the would-be assassin. After three days of hearings, the committee unanimously exonerated him of all suspicion. Every senator on the floor voted to accept the report, ending a most regrettable incident in both Jackson's and Poindexter's lives.

Thomas Hart Benton portrayed as a beetle carrying the burden of the expunging resolution

1837
JANUARY 16

Senate Reverses Censure of President

On January 16, 1837, the Senate voted to expunge from its *Journal* a resolution of censure against the president. Three years earlier, this body administered an unprecedented rebuke to President Andrew Jackson in a resolution declaring that he had "assumed upon himself authority and power not conferred by the Constitution and the laws, but in derogation of both."

This conflict began in 1832 when the chief executive vetoed legislation to renew the federal charter of the Bank of the United States. Since 1816, this private financial institution had exercised exclusive control over the government's deposits. Jackson and his Senate supporters, led by Missouri Democrat Thomas Hart Benton, argued that the bank was unconstitutional. They also believed that it aided commercial interests in the Northeast at the expense of the rest of the nation. After Jackson defeated Henry Clay, a strong bank ally, in the 1832 presidential election, he withdrew government funds from the bank. Subsequently, Jackson refused a Senate request for bank-related documents that he considered privileged. This prompted the Senate's anti-administration majority in 1834 to censure the president.

Senator Benton worked tirelessly over the next three years to have this blot removed from Jackson's record. Finally, on January 16, 1837, as the ailing president was preparing to leave office, the Democrats, with a new majority in the Senate, achieved Benton's wish. By a vote of 24 to 19, the Senate directed its secretary to draw heavy black lines around the censure notation in its 1834 *Journal*. The Democrats thrilled to their great symbolic victory, while Henry Clay, dressed in black to mourn the Constitution, concluded, "The Senate is no longer a place for any decent man."

1841
JUNE 21

First Extended Filibuster

On June 21, 1841, the Senate began its first extended filibuster. To be sure, this was not the first occasion for the use of dilatory tactics in the Senate. In 1789, the first year of the Senate's existence, such methods were employed by those opposed to locating the nation's permanent capital along the Susquehanna River. Again, in 1825, after listening to Senator John Randolph speak for more than thirty minutes, an editor reported that he "had been told that the bankrupt bill was before the Senate—but, during the time stated, he [Randolph] never mentioned, or even remotely alluded to it, or any of its parts, in any manner whatsoever." In fact, dilatory debate was frequent enough that by 1840 Henry Clay of Kentucky urged adoption of a rule that would allow a simple majority to bring debate to a close. Filibustering as a legislative tactic was not openly acknowledged until 1841, when Democrats and Whigs "squared off" over the establishment of a national bank.

Since the mid-1830s, Whigs in the Senate had strongly pressed for bank legislation, but Democratic presidents Andrew Jackson and Martin Van Buren had blocked any hope of success. When the Whig-supported John

Tyler rose to the presidency in 1841, Clay and his supporters sought passage of a measure that would centralize the nation's banking operations. A Select Committee on Currency, which Clay chaired, reported such a bill to the Senate on June 21.

Although the Whigs had a seven-vote majority over the Democrats, a coalition of states' rights Whigs and antibank Democrats decided to discuss the bill at length. When John C. Calhoun objected to Clay's attempts to exercise iron control over Senate proceedings, Clay indignantly vowed to ram through a provision for majority cloture. The opposition countered with the Senate's first acknowledged filibuster, which lasted fourteen days and resulted in the defeat of Clay's bill.

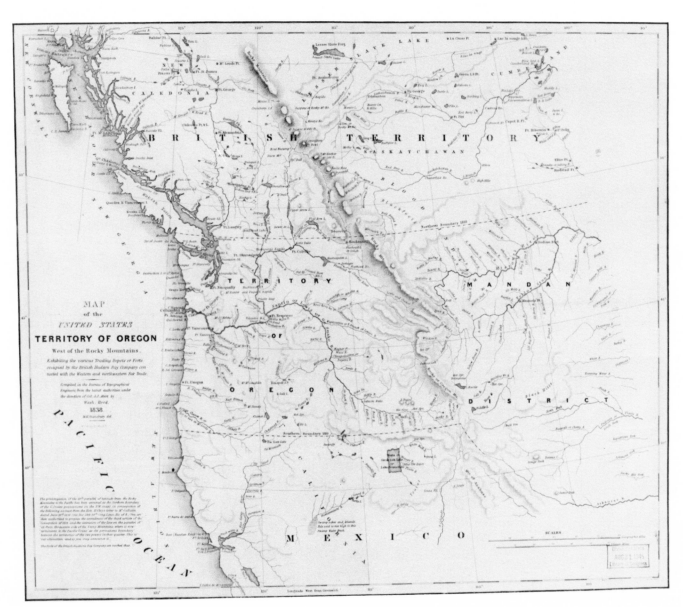

A map of the Oregon Territory

Senator Promotes Settlement of Oregon

On December 16, 1841, Senator Lewis Linn, a Missouri Democrat, introduced a bill providing for settlement of the Oregon Territory. For this action and his related unyielding efforts on behalf of American expansion, the states of Kansas, Missouri, Iowa, and Oregon each subsequently honored Senator Linn with the establishment of a Linn County. Few senators, apart from the likes of Clay, Webster, and Calhoun, have been so memorialized.

As a Missourian, Senator Linn had a particular interest in promoting settlement of Oregon. St. Louis and Independence served as the usual jumping-off points for pioneers headed west, and among those who made the journey were many of his constituents. What made his legislation of particular interest was its provision for a grant of 640 acres of land to each white male inhabitant of the territory over the age of eighteen who would cultivate the land for five consecutive years.

Under an 1818 agreement, the United States and Great Britain jointly occupied the Oregon Territory. By the late 1830s, members of the Senate were coming under increased pressure from anxious settlers to establish military occupation and a territorial government in Oregon, or risk losing it to the British. Supporters of settlement, led by Senator Linn, distributed at government expense survey reports that described fertile valleys, easy travel conditions, and a lucrative trade in furs, timber, and fisheries.

In February 1843, the Senate passed the Linn bill by a two-vote margin. Although the measure subsequently failed in the House, it triggered an extensive migration that year. The Oregon territorial boundary was finally settled by treaty with the British in 1846. The land donation provision Linn devised attracted great attention throughout the western states and became the basis of later federal land policy, culminating in the 1862 Homestead Act.

Lewis L. Linn of Missouri

1842
MARCH 31

Henry Clay Quits the Senate

When we think of the Senate's early years, we conjure up images of fiery oratory and impassioned debate. One such memorable event occurred on March 31, 1842. The occasion was Senator Henry Clay's retirement from the Senate, bringing to a close, at least for the time being, a congressional career that had spanned nearly forty years.

Henry Clay chose to leave the Senate for several reasons. The sixty-three-year-old senator had been suffering from poor health—both physically and financially. His relations with long-time rivals John C. Calhoun and Daniel Webster had become unusually acrimonious. Two years earlier, he had been passed over for the Whig party's presidential nomination and he was determined, as that party's most prominent leader, to consolidate his leadership, unite his party, and plan his 1844 presidential campaign from the comfort and security of his estate at Lexington, Kentucky.

One biographer has called Clay's valedictory address "an epoch in the history of the Republic." "At the time of my entry into this body, which took place in December 1806," Clay began in a voice trembling with emotion:

I regarded it, and still regard it, as a body which may be compared, without disadvantage, to any of a similar character which has existed in ancient or modern times. . . . And now, in retiring, I beg leave to deposit with it my fervent wishes, that all the great and patriotic objects for which it was instituted, may be accomplished—that the destiny designed for it by the framers of the Constitution may be fulfilled—that the deliberations, now and hereafter, in which it may engage for the good of our common country, may eventuate in the restoration of its prosperity, and in the preservation and maintenance of her honor abroad, and her best interests at home.

When Clay concluded, Calhoun—tears streaming down his face—silently crossed the chamber, and the two adversaries embraced. Clay's retirement proved to be premature, for he returned in 1849 and served until his death in 1852.

Facing page:
Henry Clay of Kentucky by
John Neagle

87

Senate Rejects a Cabinet Nominee Three Times

It is a very rare occasion when the Senate rejects a cabinet nomination, but on March 3, 1843 the Senate turned down a cabinet nominee—not just once—but three times.

What precipitated such a senatorial rebuke? Essentially, the Whig-dominated Senate was at loggerheads with the independent-minded president, John Tyler. Tyler, a Democrat turned Whig, was the first vice president to succeed to the presidency upon the death of a president. In the White House, he vetoed much of the Whigs' legislative program and won the party's enmity.

On the night of March 3, 1843, Tyler came to the Capitol to sign legislation and submit last-minute nominations at the end of the Twenty-seventh Congress. For his secretary of the treasury, the president nominated Representative Caleb Cushing of Massachusetts. Although a Whig, Cushing had been sharply critical of Senate Whigs and a strong supporter of President Tyler. Liking neither the president nor his nominee, the Senate rejected Cushing by a vote of 19 to 27.

President Tyler was so outraged by the Senate's action that he sent his secretary back into the chamber with a notice that he had renominated Cushing for the same post. What the president hoped to accomplish is hard to fathom, for the second vote went even more heavily against him. This time, Cushing lost by a 10 to 27 vote. This defeat further inflamed the president's anger, and he returned Cushing's nomination for a third time, only to lose by an embarrassing 2 to 29. At last, even Tyler had to bow to the inevitable and nominate another candidate.

Caleb Cushing was the second cabinet nominee ever rejected for confirmation; since 1843 the Senate has turned down only seven others.

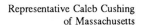

Representative Caleb Cushing
of Massachusetts

Samuel Morse with his telegraph

1844
MAY 24

The Senate and the Telegraph

Over the years, the United States Senate has served as a forum for the unveiling of new ideas, programs, and even inventions. One notable debut of a significant invention occurred on May 24, 1844, when Professor Samuel F.B. Morse successfully tested his "magneto-telegraph" from a ground-floor room in the Senate wing of the Capitol.

Morse had first tested the telegraph from one end of the Capitol Building to the other, sending senators from one terminal to the other and using the machine to announce their arrival in advance. But to prove that his invention was more than a parlor game, he needed to test it over a longer distance. With the help of a thirty-thousand-dollar congressional appropriation, Morse had wires strung forty-four miles, along the railroad tracks that ran from Washington to Baltimore.

On the appointed day, he invited senators and representatives to be present as he transmitted the first message over the telegraph. We all remember from our history books Morse's famous message that day, "What hath God wrought!" What we may not remember is the message that returned from Baltimore. There the Democrats were holding their national convention, and operators in Baltimore immediately began relaying the latest convention news.

The assembled politicians in Washington were fascinated to hear that the convention nominated for president the first "darkhorse" candidate, former House Speaker James K. Polk. For vice president the convention chose Senator Silas Wright. Professor Morse telegraphed back to Baltimore, "Mr. Wright is here and says . . . that he cannot accept the nomination." But the convention did not trust the new invention and again sent its message. Again, Wright declined. It was not until he sent a handwritten letter, by a special messenger on horseback, that the convention accepted his refusal and nominated former Senator George M. Dallas.

1844
JUNE 8

Senate Rejects Texas Treaty

On June 8, 1844, the Senate rejected a treaty that would have annexed Texas into the Union. It seems strange to us now that the Senate would reject such a vast and desirable territory, but there were good reasons at the time.

Texas won its independence from Mexico in 1836 and offered to join the United States. But several problems stood in the way: Texas and Mexico disputed their mutual border; Mexican President Santa Anna had let it be known that he would view annexation of Texas as an act of war; and abolitionists feared that Texas' territory would be split into five states, thus tipping the carefully preserved balance in the Senate in favor of slaveholding states.

Nevertheless, Secretary of State John C. Calhoun negotiated a treaty of annexation with the Republic of Texas, which he submitted to the Senate on April 22, 1844. Calhoun warned that annexation was necessary to prevent Great Britain from using its commercial position in Texas to persuade

An 1844 cartoon reflecting the heated debate over the annexation of Texas

Texans to abolish slavery. Abolitionists cited Calhoun's arguments as proof of their suspicion that Texas annexation was really a slaveholders' plot.

Missouri's Senator Thomas Hart Benton sought a compromise. He offered a resolution that would have annexed Texas only if the disputed territory on the Rio Grande was left to Mexico and if the remainder was equally divided between slaveholding and nonslaveholding regions. To admit Texas otherwise would only provoke a war with Mexico and stimulate a sectional struggle that could lead to an American civil war. When Benton's motion lost by a narrow margin, Benton and six other Democrats joined all of the Senate's Whigs to defeat the treaty, 16 to 35. Two years later, Texas won admission to the Union, but the consequences were exactly as Senator Benton had warned.

1845
MARCH 20

Executive Session Adjourns

On March 20, 1845, the Senate approved the nomination of Frederick T. Bush as consul to the port of Hong Kong and then adjourned. This ended a session that lasted only twelve days. Aside from brief *Journal* entries outlining Senate activities, no record of that session's secret proceedings exists. At the other end of the Capitol, dust gathered in the House chamber, and its members were not expected in town until December.

Why did this session conclude so quickly? Why was it held in secret? Where was the House? These questions, reasonable to us today, would not have occurred to mid-nineteenth century senators.

An answer lies with procedures established at the time the Constitution was adopted and ratified. Under the Constitution, Congress was required to meet at least once a year on the first Monday in December, although members' terms began on the previous March 4. The Constitution also gave the Senate the unique power to advise and consent to presidential nominations.

These constitutional requirements help explain what the Senate was doing in town for that brief session in March 1845. The term of President James K. Polk started on March 4. On that date, the president submitted his cabinet nominations to the Senate for action.

To exercise these constitutional responsibilities, the Senate customarily met for a few days at the start of each new presidential term, while the House could wait until December to convene. Under procedures in effect from 1789 until 1929, the Senate conducted all of its so-called executive business behind closed doors, allowing its members to speak freely to avoid incurring presidential wrath for opposing certain nominees. Between 1789 and 1933, the Senate held thirty-six of these special sessions. Ratification of the Constitution's Twentieth Amendment made them unnecessary, for it moved the beginning of the congressional term from December back to January, more than two weeks before the start of the presidential term.

1846
MAY 12

Senate Votes to Go to War with Mexico

On May 12, 1846, the Senate voted, 40 to 2, to declare war on Mexico.

One day earlier, President James K. Polk had reported to Congress that Mexican troops had crossed the Rio Grande into territory claimed by both nations and had attacked a small detachment of U.S. cavalry, killing eleven and capturing the rest. Polk charged that, by this action, Mexico had "shed American blood on the American soil. War exists by the act of Mexico herself." The House responded immediately, voting 174 to 14 to declare war and authorizing a ten-million-dollar appropriation and a call for fifty thousand volunteers to fight the war.

Many northerners opposed war with Mexico, believing that the South was promoting the war to seize more territory for the spread of slavery. Ironically, the chief opponent of the war in the Senate was the South's leading spokesman, South Carolina's John C. Calhoun. Calhoun was troubled by the president's message and did his best to slow down the rush toward war. He objected to the declaration's preamble, which stated that war already existed, on the constitutional grounds that only Congress could declare war. On May 12, when both the Foreign Relations and Military Affairs committees favorably reported the war bill, Calhoun and a few Whigs led the opposition during the floor debate. The government's haste had plunged him into "a state of wonder and deep alarm," Calhoun said. He feared that future presidents would follow Polk's actions in similarly forcing Congress into a declaration of war; that the nation was unprepared militarily to fight; and that war with Mexico would adversely affect America's relations with other nations. But President Polk clearly had the votes on his side. When the vote came, only two senators voted no, while Calhoun and a few others abstained.

1847
DECEMBER 24

Senator John Fairfield Dies

The Senate, throughout its history, has customarily found itself in session during the winter holiday season, a time when members would rather be with their loved ones. On December 24, 1847, freshman Maine Senator John Fairfield, a man of exceptional promise, died suddenly. His unexpected death as a consequence of a minor operation was apparently due to the bungling or quackery of the surgeon.

Back in Maine, his family, to whom he was devoted, was unaware of this sad turn of events. On Christmas Eve, his wife and children eagerly awaited his arrival. Among the senator's chief legacies to us today are the warm, almost daily letters he sent home to his family from the time he first arrived in Washington as a representative in 1835. These letters, in their published form, contribute greatly to our knowledge of Washington life in the 1830s and 1840s. From them we learn that Fairfield experienced particular frustration at being separated from his family throughout the legislative year. After his struggles to find a reasonably priced boardinghouse in the capital, he

John Fairfield of Maine

wrote his wife, "I had no idea before being put to the trial how hard it would be for me to quit you and ours." He had barely arrived in Washington as a new member when news reached him of the early birth of his third son, and he wrote his wife of his sorrow at not being by her side.

Fairfield was born in Maine in 1797. After attending Bowdoin College, he embarked on a promising legal career. Twice elected to the House, he resigned in 1838 to become governor of Maine. He resigned that position in 1843 to become a senator. At the time of his death, the Maine senator was being watched closely by the senior members of his party as a potential leader. Fairfield had written movingly of his colleagues who died in office, and he attended each funeral. Now it was his colleagues' turn to inform Mrs. Fairfield of her husband's untimely death in office at the age of fifty.

1848
MARCH 10

Senate Approves Treaty of Guadalupe-Hidalgo

On March 10, 1848, the United States Senate approved one of the most significant treaties in our nation's history. The Treaty of Guadalupe-Hidalgo terminated the war with Mexico, which had begun in 1846 with a dispute over the border between Texas and Mexico, and which had ended with the American occupation of Mexico City.

Following the American victory, Mexico agreed, for the sum of fifteen million dollars and repayment of three million dollars in its debts, to cede to the United States 600,000 square miles of territory. This vast territory, comparable only to the Louisiana purchase, included all of the present-day states of California, Arizona, New Mexico, Nevada, Utah, and Colorado, as well as recognition of Texas' border at the Rio Grande River.

Despite the immense advantages of this treaty, some senators thought it could be improved and offered numerous amendments when the pact reached the Senate. These amendments ranged from a proposal to disavow so much annexation of new territory to one that would move the boundary even further south into Mexico. Amendments to ban slavery from the new territories were also introduced. The Senate rejected most of these amendments and also removed two articles in the treaty, relating to the validity of Mexican land grants and the rights of the Catholic Church in the acquired territories. With these adjustments, the Senate consented to the treaty by a vote of 38 to 14.

Adoption of the treaty of Guadalupe-Hidalgo launched a whole new chapter in the history of the American West. It also confronted Congress and the nation with the unresolved question of whether the new territory would be free or would be open to slavery. The settlement of this question would require another decade of debate and a bloody civil war.

1848
MARCH 26

The Senate Arrests a Reporter

In March 1848 the Senate approved the Treaty of Guadalupe-Hidalgo, ending the war with Mexico. Just two weeks after that vote, the Senate appointed a select committee to investigate how the *New York Herald* had obtained and published a copy of the treaty, since the Senate had not yet lifted its injunction of secrecy.

The committee called the *Herald*'s Washington correspondent, John Nugent, to testify. Nugent swore that no senator, member of a senator's family, or officer of the Senate had given him the treaty. In fact, historians suspect that the leaker was Secretary of State James Buchanan, who was anxious for the treaty to be published. As for Nugent, he regarded publication of the treaty as proper and felt himself under no obligation to name his source. The committee felt otherwise and placed Nugent under arrest until

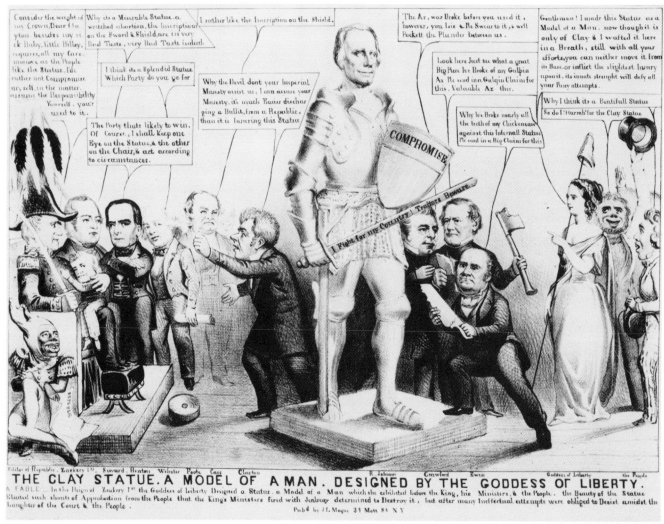

A depiction of the conflict over Clay's compromise

he would answer their questions. During the month from March 27 to April 28, 1848, Nugent was held in a Capitol committee room and occasionally brought before the Senate as a whole to answer questions. "I do not object to that question on the grounds that it will [in]criminate me," he replied at one point. "I consider myself in honor bound not to answer it."

While a Capitol Hill prisoner, Nugent continued to send dispatches to the *New York Herald*. At the same time, the *Herald* ran regular editorials denouncing the senatorial imprisonment of its reporter. Nugent apparently did not suffer terribly. During the day, his committee room was a comfortable cell, and at night the sergeant at arms took him home for a good night's sleep. At last, as the session drew to a close, the Senate released an unrepentant John Nugent from captivity. No amount of intimidation, they discovered, would force a reporter to divulge his sources.

1850
JANUARY 29

Henry Clay and the Compromise of 1850

On January 29, 1850, in the old crimson and gilt Senate chamber, seventy-three-year-old Henry Clay, "weak in body but strong in spirit," arose to deliver one of the greatest speeches of his career. His colleagues, even his enemies, were held in the spell of his personal magnetism. On this occasion, Clay enlisted the spirit of George Washington to his cause. Lest the power of words alone fail to move his audience, he struck an impressive, if macabre, note by exhibiting a fragment of Washington's coffin. Adding to the drama on that day, was the fact that all knew the aging Clay—Harry of the West, the Kentucky Hotspur, the Great Pacificator, the Old Prince—was dying, and that this would very likely be his last crusade.

What cause drew Clay out of retirement in Kentucky? He had already delivered a stirring valedictory in the Senate chamber in 1842. Besides having been a senator on three separate occasions beginning in 1806, he had been a representative, Speaker of the House, secretary of state, and perennial Whig presidential candidate. Clay, the Great Compromiser, one of the masterminds of the Missouri Compromise of 1820–1821, came out of retirement in a desperate attempt to save the nation from the disaster of disunion. Beginning with his speech on January 29, 1850, Clay introduced the complex series of resolutions that became known as the Compromise of 1850. Clay hoped that the measures he espoused, which were largely adopted, would settle the sectional struggle threatening disunion. He died in Washington in June 1852 believing they had.

Daniel Webster Speaks for the Union

On March 7, 1850, one of the most famous speeches in the nation's history was delivered on the Senate floor. During the dramatic debates that took place in 1850 over the issues of slavery and secession, Senator Daniel Webster of Massachusetts eloquently responded to the classical southern argument advocated by Senator John C. Calhoun of South Carolina. Calhoun, who felt states existed as sovereign entities within the Union, contended that southern states had the right to uphold the institution of slavery. Webster, although he was morally opposed to slavery, felt a strong obligation to preserve the Union at any cost, even if this meant forsaking abolitionism. Persuaded by his old rival, Senator Henry Clay of Kentucky, Webster decided to argue on behalf of a compromise that might appease both the North and the South.

Generations of Americans have memorized portions of Webster's stirring speech, particularly its opening lines:

Mr. President—I wish to speak today not as a Massachusetts man, nor as a Northern man, but as an American, and a member of the Senate of the United States. . . . I have a part to act, not for my own security and safety, for I am looking out for no fragment upon which to float away from the wreck, if wreck there must be, but for the good of the whole, and the preservation of all. . . . I speak today for the preservation of the Union: "Hear me for my cause."

Webster's Seventh of March speech caused an uproar among New England abolitionists, free-soilers and reformers. They felt betrayed by their spokesman, whom they had admired as a god. Likewise, southern secessionists viewed Webster's and Clay's compromise as abhorrent. Eleven years later, the Union, whose preservation Webster had so eloquently advocated in his speech, was at war.

A detail from *Daniel Webster Addressing the U.S. Senate on the Compromise Measures, March 7, 1850*

William Henry Seward
of New York

1850
MARCH 11

William Henry Seward's "Higher Law" Speech

In the emotion-charged decades that preceded the American Civil War, the Senate, with its even balance of northern and southern members, served as the principal arena for debate over the slavery issue. The theater-like setting of the old Senate chamber resounded to the powerful oratory of vigorous sectional spokesmen. By 1850, the recent invention of the telegraph and the development of a reliable shorthand reporting system made it possible to transmit these addresses rapidly to newspapers across the nation.

On March 11, 1850, William Henry Seward, a New York Whig serving his first year in the Senate, delivered a carefully prepared speech that instantly made him a national figure. Seward argued against any compromise that would permit slavery in the territories recently acquired in the war with Mexico. He accurately warned that the slave system would either be removed by "gradual voluntary effort, and with compensation," within the framework of the Union, or the Union would be thrown into a violent civil war that would lead to complete and immediate emancipation.

In a phrase that became forever associated with the substance of his dramatic speech, Seward declared, "There is a higher law than the Constitution which regulates our authority over the domain and devotes it to the same noble purposes." He argued that the Senate, in discharging its duties, must take into account not only its specific constitutional responsibilities, but a broader moral obligation as well. In this tension-filled climate, Seward's "higher law" address provided the spark that ignited a violent explosion. Proslavery forces immediately and incorrectly cast Seward as a dangerous radical who advocated lawlessness. In this controversy, the nation took another long step toward the disunion and war that Seward had predicted.

1850
MARCH 31

Death of John C. Calhoun

On April 1, 1850, Senator Andrew Butler of South Carolina entered the Senate chamber and, in a voice choked with emotion, announced the death of his colleague John C. Calhoun. Calhoun had died the day before, Sunday, March 31, at 7:30 a.m. His death came as no surprise—he had been failing for weeks and looked, said colleagues, like the specter of death himself. Still, the news was a blow.

Senator Butler praised Calhoun's life and accomplishments and noted that his name carried associations that "reached the heart of the Nation." Henry Clay of Kentucky rose next to laud his long-time adversary, declaring, "I have seen him surpassed by no one . . . I am his senior only in years." Daniel Webster of Massachusetts, who had vigorously attacked Calhoun's Fourth of March address less than a month before, followed Clay, saying, "We shall carry with us a deep sense of his honor and integrity, his amiable deportment in life, and the purity of his exalted patriotism."

While Webster paid tribute to his old foe Calhoun, Thomas Hart Benton of Missouri turned his back, refusing to listen. As a senior senator, Benton should have at least found a few words to utter about his long-time colleague. Webster even prodded him to do so. But Benton refused. He had said of Calhoun that his doctrines were treasonous and that he, Benton, "could make no distinction between the treason and the traitor." The day's business ended with the adoption of a resolution providing that each senator would wear a black armband for one month to mourn the death of a distinguished colleague.

The following day, April 2, funeral services for Calhoun were conducted in the Senate chamber. President Zachary Taylor attended, along with scores of government dignitaries. Among the pallbearers were Webster and Clay. Each had less than three years to live. With the death of John C. Calhoun, the Golden Age of the Senate began to fade.

1850
APRIL 17

Benton-Foote Confrontation

On April 17, 1850, a most dramatic confrontation took place on the floor of the old Senate chamber between Thomas Hart Benton of Missouri and Henry Foote of Mississippi. Both men were known for their violent tempers. Foote especially had a penchant for personal feuds. He took part in four duels, being wounded in three. During the previous session of the Senate, Foote had scuffled with Simon Cameron of Pennsylvania and promised John Hale of New Hampshire that he would "hang him from the highest tree if he ventured to set foot in Mississippi."

Throughout March 1850, debate raged in the chamber over Henry Clay's proposed compromise and its implications for the issue of slavery. During the debates, Foote went out of his way to annoy the aging Benton. On March 26, Foote directly challenged Benton and inquired whether Benton wished to "patch up his reputation for courage, now greatly on the wane."

The feud between the two senators reached a climax on April 17 when Benton attacked the doctrines of the late Senator John C. Calhoun, dead less than three weeks. Foote, a protégé of Calhoun's, leapt to his feet and charged that the "late, illustrious Senator from South Carolina" was being denounced by "a gentleman who . . ." Foote failed to finish as Benton advanced menacingly down the aisle toward him. Foote began to retreat and drew a pistol from his coat. Benton, who was being restrained by Henry Dodge of Wisconsin, pulled himself free and shouted: "I have no pistols. Let him fire. Stand out of the way. Let the assassin fire." Pandemonium broke loose in the chamber. Daniel Dickinson of New York took possession of the pistol, and Benton and Foote, still seething, were returned to their seats.

A special Senate committee later absolved Foote of "premeditated use of his weapons" but criticized the introduction of personal feuds into the Senate chamber.

An 1850 cartoon mocking the rivalry between Henry Foote of Mississippi and Thomas Hart Benton of Missouri

1850
APRIL 17

First Woman in the Senate Press Gallery

On April 17, 1850, the first woman reporter was admitted into the Senate press gallery.

Jane Gray Swisshelm, a fervent abolitionist, convinced editor Horace Greeley to publish her occasional letters from Washington in the *New York Tribune*. Once in Washington, she set about convincing Vice President Millard Fillmore to grant her access to the press gallery. The vice president thought this was a terrible idea. He warned her that she would find the company of the male reporters unpleasant and that her presence would attract excessive attention. But Mrs. Swisshelm had so set her mind on her objective that Millard Fillmore capitulated.

On April 17, Mrs. Swisshelm took her seat in the press gallery in the old Senate chamber, and she was not disappointed in the scene below. "If you had only been here to see!" she wrote back to editor Greeley. "Such a scene as our Senate Chamber did present an hour ago!" During the debate over the Compromise of 1850 that day, Mississippi Senator Henry S. Foote pulled a pistol to protect himself from the wrath of Missouri Senator Thomas Hart Benton. "Stand out of the way and let the assassin fire!" Benton had shouted melodramatically, before the two men were separated. "Here was all confusion," she wrote, "the President's [gavel] going but scarcely heard, the men in the gallery swearing, the members of the floor rushing up and calling all manner of order and disorder."

"I sat in the reporters' gallery, directly opposite the gentlemen," Mrs. Swisshelm recorded, "and saw it all." Although the press gallery largely remained a male bastion until the twentieth century, an increasing number of women journalists today follow in her path, sitting in the press galleries and seeing it all.

1850
JULY 22

Daniel Webster Resigns From the Senate

On July 22, 1850, Daniel Webster resigned from the Senate to become secretary of state in the cabinet of President Millard Fillmore. One of the most outstanding members in the body's entire history, Webster, the great orator, joined with Henry Clay, the brilliant tactician, and John C. Calhoun, the gifted theorist, to lead the Senate through its Golden Age.

Webster capped his thirty-seven-year public career amidst the bitter conflict that marked the tumultuous year of 1850. While the Senate was embroiled in the controversial slavery issue and the nation tottered on the brink of disunion, the Massachusetts senator did his best to restore peace and order. Beginning with his famous Seventh of March speech, he urged a compromise between southern and northern views. Webster emphasized the importance of maintaining the union between the states above and beyond any conflict that might threaten this sacred bond, such as slavery and possible secession.

As the debate raged, Webster's resonant voice could be heard echoing throughout the crimson and gold old Senate chamber. He said: "My object is peace [and] reconciliation. I am against local ideas, North and South, and against all local and narrow contests." The end of Webster's Senate career was brought about by the unexpected death of President Zachary Taylor on July 9, 1850, and by his decision to join the new president's cabinet. On July 22, in the final speech of his long career, Webster called earnestly for the end of the strife that had plagued the Senate and, in words that retain their rich meaning even today, he proclaimed: "I mean to stand upon the Constitution. I need no other platform. I shall know but one country. No man can suffer too much, and no man can fall too soon, if he suffer or if he fall in defense of the liberties and constitution of his country."

1852
JUNE 5

William R. King of Alabama

First Incumbent Senator Nominated for Vice President

On June 5, 1852, for the first time, an incumbent U.S. senator was chosen to run for the vice presidency. That man was Senator William R. King of Alabama. A former president pro tempore of the Senate, King ran as vice president in the election of 1852 on the Democratic ticket headed by Franklin Pierce.

On one hand, we might be surprised to find that national elections had been held for over sixty years without a senator running for vice president, but we should note that five former senators had previously run for vice president—a sixth, former Senator William A. Graham of North Carolina, was King's opponent in 1852. And several other senators had declined the honor.

Since King's nomination, twenty-four sitting U.S. senators have run for vice president on major and minor party tickets—twelve of these, including King, won their elections.

In recent times, it has become almost standard procedure to nominate a senator for vice president. From 1944 to 1988, in every election except one, at least one vice presidential candidate was an incumbent or a recently serving former senator. The sole exception occurred in 1984.

On several occasions, both major party vice presidential candidates were senators. This first happened in 1860, when Senator Hannibal Hamlin ran with Abraham Lincoln on the Republican ticket while Senator Joseph Lane ran with John C. Breckinridge for the Southern Democratic party. In 1928 the Republican majority leader of the Senate, Charles Curtis, ran for vice president against the Democratic minority leader of the Senate, Joe Robinson.

In 1952, Senators Richard Nixon and John Sparkman paired off against each other. In 1976, some of us recall when the vice presidential candidates were Senators Walter Mondale and Bob Dole. And, once again, in 1988, two senatorial contenders, Lloyd Bentsen and Dan Quayle, vied for the vice presidency.

An 1852 lithograph depicting the funeral procession of Henry Clay

1852
JUNE 29

Henry Clay Dies

On June 29, 1852, Senator Henry Clay died of tuberculosis at age seventy-five in Washington, DC.

As one biographer has written, "No man in American public life has had more ardent supporters or more bitter enemies than Clay, and no one has depended more for his happiness on the friendship of the people." Known by many as the "Great Compromiser," Clay played a prominent part in directing and influencing both domestic and foreign policy during his forty-six years of public service. Practicing law in his early years, Clay earned a reputation for being a spirited advocate and supporter of the West. The people of Kentucky embraced him early, and the state legislature elected him to the Senate at the age of twenty-nine. While beginning and ending his political career as a U.S. senator, he also served in the House—becoming speaker on the first day of his first term—and as secretary of state during the administration of John Quincy Adams.

Clay's impressive funeral reflected the nation's profound sorrow at his passing. It began as a simple procession from his hotel on Pennsylvania Avenue to the Capitol. Here, his coffin was carried into the old Senate chamber for a funeral service in the presence of the president, the vice president, the cabinet, and members of the Senate and House. Then his coffin was placed in the Capitol's Rotunda. Clay thus became the first American so honored. On July 2, his body was taken to Philadelphia where, after a torchlight parade, it lay in Independence Hall. His remains were then transported to five other major cities before burial in Lexington, Kentucky.

Six other Americans have lain in state in the Capitol Rotunda in tribute to their service as U.S. senators. They are Charles Sumner, John A. Logan, Robert Taft, Everett Dirksen, Hubert Humphrey, and Claude Pepper.

1853
MARCH 24

Vice President William King

On March 24, 1853, William Rufus de Vane King was sworn in as vice president of the United States. What makes this otherwise routine event significant is that he took his oath in Cuba. King is the only vice president to have been sworn in outside the United States, and it had taken a special act of Congress to authorize this unusual oath-taking.

William King was born in North Carolina in 1786. When he was just twenty-four years old, he was elected to the first of three terms in the House. In 1818, he moved to Alabama and immediately became active in politics there. When Alabama became a state in 1819, King was one of its first two senators. He was reelected in 1822, 1828, 1834, and 1840. King served in the Senate for twenty-five years, six of them as president pro tempore, before he resigned in 1844 to become minister to France. While in the Senate and even in France, King had pursued the Democratic vice presidential nomination, but it had always eluded him. King was again elected to the Senate in 1848.

In the summer of 1852, Democrats chose King as the running mate of Franklin Pierce, and the pair easily won election that fall. King resigned from the Senate in December and went to stay at a Cuban sugar plantation, hoping to seek relief from the tuberculosis that plagued him. When it became clear that King was too weak to return for the March 4, 1853, inauguration, the special act was passed permitting him to be sworn in where he was. After taking the oath, King was determined to go home to exercise the powers of the office he had sought for a decade and a half. Although very feeble, he left Cuba in early April and reached his plantation, "King's Bend," in Alabama on April 17. He died the next day.

1854
APRIL 25

Senate Approves the Gadsden Purchase

Throughout the nation's history, there have been notable occasions when a major shift in American priorities has become dramatically apparent in the deliberations of the U.S. Senate. One of these instances occurred on April 25, 1854, as the Senate reluctantly consented to the ratification of a treaty with Mexico.

During the previous decade, the nation had concentrated on the expansion of its empire. Between 1845 and 1848, the United States, by acquiring Texas, Oregon, California, and the Southwest, had virtually doubled its territory. There was talk in the early 1850s of annexing Canada, seizing Cuba, and planting an American colony in slaveholding Brazil.

Under the influence of this spirit of Manifest Destiny, President Franklin Pierce in 1853 authorized the U.S. minister to Mexico, James Gadsden, to buy as much Mexican territory as possible for fifty million dollars. A former president of a South Carolina railroad, Gadsden hoped to create a southern rail system that would run to the Pacific and securely tie the West to the South, ensuring the latter section's economic survival. Essential to this plan was the acquisition of a triangular section of land amounting to 54,000 acres adjacent to the U.S. border in northwestern Mexico.

The Senate heatedly debated the Gadsden Purchase treaty early in 1854. Free-state senators strongly opposed the pact, fearing it would provide more territory that might be opened to slavery. Initially, the Senate rejected the treaty. Approval came only after its supporters agreed to trim the land area to the minimum necessary for the railroad and to reduce the purchase price to ten million dollars. For the first time in history, the Senate had refused to accept land ceded to the United States—a major turning point, as the divisive issue of slavery curbed senators' appetites for further expansionist adventures.

Senate Passes Kansas-Nebraska Act

On May 3, 1854, the Senate passed a bill designed to settle a difficult sectional issue. The resulting law instead divided the nation even more deeply, pushed the United States closer to civil war, and inspired the creation of the Republican party.

Just four years after the Compromise of 1850 had attempted to solve the question of whether slavery would be permitted into the new western territories, Illinois Senator Stephen Douglas reopened the issue when he introduced the Kansas-Nebraska Act. As chairman of the Committee on Territories, and as a booster of Chicago as a central commercial and transportation depot, Douglas promoted the construction of a transcontinental railroad system. But before the railroad could be built the territories would have to be organized, and before the territories could be organized both the North and South would have to be satisfied that their interests were protected. How could slaveholding and antislavery interests be reconciled? Senator Douglas thought that he had found the answer in "popular sovereignty," letting the residents of the territories decide the issue for themselves rather than letting Washington dictate a solution.

To enact popular sovereignty for Kansas and Nebraska, however, Douglas' bill provided for the repeal of the Missouri Compromise, which had prohibited the spread of slavery above the thirty-sixth parallel. Seeing this as a violation of an almost sacred pledge, antislavery members of Congress objected vigorously to the bill. Nevertheless, under Douglas' skillful legislative leadership, the bill passed the Senate by a vote of 37 to 14. Little did Stephen Douglas suspect that his legislative triumph had spelled his political doom. The Kansas-Nebraska Act made sectional reconciliation impossible and undermined Douglas' presidential ambitions.

Stephen A. Douglas of Illinois

Sumner's "Crime Against Kansas" Speech

On May 19, 1856, with the galleries of the old Senate chamber filled to capacity, Charles Sumner of Massachusetts took the floor to begin his long-awaited address on the question of statehood for Kansas. These remarks later became known as his "Crime Against Kansas" speech.

Sumner, a strident abolitionist who opposed the extension of slavery into the potential new state, wasted little time in getting to his point. "A crime has been committed," he thundered, "which is without example in the records of the past. . . . It is the rape of a virgin territory, compelling it to the hateful embrace of slavery." The learned Sumner used quotations from Cervantes, Cicero, Dante, and Milton to attack his fellow senators, notably Stephen Douglas of Illinois and Andrew Butler of South Carolina. Following the speech, which he concluded the next day, several senators took the floor to respond. In a heated exchange, Douglas charged that Sumner added nothing new to the debate on Kansas but "personal assaults," "obscenity," and "gross insults." "Mr. President," Sumner retorted, "again the Senator has switched his tongue, and again he fills the Senate with its offensive odor."

Newspapers in the North hailed the "Crime Against Kansas" speech, while it was castigated in the South. South Carolina especially took offense at Sumner's address, claiming that the honor of both the state and Senator Butler had been violated. Sumner's friends feared for his safety, with good reason.

Charles Sumner Beaten in Senate Chamber

On May 22, 1856, Massachusetts Senator Charles Sumner was brutally beaten while seated at his desk in the Senate chamber. This dramatic event in the Senate's history stands as a symbol of the terrible tensions that existed in the United States during the decade before the Civil War.

An outspoken opponent of slavery, Sumner had delivered a heated address on the "Crime Against Kansas," denouncing efforts of proslavery forces to inject slavery into the Kansas Territory. One of the victims of Sumner's tongue-lashing was South Carolina's aging Senator Andrew Butler. Deeply offended by Sumner's remarks, Senator Butler's kinsman, South Carolina Representative Preston Brooks, determined to avenge his family's honor.

Waiting until after the Senate had adjourned, Brooks approached the senator at his desk, where he was franking copies of the offending speech. Calling the speech "a libel on South Carolina, and Mr. Butler, who is a relative of mine," Brooks lifted his cane and brought it down upon Sumner's head, neck, and shoulders, over and over, harder and harder, until the cane shattered into pieces. Seeking to escape his assailant, Sumner tried to rise from his desk, ripping up the heavy screws that bolted it to the floor. Blinded by blood, he staggered down the center aisle of the Senate chamber.

This incident ended within a minute, but its repercussions were felt for years. The South made a hero out of Preston Brooks, while the North rallied behind Sumner as a martyr. Censure efforts against Brooks failed in the House, but the young congressman died shortly thereafter. Sumner absented himself from the Senate for three years. His supporters said he was recuperating; his opponents said he was afraid to come back. In any event, his empty chair remained a visible reminder of the nation's sectional division.

The assault on Senator Charles Sumner of Massachusetts

1858
MARCH 23

Senate Votes on Admission of Kansas

On March 23, 1858, the Senate voted to admit the state of Kansas to the Union under the terms of the Lecompton Constitution. This vote had been preceded by two years of the most bitter debates the Senate had yet witnessed. Charles Sumner's stinging "Crime Against Kansas" speech, and his caning at the hands of Representative Preston Brooks in 1856, served as a preface to this important day and vote.

At issue was the extension of slavery into Kansas. Proslavery forces, meeting in Lecompton, Kansas, had drawn up a constitution permitting slavery. President Buchanan, eager to placate the South, recommended that Kansas be admitted to the Union with the Lecompton Constitution. Enraged by what he regarded as Buchanan's betrayal, Senator Stephen Douglas of Illinois led a revolt of northern Democrats who supported the free-state partisans and opposed the extension of slavery.

Douglas threw himself into the Senate debates over Kansas. At seven o'clock on the evening of March 22, as a "prodigious multitude" crowded the old Senate chamber, he appeared on the floor to make his final speech against the Lecompton bill. Douglas spoke for three hours but to no avail. The next day, March 23, when the decks were cleared for final action on the bill, 33 senators upheld the admission of Kansas under the Lecompton constitution, 22 opposed it.

Mr. President, the House refused to comply, and the issue of Kansas remained alive for three more years. Not until January 1861, after the South had seceded, was Kansas finally admitted to the Union, becoming the thirty-fourth state.

1858
APRIL 10

Death of Thomas Hart Benton

On April 10, 1858, one of the giants of the Senate's Golden Age died after the most desperate race of his career. In the face of a long and painful illness, Thomas Hart Benton of Missouri drove himself to complete his memoirs of thirty years in the Senate. His *Thirty Years' View* remains one of the most remarkable political memoirs in American literature.

Benton, a Democrat, was first elected to the Senate in 1820. For the next three turbulent decades, he was involved in every major issue that erupted on the Senate floor. His name, like those of Clay, Webster, and Calhoun, was known throughout the land. When Benton opposed the Compromise of 1850, he failed to win reelection. After one term in the House, he was defeated again. Benton had long considered writing a book on his experiences, and, in retirement, he threw himself into the project. Month after month he labored, dunning, cajoling, and pleading with colleagues for reminiscences and critiques. "Scrawl away without restraint," he urged former President Martin Van Buren.

Benton was already suffering from cancer when volume one of *Thirty Years' View* was published in the spring of 1854. Enemies labeled it a "huge monument of self-eulogy," but none could deny the grand sweep of Benton's prose and vision. Benton was well into volume two when his Washington house burned to the ground, destroying his books, papers, and the nearly finished second volume. He had invested too much of himself into the project to stop, and throughout 1855 he furiously rewrote huge passages from memory. In 1856, volume two appeared.

By then bedridden, Benton drove himself to complete his final project, the monumental *Abridgment of the Debates of Congress.* He finished the sixteenth and final volume on April 9, 1858, and whispered, "I am comfortable and content." The next morning Thomas Hart Benton died at the age of seventy-six amid the documents of the Congress he loved.

Thomas Hart Benton of Missouri

Abraham Lincoln debating Stephen Douglas

1858
JULY 24

Lincoln-Douglas Debates

On July 24, 1858, Abraham Lincoln challenged Stephen Douglas to a series of debates that would highlight one of the legendary Senate races in our history. In an era when senators were elected by state legislatures and popular campaigns were unheard of, Lincoln and Douglas traveled an astounding ten thousand miles across the state of Illinois, speaking before huge crowds complete with bands, banners, and other campaign trimmings. Their seven debates attracted national coverage and became a forum for the discussion of slavery.

Douglas, the Democratic Little Giant, was a twelve-year veteran of the Senate and chairman of its powerful Committee on Territories. He was well known for introducing the Kansas-Nebraska bill, and promoting the doctrine of popular sovereignty. The tall, awkward Lincoln had served one term in the House. As a member of the newly established Republican party, Lincoln was among the first to articulate its position on slavery. Although not an abolitionist, he was opposed to slavery in the new territories, calling it a "moral, social and political wrong," inconsistent with democratic principles.

In the critical debate at Freeport, Illinois, Lincoln cornered Douglas by asking him if people could in any lawful way exclude slavery prior to the formation of their state constitutions. If Douglas answered "yes" he would go against the Supreme Court's recent *Dred Scott* decision; if he said "no," he would contradict his own stand on popular sovereignty. Douglas evaded the question, cleverly responding that slavery could not exist anywhere without police enforcement, so territories could discourage slavery by failing to pass the necessary legislation.

Douglas won the Senate race, but his attempt at a compromise position on slavery destroyed his popularity. The debates launched Lincoln into national politics and paved the way for his election to the presidency in 1860.

1858
DECEMBER 9

Stephen Douglas Removed as Committee Chairman

On December 9, 1858, the Senate Democratic caucus removed Stephen Douglas as chairman of the Committee on Territories. Only twice in the history of this institution has a senator been summarily stripped of his chairmanship (the other being Charles Sumner, as chairman of the Foreign Relations Committee).

Stephen Douglas stood among the most powerful and influential senators during the decade before the Civil War. In 1850, after Henry Clay had failed, Douglas had forged the compromise that saved the Union. Four years later, in an effort to organize the Kansas-Nebraska territory, Douglas had attempted to solve the vexing issue of slavery in the territories by promoting popular sovereignty, that is, by letting the settlers vote to decide whether their territories would admit or prohibit slavery. It was the public explosion that followed the Kansas-Nebraska bill that led directly to the formation of the Republican party.

In 1857 the Democratic Douglas found himself at odds with the Democratic administration of James Buchanan. He believed that Buchanan's support of proslavery factions in Kansas was undermining his concept of popular sovereignty. His break with Buchanan alienated him from southern Democrats at the same time that he was under assault from the new Republicans. In 1858, Abraham Lincoln challenged Douglas for his Senate seat. When he narrowly defeated Lincoln, Douglas returned to the Senate to find that the Buchanan wing of the Democratic caucus had stripped him of his chairmanship.

A hard man to keep down, Stephen Douglas rallied from these adversities to win the Democratic nomination for president in 1860, only to lose the election to his old rival, Abraham Lincoln.

1859
SEPTEMBER 13

David Broderick of California

Senator Broderick Shot in a Duel

On September 16, 1859, a senator died in California. What made this death remarkable was the fact that the senator, David Broderick, had been shot three days earlier in a duel with David Terry, the former chief justice of the California Supreme Court. A number of early nineteenth-century senators, including Andrew Jackson, Henry Clay, and Thomas Hart Benton, had attempted to settle personal grievances on the dueling ground, and some had actually killed their opponents, but no sitting senator, before or after Broderick, would himself meet so barbaric an end.

Broderick, a tough, self-made Democrat, had migrated to California in 1848. Also moving to California that year was Congressman William Gwin of Mississippi, a patrician lawyer and physician. Both men quickly became embroiled in the turbulent politics of the region: Gwin, a slave owner, leading the "chivalry" or proslavery wing of the California Democrats, while Broderick's faction vigorously opposed the extension of slavery into California. When California became a state in 1850, the legislature sent the two enemies to the Senate, where they constantly traded insults on the floor.

Back in California in the summer of 1859 to campaign for local candidates, Broderick loudly announced in a hotel dining room that one of Gwin's closest allies, Chief Justice Terry, was corrupt and unfit for office. Terry immediately resigned from the bench and challenged Broderick to a duel. Their first attempt on September 12, was interrupted by the police, but the next morning at sunrise the two men faced each other on a secluded beach beside the Pacific. At the command to fire, Broderick prematurely touched the hair trigger, firing his bullet into the sand at Terry's feet. Terry coolly aimed, fired, and shot Broderick in the chest. Broderick lingered in great pain for three days until he died on September 16.

Facing page, the east front of the Capitol, photographed about 1863 during the installation of the *Statue of Freedom*

CHAPTER V
War and
Reconstruction
1860–1889

1860
FEBRUARY 2

Jefferson Davis and Presidential Politics

On February 2, 1860, Senator Jefferson Davis of Mississippi introduced six politically explosive resolutions in this chamber. Together, they constituted what one historian termed "a grim sectional manifesto . . . a platform of theories built to sustain the drama of secession."

In these measures, Senator Davis confronted the federal government's role in protecting slavery in the nation's territories, with the intention of placing the national Democratic party on record in support of slaveholders there. As one of ten Senate Democrats who aspired to their party's 1860 presidential nomination, Davis believed his action would increase chances that a southerner would obtain that nomination at the party convention, less than three months away.

In 1860 the southern Democrats, who followed Davis, dominated their party's congressional wing. Supporters of Illinois Senator Stephen Douglas, leader of the northern bloc and himself a contender for the Democratic presidential nomination, found their strength in the party's state organizations. Douglas and other moderates sought to sidetrack the Davis resolutions, fearing that, if the feuding northern and southern wings of the party could not maintain some semblance of unity during the 1860 campaigns, the presidency would certainly fall into the hands of the newly established Republican party.

In introducing his resolutions, Davis hoped to force the Senate Democratic caucus to support slavery in the territories as party doctrine. He argued that the party's northern wing should have no influence because its members represented states that were certain to vote Republican. Subsequently, Senate Democrats adopted the Davis resolutions. The resulting uproar within the party contributed to a crippling deadlock at the April convention and became another major step on the road to the Civil War.

1860
DECEMBER 20

Senate Establishes Committee of Thirteen

On December 20, 1860, the Senate established its so-called Committee of Thirteen in a last-ditch effort to prevent the breakup of the Union. This action occurred on the same day that South Carolina voted for secession. Unlike its unwieldy House counterpart—the Committee of Thirty-Three, with one member from each state—the Senate panel contained a more balanced and illustrious group of members. They included Kentucky's John Crittenden, New York's William Seward, Illinois' Stephen Douglas, and Mississippi's Jefferson Davis.

From its inception, however, the committee faced insurmountable odds against success. With four states virtually out of the Union, it had to focus on reconstruction rather than on simply stopping secession. The committee's doom was sealed when members adopted Jefferson Davis' proposal that no action would be taken except by a dual majority of the five Republicans and eight other committee members. This came in recognition that no compro-

Jefferson Davis of Mississippi

mise proposals, particularly requiring amendment of the Constitution, could succeed without strong bipartisan and bisectional support.

The committee met four times between December 22 and 28. John Crittenden, following in Henry Clay's conciliatory tradition, presented a package of constitutional amendments. Acceptance of these compromise plans would require the Republican party to abandon its intention to prohibit slavery in the territories—the basis on which it had been founded and had just won its first presidential election. Taking their cue from President-elect Lincoln, Republican senators rejected all proposals.

On New Year's Eve, the committee reported to the full Senate that it had been unable to agree on "any general plan of adjustment." Louisiana's Senator Judah Benjamin sounded the panel's death knell in the final hours of 1860. "The day for the adjustment has passed," he declared. "If you would give it now, you are too late. We desire, we beseech you, [to let our] parting be in peace."

1861
JANUARY 21

Jefferson Davis' Farewell Address

This chamber has witnessed many dramatic events in the 130 years that it has served as the Senate's meeting place. The joys and the sorrows that engage our nation invariably make their way to this room. One of the most heart-rending moments in the Senate's entire history occurred here on January 21, 1861.

On that day, Senator Jefferson Davis and four of his colleagues from Mississippi, Alabama, and Florida came to take their leave of the Senate. Days earlier, their states had voted to follow South Carolina in severing ties with the Union. Following decades of compromise measures to ward off the impending crisis of "secession," the election of Abraham Lincoln signaled to many Americans the end of that road. As fear of coming disaster gripped the nation, all eyes turned to the Senate chamber.

With the galleries jammed and all available floor space occupied, the five senators, one by one, expressed sadness at the course events had taken and prayed that the departing states would be allowed to go in peace. Jefferson Davis was the last to speak. Before the hushed audience, he quietly recited the theory he believed supported his state's decision to leave the Union. Citing the Declaration of Independence, Davis asserted: "We tread in the path of our fathers when we proclaim our independence, and take the hazard. This is done not in hostility to others, not to injure any section of the country, not even for our own pecuniary benefit; but from the high and solemn motive of defending and protecting the rights we inherited, and which it is our sacred duty to transmit unshorn to our children."

When he finished, the chamber was silent but for the muffled sound of sobbing. All fifty-eight remaining senators in solemn despair rose as the five departing members slowly made their way up the center aisle and out these swinging doors.

1861
APRIL 22

The Massachusetts Regiment in the Senate

On April 22, 1861, the Senate chamber was occupied by the young recruits of the Sixth Massachusetts Regiment on their way south to face Confederate troops. Soldiers were housed in the Capitol throughout the early days of the Civil War after President Lincoln called up 75,000 state militia volunteers. Quarters for such a large contingent were difficult to find in Washington and, at times, the Capitol housed as many as 3,000 troops.

The Sixth Massachusetts Regiment arrived in Washington by train a little after 5 p.m. on April 19. The troops marched, along with throngs of cheering well-wishers, to New Jersey Avenue and then to the Capitol. Despite the warm spring weather, the recruits still wore their heavy winter uniforms and knapsacks and "presented a thoroughly soldierly appearance." Entering the Rotunda by the east portico, they were directed to their quarters in this very chamber, where they collapsed, exhausted by the preceding twenty-four hours. In Baltimore, they had been pelted with bricks and paving stones by angry mobs of southern sympathizers. Thirty soldiers were injured, and ten citizens and soldiers were left dead.

No food awaited the troops when they arrived in this chamber. They had to wait well into the night for a meal. Grateful for any place to rest, the soldiers used the cushioned chairs in the gallery, the floor of the Senate chamber, and the couches in the surrounding rooms as beds. During their stay, the chamber was filled with a smell of bacon, as the men cut chunks of meat from large slabs hanging in the Marble Room and roasted them in the fireplaces. Throughout the remaining days of April and into May, the Sixth Regiment could be seen each day marching through the city streets. The *Washington Star* commented that the boys from Massachusetts found their Capitol quarters more than adequate.

1861
JULY 10

Resolution to Expel Southern Senators

On July 10, 1861, New Hampshire Senator Daniel Clark submitted a resolution calling for the expulsion of ten senators. Under normal circumstances, this would have been an unthinkable action. In July 1861, however, circumstances were anything but normal as the Senate and the nation faced a constitutional and military cataclysm of unprecedented magnitude. Six months earlier, senators from Florida, Alabama, and Mississippi had dramatically walked out of the chamber as southern states withdrew from the Union. In April, Fort Sumter had fallen, and President Lincoln quickly issued a call for 75,000 volunteer militiamen. One regiment of Union soldiers had actually been housed in the Senate chamber for several weeks prior to the July 4, 1861 convening of the Thirty-seventh Congress.

Senator Clark's resolution named ten southern senators: two each from Arkansas, North Carolina, Texas, and Virginia, and one each from South Carolina and Tennessee. The New Hampshire senator charged that all had participated in a conspiracy against the "peace, union and liberties of the people and Government of the United States."

A few moderate voices opposed expulsion, arguing that the senators had only followed the directions of their states, but they were drowned out by the passions of war. Clark would hear none of the arguments for mitigation. The southern senators, he declared, had "taken up arms against the government. Their guns are now within the sound of your capital; and shall we sit here in the Senate and deliberate and doubt whether we shall turn out of this Senate the very men who are ready to explode those guns against your capital? . . . Let them be ejected from the councils of the nation."

Clark's rhetoric carried the day. On July 11, the Senate, by a vote of 32 to 10, expelled the ten southern senators.

"Secession Exploded," 1861

First Battle of Bull Run

On July 21, 1861, the first battle of the Civil War took place in Virginia. Members of Congress expected a quick and decisive Union victory, but, instead, several senators were caught up in the disorderly retreat from the Union debacle at the Battle of Bull Run.

Patriotic excitement about the impending confrontation built to fever pitch in Washington in the days before the battle. In a festive mood, senators and private citizens hurried to obtain passes to view the battle; every carriage in town was hired for the Sunday excursion to Manassas. On the morning of the twenty-first, a jolly caravan, including Senators Henry Wilson, Ben Wade, Lyman Trumbull, Ambrose Burnside, and Zachariah Chandler, rolled across the long bridges into Virginia. Their carriages were laden with spyglasses, rifles, revolvers, huge picnic lunches, and bottles of wine.

THE FIRST BATTLE OF BULL RUN, Va. SUNDAY AFTERNOON, July 21, 1861.

RETREAT OF THE FEDERAL ARMY UNDER Col. McDOWELL UPON CENTREVILLE.—THE RESERVE DIVISION OF Col. MILES COVERING THE RETREAT AND REPELLING THE CONFEDERATE CAVALRY.

PANIC AMONG THE TEAMSTERS AND CIVILIANS, AND GENERAL STAMPEDE TOWARDS ARLINGTON HEIGHTS.

The Union retreat at Bull Run

By the afternoon, the carriages were "drawn up like those of spectators at a country race," on a hill overlooking Bull Run. As the first cannons roared, the confident spectators entertained thoughts of seeing the rebels "run to Richmond." Their pleasant Sunday excursion quickly turned sour, however, as it became clear that the Union forces had been routed and were making a panic-stricken retreat to Washington.

In the confusion, most of the chastened senators made equally ignominious retreats to the Capitol. Senator Wilson returned to Washington riding a stray army mule. Near Fairfax, Senators Wade and Chandler had halted some fleeing soldiers and Wade, brandishing a rifle, unsuccessfully tried to convince them to turn back. Senator Burnside rode back to town with "disaster written on his eyes" and missing his hat. Senator James Grimes, who came within a minute of being captured by the Confederates, perhaps best summed up the effect of the disastrous retreat when he resolved that this was "the last battlefield he would ever visit voluntarily!"

1861
AUGUST 6

Legalizing Wartime Acts of the President

On August 6, 1861, the Senate and House completed action to legalize the acts President Abraham Lincoln had undertaken during the early months of the Civil War.

Why, we might ask, did Congress need retroactively to endorse and make legal the president's actions? The answer is that, during the nineteenth century, Congress generally only met for a few months each year. As was the usual practice, the old Congress had ended on March 4, 1861, and the new Congress was not due to meet until the first Monday in December.

As the North and South moved inexorably toward civil war during the spring of 1861, President Lincoln might have called Congress into session at any time, but he preferred the freedom of action that the congressional adjournment provided.

Even after the bombardment of Fort Sumter, when President Jefferson Davis called the Confederate Congress into session, Lincoln relied upon his authority as commander in chief to issue executive orders that expanded the army and navy beyond the numbers authorized by law.

He suspended habeas corpus in border states—especially in nearby Maryland—where Confederate sympathies ran high. He blockaded southern ports, issued a call for three-year volunteers, and spent federal money for military supplies without congressional approval or appropriation.

Lincoln called Congress back into special session on July 4, 1861, by which time his initial wartime actions were already accomplished facts. Since the Republican party had won majorities in both houses, he was confident that the House and Senate would support his bold moves. Even though two-thirds of the Democrats and border-state Union party members abstained from voting, the Congress approved his executive actions "as if they had been done under the previous express authority" of Congress.

Edward Baker of Oregon

1861
OCTOBER 21

Senator Baker Killed at Ball's Bluff

At sunset on October 21, 1861, a newspaper correspondent heard the insistent clicking of the telegraph inside General George McClellan's headquarters and then watched as President Abraham Lincoln stumbled out, with tears rolling down his cheeks. Over the wire had come news that Colonel Edward Dickinson Baker, a senator from Oregon and close friend of the president's, had been killed earlier in the day at the head of his battalion in the disastrous Union defeat at Ball's Bluff.

Baker, a Republican, had only come to the Senate in 1860, but because of his long friendship with the president that began when both were aspiring politicians in Illinois, he had quickly risen to social and political prominence. On Inauguration Day in March 1861, he rode with the newly elected president in an open coach from the Willard Hotel to the Capitol, where he introduced Lincoln to the waiting throng. In August 1861, Baker won national attention as an actor in a dramatic scene on the Senate floor. On August 1, just days before the Thirty-seventh Congress adjourned, Senator John Breckinridge of Kentucky, who had opposed all war measures, addressed the Senate. The main Senate doors swung open to reveal Senator Baker in full uniform. He had been dividing his time between the Senate and his men in the field and had arrived in time to hear the final lines of Breckinridge's speech. Laying his sword across his desk, Baker listened in silence. Then, with his face glowing under his silver hair, he sprang to his feet to assail the sentiments of Breckinridge as "words of brilliant, polished treason." Baker's eloquent attack focused attention not only on Breckinridge, who would soon join the Confederacy, but on himself.

Two months later, Baker was dead, killed fighting for the Union he had eloquently upheld. His funeral, attended by President Lincoln, attracted thousands. His dramatic career, and the invocation of his memory, became a potent political touchstone for Union orators throughout the war.

1862
FEBRUARY 5

Senator Jesse Bright Expelled

On February 5, 1862, the Senate expelled Indiana's Democratic Senator Jesse Bright on grounds of disloyalty to the United States. Bright, the body's most senior Democratic member and a former president pro tempore, had earned a reputation for his knowledge of Senate procedures and for his forthright manner. Other senators regarded him as capable of unswerving friendship to those who shared his proslavery views and as "an enemy who knew how to inflict punishment" on those who did not. One of his key adversaries was Massachusetts Senator Charles Sumner, a dedicated abolitionist. When the Democrats controlled the Senate in the 1850s, Bright as president pro tempore saw to it that Sumner received no committee assignments.

In mid-1861, in the early weeks of the Civil War, Union forces captured a Confederate arms merchant. Among his belongings they found a letter of introduction from Senator Bright to "His Excellency Jefferson Davis, President of the Confederacy."

When the Senate convened in December 1861, a resolution was introduced calling for Bright's expulsion. The Indiana senator argued that he did not recall writing the incriminating letter but that he considered it appropriate to introduce a man who had been his friend to Davis, who had been his Senate colleague. In opposition, Charles Sumner delivered a dramatic and damaging speech, demanding that the Senate purge itself of such traitors.

The proceedings, which occupied the Senate intermittently for more than six weeks, ended on February 5 in a chamber filled to capacity. Although the Judiciary Committee had recommended that Bright retain his seat, the Senate, by a vote of 32 to 14, disagreed. Of the fifteen senators who have been expelled over the course of the Senate's history, all but one were removed during the Civil War as partisans of the Confederacy.

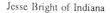

Jesse Bright of Indiana

A railroad company advertisement for farmland

1862
MAY 20

Homestead Act Becomes Law

On May 20, 1862, President Abraham Lincoln signed into law the Homestead Act, granting free family-sized parcels of public land to actual settlers after five years' residence. The bill was the culmination of nearly four decades of controversy.

As early as 1825, Senator Thomas Hart Benton of Missouri moved that an inquiry be made into the expediency of donating lands to settlers. In a message to the Senate in 1832, President Andrew Jackson expressed the opinion that "the public lands should cease as soon as practicable to be a source of revenue." In 1846, Representative Andrew Johnson of Tennessee introduced a bill in the House calling for free land for settlers. But when a general bill for free land actually came to a vote in Congress in 1852, it was defeated in the Senate.

The "homestead" issue took on sectional tones in the Senate debate. Southern senators opposed the bill, fearing it would result in the populating of territories with antislavery settlers. Eastern senators were afraid a homestead bill would accelerate western movement and lower land prices in the East. Western senators were the most consistent supporters until the issue was taken up in 1860 by the new Republican party. That year, a homestead bill was passed by the House and Senate but vetoed by Democratic President James Buchanan. The attempt to override the veto failed by a small margin.

In the absence of the mostly Democratic southern senators who withdrew in January 1861, the Republicans in the Senate, by a vote of 33 to 7, were finally able to push through the Homestead Act on May 6, 1862. By any standard, this was one of the most significant pieces of legislation ever to emerge from the United States Senate.

1864
AUGUST 5

The Wade-Davis Manifesto

On August 5, 1864, Senator Benjamin Wade of Ohio and Representative Henry Davis of Maryland issued a document known as the Wade-Davis manifesto—a classic defense of congressional prerogatives. The manifesto, a sulphurous harangue against President Abraham Lincoln, exhibited the intense passions and competition to direct the reconstruction of the South following the Civil War. Rarely has a president been attacked as vehemently and as openly by members of his own party, especially in an election year.

In the spring of 1864, after a string of Union victories, an increasingly influential faction of senators known as the Radical Republicans began to plan for the restoration of the seceded states. Anticipating their actions, President Lincoln unveiled his own Reconstruction plan. No matter how compassionate or vindictive Lincoln's plan had been, it could not have pleased the Radicals, who believed Congress—not the chief executive—should formulate such policies.

Countering the president's move, Wade and Davis introduced their own proposal for congressional Reconstruction and skillfully maneuvered it through the Senate and House. Although the Wade-Davis bill differed significantly from the president's plan, the Radicals believed he would feel compelled to sign it. They were mistaken. On July 4, 1864, the last day of the session, after signing other acts in the President's Room adjacent to the Senate chamber, Lincoln placed the measure in his pocket and returned to the White House.

Lincoln's refusal infuriated Wade. He spent the next four weeks hammering out the blistering manifesto, which began with the stinging words, "a more studied outrage on the legislative authority of the people has never been perpetrated." The Wade-Davis bill and the manifesto it spawned proved to be the opening salvos in a bitter struggle between the president and Congress over who would guide the reconstruction of the South.

1866
JULY 25

Election of Senators by State Legislatures

On July 25, 1866, Congress passed an act regulating the time and manner by which state legislatures would elect members of the United States Senate.

The Constitution had assigned this responsibility to the individual state legislatures without specifying how and when elections of senators should take place. For more than seventy-five years, the states acted independently, generally electing senators by concurrent votes of the two houses of the state legislature. But this practice not infrequently led to deadlocks between the two houses, and Senate seats went embarrassingly vacant. The new state of California, for instance, was unable to elect a senator on three occasions in the 1850s. Changes in party majorities in the legislatures sometimes resulted in two senators from different parties claiming the same seat.

As a result of this scandalous situation, a bill was introduced in the Senate, as provided by Article I, section 4 of the Constitution, to set the time and manner for electing senators and the form of their credentials. For five years, the bill languished in the Judiciary Committee, while the Senate was preoccupied with the larger issues of the Civil War. But in 1866, after another troublesome election in the New Jersey state legislature, the measure was revived. This bill provided that, on the first Tuesday after the meeting and organization of a legislature when a senator was to be elected, the two houses were to meet separately and vote for a senator. On the following day, the two houses would meet jointly and the results of the voting be compared. If both houses did not give a majority to the same man, then the joint assembly would meet every succeeding day at noon and take at least one vote a day until they agreed upon someone.

This measure became law on July 25, 1866, but had little effect in discouraging deadlocks. The problem festered for another half century, until it was solved by an amendment to the Constitution providing for election of senators directly by the people.

Senate Approves Alaska Purchase

On April 9, 1867, the U.S. Senate approved the Alaska treaty. Under the terms of this treaty, the United States paid the Russians $7.2 million for a territory twice the size of Texas. Averaging about two cents an acre, the Alaska purchase was one of the greatest real estate deals in world history. But this bargain was not fully appreciated at the time.

The Russians, eager to unload their unprofitable colony, let Secretary of State William H. Seward know they were ready to negotiate its sale, and he jumped at the opportunity. Seward was an ardent expansionist, who envisioned the United States someday extending over the entire continent of North America. With a vast western territory still largely unoccupied, most Americans could not see the need to purchase Alaska, which for all they knew was "a city, an animal, or a new kind of drink." The newspapers laughed at "Seward's folly" and "Seward's icebox." The able secretary of state, however, convinced the Senate of Alaska's valuable natural resources and strategic location for American interests in the Pacific, and the Senate approved the treaty by a vote of 37 to 2.

It took the House of Representatives another year to appropriate the funds to make the purchase, and when it did, rumors spread that the Russian ambassador had used some of the money as bribes to win the support of various congressmen and journalists. A congressional investigation failed to substantiate these charges, but the bitter taste left by the Alaska scandal lingered for years. Thus, one of the most successful land deals in our history helped to turn Americans away from further expansionist efforts.

Alaska Purchase Treaty of 1867,
signed by Czar Alexander II

1868
JANUARY 14

Senate Rejects President's Removal of Cabinet Officer

Early in 1867, Congress passed the Tenure of Office Act over President Andrew Johnson's veto. Drawing on the Senate's constitutional right to consent to cabinet nominations, this act gave the Senate the authority to block the removal of cabinet officers. That provision was specifically designed to keep Secretary of War Edwin Stanton in office. Appointed by President Lincoln, Stanton had fallen into disfavor with President Johnson because of his sympathy with the Reconstruction aims of congressional Republicans. The so-called Radical Republicans in Congress sought to impose stringent requirements on former Confederate states seeking to reenter the Union. As secretary of war, Stanton controlled the army, the only instrument with sufficient power to enforce Congress' Reconstruction policies.

President Johnson believed that the Supreme Court, given the opportunity, would strike down the offensive Tenure of Office Act. Accordingly, he dismissed Stanton in July 1867 while the Senate was out of session and replaced him, by recess appointment, with the widely popular General Ulysses Grant. When the Senate reconvened in December 1867, the president reported his suspension of Stanton and asked its consent. Johnson thought he had Grant's pledge to hold onto the office, regardless of the Senate's action, until the Court ruled on the Act's constitutionality.

On January 13, 1868, the Senate, by a vote of 35 to 6, reinstated Stanton as secretary of war. On the fourteenth, General Grant turned over the key to the War Department to Stanton. Not wishing to defy the Senate, Grant refused to conduct the fight for his post that would place the matter before the Supreme Court, and thus he deprived a bitterly angry president of the opportunity to replace Stanton. This accelerated the chain of events that, within several months, led to Johnson's Senate impeachment trial.

Secretary of War Edwin Stanton

1868
MARCH 30

The Johnson Impeachment Trial

On March 30, 1868, this chamber was a courtroom, the senators were the jury, and on trial was the president of the United States. In February, Radical Republicans in the House had pushed through eleven articles of impeachment against President Andrew Johnson. The resulting trial in the Senate had officially begun on March 5, but the next three weeks were largely filled with sober statements and the presentation of exhibits. Everyone knew that the real verbal pyrotechnics would begin on March 30, when Representative Ben Butler of Massachusetts, the most notorious of the House managers, opened arguments for the prosecution.

The galleries were filled to overflowing that day. Senators were besieged by constituents clamoring for the little yellow admission tickets. Long before the appointed hour of 12:30 p.m., the senators were in their seats. The chief justice entered, followed by the House managers and most of the House of Representatives. The crowds were not disappointed. Butler was a physically unattractive man, with a reputation, personality, and vicious speaking style to match. For three long hours, broken only by one ten-minute recess, he hurled bitter denunciations and vile accusations at the absent Johnson. The sun began to set before Butler finally brought his harangue to a close and sat down.

The Radicals were jubilant over Butler's performance. Their joy, however, was short-lived. In the days that followed, the hollowness of their charges became increasingly apparent. In mid-May, test votes on Articles II, III, and XI produced identical results—35 "guilty" to 19 "not guilty" votes. Thirty-six "guiltys" were necessary for conviction. To head off further defeats, the Radicals moved on May 26 to adjourn *sine die*, abruptly ending the impeachment trial of President Andrew Johnson.

Spectators rushing for the Senate gallery doors during the impeachment trial

Benjamin
Butler's
opening speech
at Johnson's
impeachment
trial

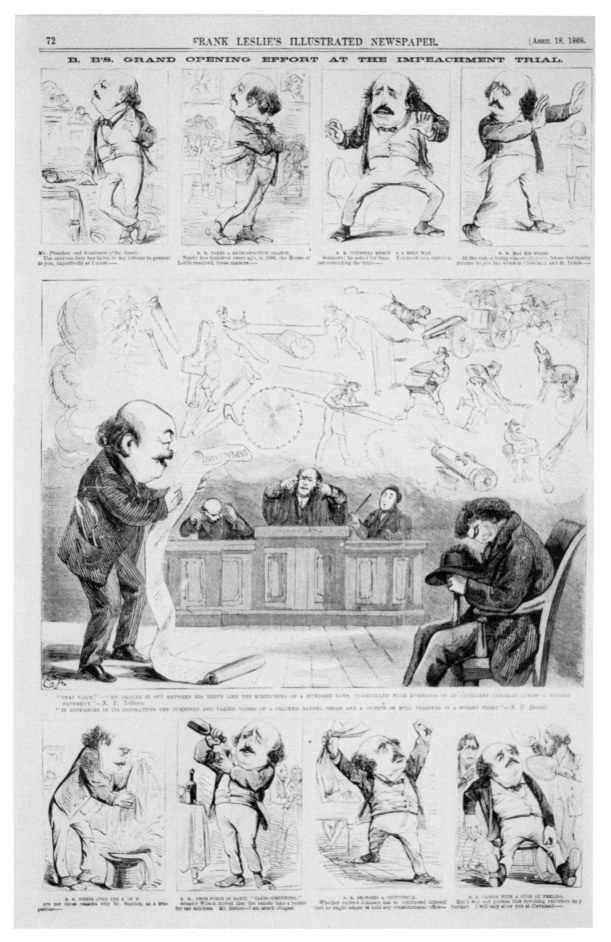

1868
MAY 16

Senate's First Vote to Remove a President

On May 16, 1868, for the first time in history, the Senate voted on an article of impeachment lodged against a president of the United States. By a tally of 35 to 19, the Senate fell one vote short of the two-thirds margin necessary to remove President Andrew Johnson from office.

During the Constitutional Convention of 1787, the delegates gave close attention to the Senate's role in impeachment trials. Several argued that the president should not be impeachable, for this would make him too dependent on the legislature. In opposition, Benjamin Franklin asserted that there must be some ultimate limitation on presidential power and that impeachment was a method of removal greatly preferable to the alternative—assassination.

The convention struggled over the definition of an impeachable offense. Early draft language identified these offenses as "neglect of duty, bribery, maladministration, or corruption." Finally, the delegates settled on "high crimes and misdemeanors" as encompassing the above terms.

Early in their deliberations, the framers wrestled with the apparent conflict of giving the Senate the power to elect the president, as was then contemplated, and also the power to remove him. At first, they tried to solve

Opening of impeachment proceedings against Andrew Johnson

131

this by having the Supreme Court and the Senate jointly conduct impeachment trials. Late in the convention, after the framers devised a special electoral college to select presidents, the way was cleared for the Senate alone to try impeachments of all federal officers, including presidents. In trials involving a president, the chief justice of the United States would preside, keeping the vice president, who would normally preside, from the impropriety of conducting a trial that might result in his own elevation to the presidency.

Although the Senate has conducted only one impeachment trial against a president, its power of removal remains a vital safeguard of our liberties.

William Pitt Fessenden Dies

On September 9, 1869, Senator William Pitt Fessenden died. In his early years, Fessenden was one of Maine's most prominent lawyers. In 1854, his antislavery views and his role in founding the Republican party earned him national prominence and a seat in the United States Senate. Fessenden, who remained in the Senate for fifteen years until his death in 1869, became a leading member of this body and one of the nation's outstanding political figures.

Historian Allan Bogue has written of Fessenden: "His level gaze, high-bridged nose, and firm lips and chin identified a man who would be intimidated by none. Although known as a genial friend and a speaker who on occasion enlivened the chamber with humorous sallies, he was also capable of devastating sarcasm and a remorseless recall and logic that left his [senatorial opponents] licking their wounds in frustrated fury."

At the outbreak of the Civil War, Fessenden became chairman of the Senate Finance Committee. In that position, he had the thankless task of raising funds to carry on the war and, in those days before the existence of a separate appropriations committee, he had a major responsibility for guiding the government's spending priorities. In an atmosphere of intense crisis and impending national disaster, he toiled long hours, in committee and on the Senate floor. Tired and apprehensive, he observed early in the war: "When a man feels as if he could cut everybody's throat and that everybody could cut his, he is in pretty bad condition. The truth is," he continued, "that nobody can be found who is equal to this crisis in any branch of the government."

Fessenden succeeded as wartime chairman of the Finance Committee through his tireless efforts to confine expenditures to war-related necessities and his avoidance of wasteful precedents. His solid character and deep intellect earned for him a secure place as one of our nation's great financial leaders.

1869
DECEMBER 8

A Senator Seeks Peace and Quiet

On December 8, 1869, the Senate adopted a resolution requiring that the Senate chamber be cleared of all unauthorized persons each day ten minutes before the time set for meeting.

In those days before the existence of separate Senate office buildings, members' desks in the chamber were often all the office space senators could claim. Increasingly, in the years immediately following the Civil War, constituents and reporters had begun crowding into the chamber, buttonholing members in the hours before the customary noon convening time. Senator Charles Drake of Missouri, for one, was sick of the increasing din. Accordingly, he proposed the successful resolution at the start of the new congressional session.

On the following day, Senator John Thayer of Nebraska, who had been absent on December 8, asked for reconsideration of the vote. He claimed he enjoyed visiting at his desk with journalists and constituents until the very moment the Senate was called to order. Thayer's action deeply annoyed Senator Drake. Perhaps, he suggested, not as many constituents visited the Nebraska senator as he received from Missouri, or perhaps not enough reporters were interested in Senator Thayer's views to have made themselves a nuisance. He, however, was tired of having to "elbow my way through a crowd of people to get to my desk. If I wish to sit down at my desk probably there is somebody occupying my seat, or if I wish to examine any papers there, I have half a dozen standing behind my back, or if I wish to talk with one person there are half a dozen within hearing distance of me."

No one rose to support either Drake or Thayer. Finally, Thomas Tipton of Nebraska moved to amend the resolution to provide that the chamber be cleared five minutes before convening, and it was quickly agreed to.

1870
FEBRUARY 25

First Black Senator

On February 25, 1870, the Senate voted 48 to 8 to seat Hiram Revels of Mississippi—the first black person ever elected to the United States Senate.

An emotional debate preceded the vote on Revels' credentials. Democrats cast doubt on the authority of the reconstruction government of Mississippi, but Republicans charged them with "hiding their anti-Negro sentiments behind a mask of technicalities." Senator Garrett Davis of Kentucky declared the seating of a black man in the Senate a "morbid state of affairs," and denied that freed slaves could even be citizens, let alone serve in the national government. Senator Willard Saulsbury of Maryland denied that the Fourteenth Amendment was a legitimate part of the Constitution and called the seating of a "negro or mulatto or octoroon in the Senate of the United States" a "great and damning outrage." Against such blatantly prejudiced arguments, the majority of the Senate stood firm and voted to seat Hiram Revels.

Revels' term in the Senate lasted only from 1870 to 1871, but during that period he spoke out in defense of freedmen's rights, in favor of enforcement of federal elections law, and in opposition to segregated schools.

If race had not been an issue, it is doubtful that any challenge would have been raised against Hiram Revels, who possessed strong qualifications and experience. He was a college graduate and an ordained minister in the African Methodist Episcopal Church. He had helped to organize black regiments during the Civil War, served as a chaplain in the Union army, as an alderman from Natchez, Mississippi, and as a state senator. After completing his short term in the U.S. Senate, he returned to become secretary of state of Mississippi and president of Alcorn Agricultural College. Of all these accomplishments, however, he will be most remembered for having integrated the U.S. Senate.

Hiram Revels of Mississippi, *seated far right*, in the Senate chamber

1871
MAY 15

The Senate Investigates Newspaper Reporters

On May 15, 1871, a Senate select committee began an investigation into the unauthorized publication in the *New-York Tribune* of the Treaty of Washington, which settled relations between the United States and Great Britain that had been disrupted during the Civil War.

Today, the Senate conducts most treaty debates in open session but, back in the late nineteenth century, such proceedings were generally held in secret—or at least they were intended to be secret. Washington newspaper correspondents rather quickly learned most of what went on inside these closed sessions and published the secret debates and votes in their papers. Periodically, some outraged senator would demand an investigation, and a select committee would be appointed to uncover the sources of the leak. But these sources invariably remained more confidential than the original secret debates.

In 1871, the select committee called *Tribune* correspondents Zebulon White and Hiram Ramsdell to answer questions about where they had gotten the treaty. Since neither journalist would break his silence, the committee ordered them held captive in the Pacific Railroad Committee room until they relented. This tactic proved futile. The two correspondents entertained guests, dined in the Senate restaurant, and otherwise lived the lives of comfortable martyrs, showing no signs of relenting. Having discovered not a clue as to who leaked the treaty, the Senate finally released the two men. Although not the first such occasion, this marked the last time that the Senate attempted to hold newspaper reporters as prisoners in the Capitol Building.

1872
APRIL 24

Last Confederate State Represented in Senate

On April 24, 1872, Matt Whitaker Ransom took the oath of office as senator from North Carolina. As a result, for the first time since 1860, every state in the Union was once again represented in the United States Senate.

Although the northern states fought the Civil War to preserve the Union, they were not eager to readmit the secessionist states once the war ended. They feared for recently freed slaves and worried that southern agrarian legislators would not support national industrial expansion. During "Congressional Reconstruction," southern states came under federal rule. Not until 1868 were the first of the former Confederate states readmitted, and not until 1872 did the last one take its place in the Senate.

Matt Ransom was an appropriate man to complete this process. Before the war he had been a lawyer and Whig politician in North Carolina. After the Whig party collapsed in 1856, Ransom, feeling no affinity for either the Know-Nothings or the Republicans, joined the Democratic party. He remained a strong Union man, however, and in 1861 was sent by his state as a peace commissioner to seek a compromise between the Confederacy and the Union. When war came, Ransom volunteered as a private and was quickly commissioned a lieutenant colonel of a North Carolina regiment. Rising to brigadier general, he fought in many battles and was several times wounded before surrendering his brigade at Appomattox. Returning to law practice after the war, he was elected to the Senate in 1872. Here he played a key role in achieving the compromise that settled the disputed presidential election of 1876 and ended military reconstruction in the South. Ransom's twenty-three years in the Senate ended in 1895 when a Populist coalition finally defeated the old soldier for reelection.

Matt Ransom of North Carolina

1873
JANUARY 31

Senate Abolishes the Frank

On January 31, 1873, the United States Senate abolished its free franking privileges. This information may come as a surprise, since in fact the Senate still sends its mail out under the frank, but let me explain how this situation came to pass.

The ability of legislators to send mail by using their signature rather than postage dates back to the British House of Commons in the seventeenth century. The Continental Congress adopted the procedure during the American Revolution, and the First Congress wrote it into law in 1789. During the nineteenth century, the press began to complain of abuses in congressional use of the frank. Some senators supposedly used the frank to send their laundry home each week; others franked barrels of china, bedding, and other household goods. Legend has it that one ante-bellum senator even attached his frank to his horse's bridle and sent the animal back home. More seriously, critics accused incumbents of flooding the mails with government documents, speeches, and packages of seed from the Agriculture Department, all designed to enhance their reelection prospects.

These charges became so widespread that in 1873 Congress abolished the frank. But the new law made no provision for payment of legitimate mailings, such as sending copies of the *Congressional Record* and other public documents that constituents might request. Thus, two years later, Congress permitted these documents to be sent out postage-free. Then there was correspondence with other government agencies; in 1883, Congress required that all executive agencies enclose franked envelopes in their official communications with the House and Senate. Because this cumbersome system still did not solve all problems of mailing, in 1891 Congress at last restored full franking privileges to its members, with specific rules designed to prevent further abuses—which probably have not worked all that well.

A senator's franking privileges

A cartoon from "Harper's Weekly," 1860

MEMBER OF CONGRESS (*who franks his clothes home to Wisconsin and has them cheaply laundered*)

"Seven cotton shirts, three flannel, six pairs of socks, one collar, five handkerchiefs, three pair drawers, two linen coats—that's all, I guess; and as the mail's just closing, that must do for to-day."

1873
MARCH 3

First Congressional Record

On March 3, 1873, Congress authorized the Government Printing Office to publish the first issue of the *Congressional Record*.

Publication of the *Record* marked the end of a long debate that had begun in the First Congress. The Constitution required that each house of Congress keep a journal of its proceedings. These journals are the minutes that the secretary of the Senate and the clerk of the House began to keep back in 1789 and still publish today. But a number of private stenographers, connected with various newspapers, attempted to record a more complete version of the debates. Stenography was a much cruder art in the eighteenth century, and many members of those early congresses felt unhappy with the published accounts of their speeches. They proposed that Congress hire its own reporters of debate. But Representative James Madison strongly opposed this plan, warning that, once reporting become official, members would suffer the task of correcting their remarks in perpetuity. Thus, reporting remained a private venture.

In 1848, after decades of complaint about shoddy and often politically slanted stenography, the Senate hired its own official reporters of debate to furnish the editors of the privately published *Congressional Globe* with verbatim transcripts of the floor proceedings. In 1855, Congress decided to pay the *Globe*'s reporters directly to perform this service. But with the increased congressional activity during the Civil War and Reconstruction, the *Globe* proved unable to publish the debates as quickly as Congress desired. Finally, in 1873, the Senate and House voted to give responsibility for publishing their debates to the Government Printing Office. Two days later, the first issue of the *Congressional Record* appeared, as it has for every day that Congress has met over the past 116 years.

1874
MARCH 11

Death of Charles Sumner

On March 11, 1874, a towering member of the United States Senate died. Charles Sumner of Massachusetts, one of the leading civil rights advocates in the nineteenth century, stood among the Senate's greatest intellects and orators. He was also one of the most controversial senators in our history.

Born in Boston in 1811, Sumner graduated from Harvard University and the Harvard Law School. He then practiced law in Boston. In 1848 he helped to found the Free Soil party, dedicated to keeping slavery out of the territories. That year he lost a race as a Free Soil candidate for Congress. But in 1851 he was elected to the Senate by a coalition of Free Soilers and Democrats, and in 1856 he was reelected as a Republican.

Sumner's passionate opposition to slavery, and his fiery eloquence, won him a severe beating in 1856, when Congressman Preston Brooks of South Carolina entered the Senate chamber and beat Sumner over the head with his cane. This violent action was a response to one of Sumner's speeches that had attacked both the southern cause and Brooks' kinsman, Senator

Andrew Butler. Sumner was absent from the Senate Chamber for three years, recuperating from his injuries. When he returned on the eve of the Civil War, he worked to persuade President Lincoln to emancipate the slaves; after the war, he led the legislative efforts to protect the civil rights of the freedmen.

When the Republicans took control of the Senate in 1861, Sumner became chairman of the Senate Foreign Relations Committee, a post he held for a decade, until the Republican Conference removed him from his chairmanship because of his opposition to President Ulysses S. Grant's plan to annex the Dominican Republic. In war and peace, Charles Sumner never hesitated to stand on principle, but he paid the price for his outspokenness.

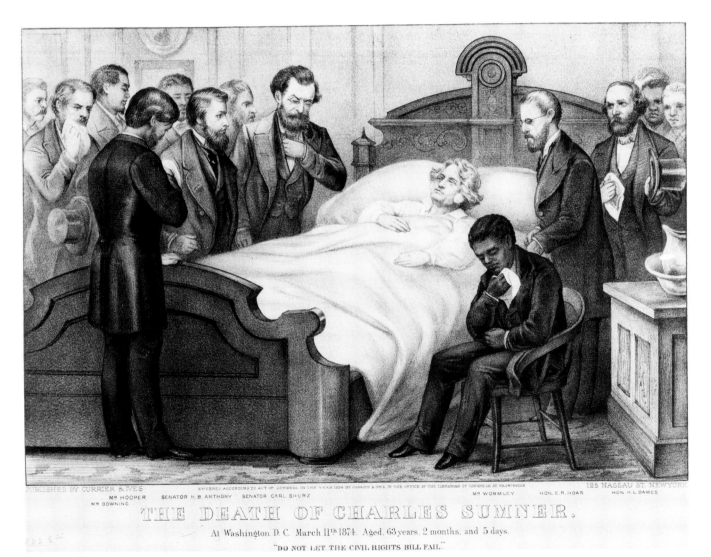

The death of Charles Sumner

1876
MARCH 14

Senate Cuts President's Salary

On March 14, 1876, the Senate took the unprecedented step of voting for a 50-percent cut in the president's salary. According to one press account, this action was not to be construed as any sort of reflection on the current president. It was rather a "measure of retrenchment and economy, likely to command the approval of the country."

The story was not that simple. In 1876 the administration of President Ulysses Grant lay mired in scandal, and the presidency as an institution enjoyed little popular esteem. To complicate matters, Congress was in a particularly touchy mood on the subject of federal salaries.

Three years earlier, the Senate and House had passed a salary act that doubled the president's compensation, which had remained at the $25,000 level established by the First Congress in 1789. At the same time, members voted to raise their own annual salaries from $5,000 to $7,500. President Grant gladly signed the measure on the final day of the March 1873 session. In the months before Congress reconvened in December, however, a firestorm of criticism swept the nation, directed at the allegedly venal members who sought to raid the treasury for their own benefit.

Early in 1874, members of the Senate and House voted to rescind their own pay raise. As the Constitution prohibited a similar action for the president during his current term of office, members had little choice but to wait until 1876 and legislate for the next presidential term.

On April 18, 1876, the president sent the Senate a veto message. In it he calculated that congressional salaries had increased by 500 percent since 1789, whereas the president's salary had only doubled. Considering the increased cost of living over the past nine decades, Grant concluded that his successor would be more than entitled to the raise. The $50,000 rate continued for the next thirty-three years.

1876
AUGUST 1

Senate Acquits Secretary of War William Belknap

On August 1, 1876, after a bitter and prolonged trial, the Senate acquitted Secretary of War William Belknap, the only cabinet member ever impeached by the House.

Despite this outcome, almost no one believed Belknap innocent. Rather, he escaped conviction on a technicality. In February 1876, just as the Whiskey Ring scandal was breaking, further tarnishing the already sullied second administration of President Ulysses Grant, the House of Representatives launched an investigation into widespread charges of corruption within the War Department. On the morning of March 2, 1876, after an insider tipped him off, Belknap rushed to the White House and thrust a hastily scribbled letter of resignation into the hands of President Grant, who accepted it with regret and surprise. Belknap had good reason for haste: the House committee was about to reveal that the secretary of war had accepted at least $20,000 in payoffs from a scheme involving a trading post in the Oklahoma

Territory. The plan was hatched by his late wife and perpetuated by his current wife, who was his late wife's sister.

By resigning, Belknap hoped to avoid impeachment by the House and trial in the Senate, fearing that the sordid dealings of his wives, leading belles of the capital, would surely be revealed. But his bold move did not work. While timely resignation had derailed impeachment initiatives against suspect officials in the past, House members, outraged by the secretary's deviousness, proceeded with a motion for his impeachment on the afternoon he resigned.

Belknap's Senate trial in the summer of 1876 proved to be the gaudy spectacle he feared. After two months of damning testimony, however, the Senate voted to acquit the former secretary of war. Senators reached this verdict not because they believed him innocent—the evidence to the contrary was overwhelming—but because they concluded that the Senate lacked jurisdiction over an individual who was no longer in office.

Secretary of War William Belknap, *seated center*

1878
APRIL 19

The Senate and the Phonograph

The human voice is perhaps the most fundamental instrument of the United States Senate. For two centuries this body has served as the stage for great national debates. Senators speak daily on issues great and small, adding our voices to the record on every issue facing this nation. Today, our proceedings are recorded both in written form in the *Congressional Record* and in audiovisual form over the C-SPAN television network. It should therefore come as no surprise that in 1878 senators were among the first to have their voices recorded on Thomas Edison's phonograph.

As a young inventor, Edison ventured down from his New Jersey laboratory on April 19, 1878, to show the world his remarkable new invention. Edison's phonograph recorded sound on wax cylinders and could immediately play back its recordings. Accompanied by a newspaper correspondent from the Senate press gallery, *Philadelphia Inquirer* reporter Uriah Hunt Painter, Edison carried his machine to the White House, where President Rutherford B. Hayes recorded a few words. The inventor marched down to "Newspaper Row," a strip of newspaper offices along Fourteenth Street, on the site of the current National Press Club, where he demonstrated this new marvel to the press.

But it was on Capitol Hill that Thomas Edison received his most skeptical audience. Here he allowed senators to speak and then for the first time listen to their own oratory. Senator James Beck, a Kentucky Democrat, recited a poem into the machine. When Edison adjusted the reproducer and turned the handle, the phonograph squawked back Senator Beck's words at him. The senator, however, concluded that Edison was a ventriloquist and insisted that the inventor leave the room so that the senator could operate the machine himself.

Thomas Edison with his phonograph, 1878

1879
JANUARY 27

James Shields

On January 27, 1879, James Shields was sworn in as the new Democratic senator from Missouri. There is nothing unusual in this event alone. It was a Senate first, however, because Missouri was the *third* state Shields had represented in the Senate; he had previously been a senator from Illinois and Minnesota.

Although Shields was the only person to represent three different states in the Senate, he began his career in this body under difficult circumstances. Immigrating to the United States from Ireland in 1823, he settled in Illinois and was elected to the Senate as a Democrat in 1849. His eligibility was questioned on the grounds that he had not been a United States citizen for the requisite nine years at the time of his election, and he was denied his seat. The Illinois legislature, however, again elected Shields for the same term, and he triumphantly claimed his seat seven days after the ninth anniversary of his naturalization. He served until 1855, when he failed in his bid for reelection.

Shields moved westward to Minnesota, where in 1858 he became one of that state's first two senators. On that occasion, his seating was challenged on the grounds that Minnesota had not been a state at the time of his election. The Minnesota delegation was finally seated, and Shields served until 1859 when, again, he was not reelected. After the Civil War, Shields moved to California, Wisconsin, and finally Missouri, where he was elected to the Senate to fill a vacancy. He served from January 27 until March 3, 1879 and declined to run for reelection. Shields died later that year in Missouri.

Throughout the Senate's history, twenty-five senators have, during the course of their careers, represented more than one state in Congress. All but two of them, however, served their other term in the House of Representatives. Only Shields and Waitman Willey, who was a senator first from Virginia and then from West Virginia during the Civil War, represented more than one state in the Senate.

SAMSON ROSCOE CONKLING ATTEMPTS TO DESTROY THE REPUBLICAN TEMPLE.
BUT HE PULLS DOWN ONLY ONE PILLAR, WHICH DESTROYS HIMSELF.

Roscoe Conkling depicted as Samson destroying the Republican temple

144

1881
FEBRUARY 23

Senator Conkling on the Senate Chamber

I think my colleagues would agree that we are all pretty comfortable in this chamber—warm enough in winter, cool enough in summer. It has not always been thus, however. On February 23, 1881, one senator took to the floor to enumerate the chamber's faults. That senator was the handsome Roscoe Conkling of New York, a man known for his volatile temper and elaborate rhetoric.

At issue that day was a bill authorizing the acquisition of land for a building for the Library of Congress, which was then wedged into cramped quarters in the Capitol. Conkling's worst enemies supported the bill, and probably for that reason alone, Conkling opposed it. Why not enlarge the Capitol to accommodate the overflowing Library, he asked. When a senator responded that the Capitol was a "perfect building," Conkling exploded.

The Capitol had been growing ever since the Congress moved to Washington in 1800, he rightly argued. The huge wing housing the new Senate chamber had been added only twenty-two years earlier. And, he thundered, that chamber was far from perfect. It was a stifling "iron box from which neither sky nor earth nor tree nor any other of nature's signs [are] visible." The place was making him sick. "Why is it that coming here in the morning and feeling very well, after a short time we feel as if a cord was bound tight around our heads over our eyes?" he asked. It was, he had determined, because the chamber was too dry, the air too stale. Senators had him to thank, he told them, for some mild relief, because, at his insistence "pan after pan" of water was set out in the basement to evaporate and humidify the chamber.

Senators were to wait another seventy years before Conkling's complaints about the chamber's climate would be satisfactorily addressed.

1881
MAY 16

Dramatic Senate Resignations

On May 16, 1881, the nation witnessed the dramatic resignations of both United States senators from New York in a showdown with the president of the United States.

Two months earlier, James Garfield had been inaugurated president. Immediately afterward, relations between the Republican president and perhaps the most prominent Republican senator, Roscoe Conkling, began deteriorating. Conkling represented the "stalwart" wing of the party that staunchly defended the patronage system. Garfield leaned more toward civil service reform. When Garfield appointed an anti-stalwart man as collector of the port of New York—a patronage-rich position—Conkling took the action as a personal offense.

As the Senate prepared for a major confirmation battle, Conkling made a bold decision and a risky gamble. He and Thomas C. Platt both submitted their resignations from the Senate. Their plan was to return to Albany to be reelected by the state legislature (as was the practice before the Seventeenth Amendment to the Constitution). Their reelection would signal New York's support for its senators in their confrontation with the president.

Fate, however, intervened. In July, while Conkling and Platt were campaigning in Albany, a deranged officeseeker who identified with Conkling shot President Garfield at a Washington train station. The president lingered for another two months before his death, becoming a national martyr for civil service reform. In that atmosphere, the New York legislature declined to reelect either Conkling or Platt, and the Senate confirmed Garfield's candidate for collector of the port of New York. In tribute to Garfield, President Chester Arthur supported enactment of the first Civil Service Act.

Although Platt returned to the Senate years later, Roscoe Conkling's political career ended when his dramatic gamble failed.

"Cowboys coming to town for Christmas," by Frederick Remington, 1889

1882
APRIL 26

Presidential Message Denounces Cowboys

On April 26, 1882, the president of the United States warned the Senate that an "alarming state of disorder" existed in the territory of Arizona, where "robbery, murder, and resistance to law have become so common as to cease causing surprise."

President Chester A. Arthur blamed these disorders on "armed bands of desperados known as cowboys," and called on Congress to enact legislation permitting federal military forces in Arizona to be employed as a *posse comitatus* to bring law and order to the frontier. To buttress his arguments, Arthur sent the Senate letters from the territorial governor of Arizona, testifying to the "insurrection, anarchy, and violence" that existed. The governor identified Tombstone as the "centre of these outrages upon public peace." Because Tombstone was "partaking of the general reckless spirit of rapid accumulation of money and property," it seemed to "wink at crime," particularly by "the thoroughly abandoned class of highway robbers and cattle thieves called 'cowboys.' . . . Hotels, saloons, restaurants, &c., where the rough 'cowboy' element spend their money freely, are both weak and wicked in their sympathy for and protection of this lawless class."

The governor appealed to Washington to send "a man of well-known courage and character, of cool, sound judgment, who, with a suitable posse of men, can . . . go forward with a firm and steady hand, bringing as fast as possible the leading spirits of this lawless class to a severe and speedy punishment."

If all this sounds familiar, it is because the same plot was repeated every Saturday at the movies of our youth. The federal marshal sent to clean up Tombstone would be Randolph Scott, Gary Cooper, Jimmy Stewart or perhaps Ronald Reagan. But in 1882 the taming of the "cowboys" was no movie; it was a real issue on the agenda of the U.S. Senate.

1882
AUGUST 7

Senate Commissions Former President to Negotiate Treaty

On August 7, 1882, the U.S. Senate commissioned a former president of the United States, Ulysses S. Grant, to negotiate a reciprocal-trade treaty with Mexico.

Ulysses Grant's fascination with Mexico dated back to his days as a young army lieutenant fighting in the Mexican War. He had been appalled at the poverty inflicted upon Mexicans by the large landowners, and for that reason he later supported the Mexican revolution led by Benito Juarez. When he left the presidency, Grant became chief executive of a company that proposed building a railroad from Texas to Mexico City, as a means of fostering free trade between the two nations.

Grant had also become a close friend of the Mexican ambassador to the United States, Matias Romero. In 1882, when Grant was commissioned to negotiate the trade agreement, Romero led the Mexican delegation, and their resulting handiwork became known as the Grant-Romero Treaty.

Agreed to in January 1883, this treaty established a list of manufactured goods and agricultural products that could be traded between the United States and Mexico free of any tariffs. Unfortunately for Grant, protectionist sympathies in Congress stymied his free-trade accomplishment. Although Grant placed his considerable prestige behind the treaty, critics charged him with negotiating primarily to promote his railroad for personal financial gain.

There was some truth to the charges. After his presidency, Grant frequently found himself in precarious financial straits, and he entered into a number of unwise business ventures. The Mexican Southern Railroad went bankrupt in 1884. That same year, the Senate approved the treaty, but with an amendment requiring congressional passage of enabling legislation.

In 1885 U.S. Grant died, and a year later the Senate formally scrapped the Grant-Romero Treaty after both houses refused to agree to the necessary legislation.

1887
MAY 29

Ben: Perley Poore

Benjamin Perley Poore Dies

On May 29, 1887, Benjamin Perley Poore died. Poore never served as a United States senator, but he was about as closely associated with this institution as any person could be without having won an election.

Ben: Perley Poore, or "Perley" as he signed his newspaper columns, was for decades the Washington correspondent of the *Boston Journal* and, at the same time, the clerk of the Senate Committee on Printing. He was also briefly the clerk of the Foreign Relations Committee. In the nineteenth century it was not at all unusual for newspaper reporters to moonlight as clerks to congressional committees and as secretaries to senators. They were in town for the same months as the Congress. They were literate men who could draft a good speech and handle constituent mail. And they always seemed to need the second salary. One supposes that they reciprocated by writing only favorable notices of the senators who hired them.

Perley became the premier patronage collector of his generation. In addition to his clerkship, he also edited the *Congressional Directory*—which he copyrighted in his own name—and the *Biographical Directory of the American Congress* and compiled *The Federal and State Constitutions* and a *Descriptive Catalogue of Government Publications*, all on government contracts. At the same time, he regularly published his gossipy news stories from Washington, which at the end of his career he compiled into a wonderful memoir: *Perley's Reminiscences of Sixty Years in the National Metropolis.*

At the age of sixty-six, the rotund and bewhiskered Ben: Perley Poore collapsed while climbing the stairs to the Senate chamber and died shortly thereafter. From the 1840s to the 1880s, he had faithfully recorded the stories of the Senate and its members, while collecting his patronage rewards.

Washington's Farewell Address

On February 22, 1888, Senator John Ingalls of Kansas became the first senator to read George Washington's Farewell Address before the Senate. By 1896, the reading had become a regular annual event. As of 1989, ninety-five senators had delivered the address, with the assignment alternating between the two political parties. At the conclusion of each reading, the appointed senator inscribes his or her name in a black, leather-bound book maintained by the secretary of the Senate.

President Washington did not publicly deliver his farewell address. Dated September 17, 1796, shortly after his decision not to seek a third term, it first appeared two days later in the Philadelphia *Daily American Advertiser*. Prepared with the assistance of Alexander Hamilton and James Madison, the document was intended as the first president's political testament to the nation. Although written ostensibly to inspire and guide future generations, the address actually set forth Washington's defense of his administration's record and embodied a classic statement of Federalist party doctrine.

Worn-out by the burdens of the presidency and the attacks of political foes, Washington feared for the safety of the nine-year-old Constitution. He believed that the stability of the Republic was threatened by the forces of geographical sectionalism, political factionalism, and interference by foreign powers in the nation's affairs. He urged Americans to subordinate sectional jealousies to common national interests. He also advised against permanent alliances with foreign powers, fearing that such connections would inevitably be subversive of America's national interest.

The first and last pages of George Washington's Farewell Address

1888
MARCH 31

Private Claims Bills

At the end of the day on March 31, 1888, assistant Senate Doorkeeper Isaac Bassett followed his daily custom of jotting down his thoughts on the day's activity. That evening he wrote: "The Senate passed *more bills* than they ever did before in the history of the Senate. Numbered one-hundred and eighty-five." At first glance, we might think that that must have been quite a day. The *Congressional Record*, however, reveals that the reason Bassett could report this great number of bills passed was because they were almost all private claims bills.

Private claims bills are intended for the benefit of an individual or group. They are used essentially as a court of last resort, because the people seeking relief must have exhausted all reasonable administrative and judicial procedures before asking Congress to intercede on their behalf. The first private claims bill was passed on September 24, 1789, and gave seventeen months of back pay to Baron de Glaubeck, a foreign officer who served America during the revolution.

In the late nineteenth century, land claims, military justice claims and pension claims were the most common types of private claims bills. Most of the 185 bills Bassett mentioned, for example, were pension claims arising from the Civil War. S. 1957, for instance, granted a pension to Virtue Smith, widow of David W. Smith, "late a private in Company A, First Regiment, Minnesota Volunteers." The 1946 Legislative Reorganization Act created the Federal Tort Claims Court to relieve Congress of the burden created by the mushrooming number of such cases. As a result, today only the small number of private claims cases not covered by the court reach the Senate each year.

1888
OCTOBER 15

Senate Nears End of Marathon Session

On October 15, 1888, the Senate of the Fiftieth Congress struggled to complete its work in the final days of what had then become its longest and perhaps least productive session.

The ingredients for stalemate were present in abundance. The Democratic party controlled the presidency and the House of Representatives, while Republicans held a slim two-vote majority in the Senate. The major issue facing Congress concerned the management of a hundred-million-dollar federal government surplus. Democrats called for lower tariffs to reduce the surplus, while Republicans sought to spend the excess funds through generous pensions for Civil War veterans.

By mid-October, both parties had nominated their presidential candidates and the general elections loomed less than three weeks ahead. As the *Washington Star* observed: "The importance of the session cannot be judged by what was actually accomplished in the way of legislation. The mere passage, or failure to pass, a new tariff is not of as much consequence. The work of the session was the designation of the policies of the two parties and the clear presentation of each for approval or rejection by the popular voice."

The thirty senators who remained in town found themselves embroiled in a heated debate over a widow's pension. As a sign of the tensions that had built up during the frustratingly over-long session, one Republican senator branded Democratic President Grover Cleveland "an infamous libeler" for vetoing the private claim of a woman injured during the Civil War. But the votes—and indeed the members—were not there to override Cleveland's veto. Five days later, only seven senators were present when Congress adjourned. Up in the press gallery, correspondents expressed their thanks over the adjournment by singing the Doxology's familiar line, "Praise God from whom all blessings flow."

Sketches of senators, 1876

Facing page, an 1897 watercolor by Walter Paris, titled, *A Stroll by the Capitol*

CHAPTER VI
Origins of the
Modern Senate
1890–1920

A "secret" session of the Senate

1890
FEBRUARY 2

Senate Investigates Leaks

In February 1890, an unusual special Senate committee was created. That panel had the responsibility of interrogating every member of the Senate to determine who was leaking information to the press about the Senate's executive sessions. Although the Senate had opened its legislative sessions to the public on a regular basis in 1795, it had continued to debate all executive business—treaties and nominations—behind closed doors.

Enterprising newspaper correspondents had little trouble reconstructing what went on in those secret sessions. In the parlance of the time, every reporter "had his own senator." That is, smart reporters cultivated good relations with at least one senator, who in turn would provide a reasonable accounting of what was said and what votes were cast. As soon as the doors were opened after an executive session, reporters sought out their sources, compiled their stories, and filed their dispatches for the next day's papers.

In 1890, Senator Joseph N. Dolph of Oregon became vexed over the repeated leakage of supposedly secret information concerning treaties. At Dolph's instigation, the Senate created a special committee, which he chaired, to uncover the source of the leaks. First the committee called newsmen, who naturally refused to divulge their sources. Then it summoned the senators themselves. The *New York Times* reported that the Senate pages scattered throughout the Capitol, calling individual senators to the committee to give testimony. Not surprisingly, no senator admitted to leaking secret session information. The Senate "smelling committee," as the press dubbed it, came to a frustrating end, no wiser than when it started. Leaks continued as before. It would be another forty years before the Senate abolished, for the most part, its secret executive sessions and held all of its debates in public.

1890
JUNE 29

The Senate Stables Boondoggle

On June 29, 1890, a *New York Times* reporter filed a story under the headline "A Very Costly Senate." Focusing on the "luxuries" enjoyed by senators at the taxpayers' expense, the article was sparked by debate over the perennial funding bill needed to keep members in ink, soap, and, in this case, horseshoes. While the reporter took aim at a variety of perquisites, he saved his deadliest fire for the Senate stables.

The stables came in for scrutiny when Senator Isham Harris of Tennessee tried to create the new position of superintendent of the Senate stables. Senator Eugene Hale of Maine successfully quashed the proposal, claiming that there were already three employees for each horse in the stables. That claim set the enterprising *Times* reporter off to inspect the stables at Delaware Avenue and C Street. Inside he found nine "Senate horses," five used to draw the Senate's wagons, and four for the riding pages, who carried messages around Capitol Hill. But he found thirteen "other horses," six of which belonged to senators, two to representatives, and the rest to various officers of the Congress. These thirteen horses were not fed, the reporter acknowledged, out of the Senate contingent fund, "out of which so much is fed." Members paid twelve dollars a month for their feed. But "for the attention that these guests of the Senate stables receive there is no charge. . . . The brushes, currycombs, cloths, and labor are all taken care of on the Senate payroll."

A quick survey of public livery stables revealed that such care would cost the average citizen no less than twenty dollars a month. "It is perfectly plain," fumed the aggrieved reporter, "that the man who is privileged to keep his horses in this stable can save the price of a pretty good horse—say $100—in a year." The reporter ferreted out the names of the owners of the thirteen "not Senate horses." It came as no surprise that Senator Harris, who had proposed the new position, was first on the list with one steed among the boarders in the Senate stables.

1890
JUNE 30

Cost to Keep a Senator in "Working Order"

On June 30, 1890, the *New York Times* published an article criticizing the Senate for its tendency toward "increased and useless expenses" for staff. The paper reported that the Senate, in its current legislative appropriations bill, sought $422,000 in funding for the salaries of 291 officers and employees. This would allow each member to have three staff assistants at an average individual salary of $1,451. By contrast, the House of Representatives requested $367,000 for 320 employees, less than one per member, at a salary 25 percent lower than for their Senate counterparts. The *Times* concluded that "while it costs $4,353 to run a senator, it costs but $1,116 to keep a representative in working order."

The issue of congressional staff funding has been around as long as there has been a Congress. Prior to the 1840s, members paid for staff assistance from personal funds. After that time, committee chairmen were authorized to hire part-time help at public expense. This led to a proliferation of committees to permit all but the most junior members on both sides of the aisle to chair a committee and thus have access to staff and to scarce office space.

In 1856, Congress authorized the employment of full-time clerks for the Senate Finance Committee and the House Ways and Means Committee. At the start of the Civil War, five years later, most of the additional major committees of the Senate and House obtained funding for full-time staff. Finally, in 1885, in part to curb the pressure to create additional committees, the Senate authorized each member who did not chair a committee to hire a clerk at six dollars per day. In 1893, three years after the *New York Times* article, the House passed a similar provision, citing an increasingly heavy work load and the need for efficiency that a permanent staff would promote.

1890
AUGUST 15

Busts of the Vice Presidents

On August 15, 1890, the last of the twenty niches that surround the Senate chamber at the gallery level was filled with the bust of Vice President Thomas A. Hendricks. Hendricks, a former representative and senator from Indiana, had served for eight months until his death in late 1885.

From the time of the chamber's completion in 1859 until March 1890, the twenty niches had remained empty. In 1886, the Senate Committee on the Library initiated a project to acquire likenesses of each vice president, in recognition of that official's constitutional role as president of the Senate. In awarding the first commissions, the committee tried to select artists associated with individual vice presidents' native states. Daniel Chester French, the nation's leading sculptor, who came from Massachusetts, won the commission for the bust of the first vice president, John Adams. Augustus Saint-Gaudens, raised in New York, portrayed Chester Arthur of that state.

In March 1890 Adams' bust was the first to be installed in the chamber. It was placed on the north wall to the left of the presiding officer's desk. Over the next five months, additional busts arrived and were located in the alternating niches according to the chronological sequence of vice presidential service. The arrival of the Hendricks bust in August completed the placements. While his was the twentieth bust installed in the chamber, Hendricks was actually the twenty-first vice president. The discrepancy is explained by the fact that the bust of the eighteenth vice president, Henry Wilson, rests just off the chamber in the Vice President's Room, where he died in 1875. Busts of succeeding vice presidents have been placed in the halls adjacent to the chamber, where they observe our deliberations from a distance.

1893
MARCH 13

Senate Committee Reorganization

On March 13, 1893, the *New York Times* carried a story about the reorganization of Senate committees following the Democratic victory in the election of 1892. The shift in majorities meant considerable change in committee structure. Whereas today the Senate has sixteen standing committees and five select or special committees, in 1893 the Republican and Democratic conferences were faced with making assignments to forty-four standing committees and sixteen select committees.

In point of fact, however, there existed about the same number of important committees then as now. The many other committees existed primarily to give each chairman a room in the Capitol and at least one staff person. The Democratic conference hoped to give every member of the party a committee chairmanship.

Thus, along with such familiar standing committees as Finance and Foreign Relations, the Senate had standing committees to audit and control the contingent expenses of the Senate; on epidemic diseases; to examine the several branches of the civil service; on fisheries; on the improvement of the Mississippi River; on private land claims; on public buildings and grounds; on transportation routes to the seaboard; and on revolutionary claims—more than a century after the Revolution. There also existed select committees on the transportation and sale of meat products; on Indian depredations; to establish the university of the United States; and to inquire into all claims of citizens of the United States against the government of Nicaragua.

The new Democratic majority also planned to allot five committee chairmanships to senior members of the Republican party, the same number that the Democrats had held when they were in the minority. That is one Senate tradition that senior members of the minority would certainly have no objection to reviving.

1893
OCTOBER 8

Senators at Lunch

Throughout our history, commentators have tried to read meaning into every action of the nation's political leaders. It is, therefore, not surprising that on October 8, 1893, the *New York Times* devoted a long column to the luncheon habits of United States senators.

In the early nineteenth century, there was only one eating place in the Capitol. A tiny room known as the "Hole in the Wall," it was located to the south of the old Senate chamber. One entered through a door in the Senate post office. The "Hole in the Wall" offered all kinds of "edibles and liquor," but specialized in oysters—raw, fried, steamed, or baked. In the 1850s, when the current Senate and House wings were added to the Capitol, more formal dining rooms were constructed. Senators then ate in the richly decorated room that is now the anteroom to the Senators' Dining Room.

The rules prohibited the sale of alcoholic beverages in the Capitol but the proprietor of the restaurant knew the tastes of his customers and kept them satisfied. The *Times* reported that in 1893 the senators enjoyed cocktails with their lunches and an occasional "cold bottle" of beer. Senator Arthur Pue Gorman of Maryland was so fond of cold lamb that it was never missing from the menu. Senator George Frisbie Hoar of Massachusetts favored the restaurant's terrapin. Senator J.C.S. Blackburn of Kentucky swore that the Senate restaurant was the only place in the world to get true deviled ham. Senator Edward Murphy, Jr. of New York always ate a plain luncheon but then refreshed himself with a strong cigar. New York's other senator, David Hill, generally passed up the more tempting dishes on the menu and dined on soup, or eggs on toast. Hill was always more preoccupied with politics than food and could often be seen waving his spoon to make a point, rather than using it as an eating utensil. That is the way senators ate a century ago.

The Senate dining room, 1886

Members of Congress debating the silver bill

1893
OCTOBER 30

Sherman Silver Purchase Act Repealed

On October 30, 1893, the Senate repealed the Sherman Silver Purchase Act after one of the most bitter filibusters of the nineteenth century. President Grover Cleveland was certain the roots of the terrible economic depression then gripping the nation lay in the decline of government credit due to the continued purchase of silver under the Sherman Act. He called the Fifty-third Congress into extra session in August and threatened to keep it in all summer until it repealed the Sherman Act.

When the extra session convened, the Senate Finance Committee, chaired by Daniel Voorhees of Indiana, reported the repeal legislation by a one-vote majority. As soon as the issue reached the floor on August 29, the long filibuster began, led by silverites—primarily western senators. One stupendous speech by Senator John P. Jones of Nevada, requiring large parts of seven days to deliver, filled a hundred pages of the *Congressional Record*. When, after several days, motions for cloture began to be offered by the pro-repeal forces, they only evoked more stormy discussions, turning the debate away from repeal toward more fundamental freedom-of-speech issues.

Voorhees decided to resort to a continuous session to break the deadlock. After the Senate convened at eleven o'clock on the morning of October 11, it remained in unbroken session for thirty-nine hours, until 1:45 a.m. on the thirteenth. But even this grueling tactic failed to break the back of the filibuster. Finally, on October 24, several anti-repeal Democrats met with administration representatives, strongly urging them to surrender, which they did, and the filibuster suddenly collapsed. On the evening of October 30, after a forty-six-day filibuster, the Sherman Act was repealed by a vote of 43 to 32. Cleveland and the gold Democrats had won, but at a high price. Their party was torn in two, and the wound would be a long time healing.

159

1894
MAY 1

Coxey's Army at the Capitol

On May 1, 1894, police arrested a man for walking on Capitol grass. This may seem an unlikely event to commemorate, but the man was Jacob Coxey, and his arrest culminated one of the most dramatic protest movements of the nineteenth century.

The United States was suffering a terrible depression in 1894, and more than two million unemployed men wandered the countryside in search of work. The federal government disclaimed any responsibility for the unemployed, but the crisis was too severe for local governments and private charities to handle. In Ohio, affluent businessman Jacob Coxey proposed that the federal government end the depression by putting unemployed men to work building public roads. Sympathetic congressmen introduced a "Good Roads bill," but Congress refused to act.

"We'll send a message to Washington with boots on," said Coxey, and he called for a march of the unemployed on Washington. On Easter Sunday, only a hundred men started the march, accompanied by half as

Jacob S. Coxey behind bars

many reporters who generally ridiculed their efforts. But, as the march progressed, it attracted greater numbers, and the desperate plight and determination of "Coxey's army" came to impress many observers.

Officials in Washington viewed the approaching marchers as an invading mob. Masses of police and federal troops were called out to protect the Capitol, and they refused to allow marchers on the grounds. Coxey slipped through the police lines. He raced for the steps, where he tried to speak, but was arrested and driven off to jail. Jacob Coxey was convicted for carrying banners on the Capitol grounds and for walking on the grass. He was sentenced to twenty days and fined five dollars. That was the price in 1894 for attempting to carry out one's constitutional right to petition Congress.

1894
JULY 22

Direct Election of Senators

On July 22, 1894, the House of Representatives voted 137 to 49 in favor of a joint resolution proposing a constitutional amendment for direct election of United States senators.

The House recognized that the constitutional system that permitted state legislatures to elect senators had deteriorated to a national scandal. The previous year, in 1893, five state legislatures had deadlocked, and in three cases—Montana, Washington, and Wyoming—these deadlocks had prevented the election of a senator, leaving those seats vacant. As the historian George Haynes wrote, "Statistics such as these can give nothing more than a hint of the stubbornness and acrimony of these contests." There were numerous charges that bribery was used to sway the votes of state legislators. Votes were delayed as legislators hid or scattered. In 1891 the Florida legislature needed thirty-five days of balloting to elect a senator. In 1893 the Oregon legislature took thirty-two days to cast fifty-eight ballots before making its choice; and the Oregon candidate who won by a majority of *one* vote was nominated only fifteen minutes earlier, immediately before the term of that legislature was due to expire.

Throughout the nineteenth century, reformers in Congress made unsuccessful attempts to amend the Constitution to change this disgraceful situation. In the 1890s the idea was revived by young Nebraska representative William Jennings Bryan, later three-time Democratic candidate for president. But in each case, senatorial opponents were able to defeat their efforts, either by burying the issue in committee or by loading it with unacceptable amendments. The situation grew steadily worse until at last an amendment was adopted in 1913.

1895
MARCH 29

Senate Chamber in Need of Renovation

On March 29, 1895, the *New York Times* noted that senators were again complaining that their chamber was badly in need of renovation. One problem was the stained glass ceiling. Sunlight poured through the colored panes, causing amusing multicolored effects on the senators' faces below. The shadows of clouds sailing overhead made the chamber look like a goldfish bowl. Not only did the glass ceiling absorb sound from the floor, but the noise during thunderstorms often forced the Senate to recess.

A more vexing problem was that of ventilation. At the time the Senate wing was completed in 1859, the *New York Herald* had boasted that "the heating and ventilation arrangements are said to be the largest in the world—those of the English House of Parliament not excepted. Every portion of the Capitol—that mountainous mass of marble—is at once ventilated and warmed by one apparatus." Unfortunately, that gargantuan apparatus did not work as well in practice as it did in theory. Senators complained of stagnant air, suffocating heat, and intolerable dryness almost from the moment they moved in.

Mr. President, senators labored on in the unimproved chamber for another half century. Not until 1949 and 1950 did this chamber undergo a thorough renovation. While the work was underway, scaffolding occasionally crowded the senators out of this chamber and down the hall into the old Senate chamber, where their predecessors met a century before. The transformation of the chamber eliminated the old stained glass ceiling, the poor acoustics, and the stale air. The result is the pleasant chamber we meet in today.

1897
FEBRUARY 20

Kansas Senator Prepares "Oratorical Eruption"

The February 20, 1897 edition of *Harper's Weekly* displayed on its cover an eye-catching illustration captioned "The Senator from Kansas Preparing an Oratorical Eruption." Senator William Peffer appears in the center of the illustration, seated at his desk in the Senate chamber. Surrounded by mountains of papers, he is attended by two young pages bearing large books. Sporting a waist-length beard, the Kansas senator appears lost in thought while drafting a major speech. This illustration reminds us that, prior to the twentieth century, the Senate chamber served as the principal office space for many senators.

A journalist and former editor of the *Kansas Farmer*, William Peffer belonged to the Populist party and served in the Senate from 1891 until March 1897. As a third-party member, he had little influence in the Senate. He was known as a persistent and somewhat tedious speaker on a wide variety of subjects. One biographer assessed him as follows: "His tall, well-rounded figure, his unusually long and wavy beard, which he combed constantly with his fingers as he talked, his heavy, dry, excessively statistical speeches,

IMPORTANT ARTICLE FROM MADRID IN THIS NUMBER.

HARPER'S WEEKLY

JOURNAL OF CIVILIZATION

Vol. XLI.—No. 2096.
Copyright, 1897, by Harper & Brothers.
All Rights Reserved.

NEW YORK, SATURDAY, FEBRUARY 20, 1897.

TEN CENTS A COPY.
FOUR DOLLARS A YEAR.

THE SENATOR FROM KANSAS PREPARING AN ORATORICAL ERUPTION.

Senator William Peffer of Kansas on the Senate floor

his absence of humor, and his deadly earnestness made him a conspicuous figure in the Senate, and one which in caricature came to typify Populism."

Soon after Peffer left the Senate, he composed these memorable lines, which are as applicable today as they were nine decades ago: "The Senate is a school. The world's history is its text book. The record of a single day's proceedings frequently shows a range of work as wide as Christendom. No man well made up can be there long, if he will but listen, without himself becoming wiser and better. His opportunities for usefulness multiply as the new days come to him; his intellectual horizon expands, his view broadens and he grows stronger."

1898
NOVEMBER 6

Gas Explosion Rocks Capitol

In the early evening of November 6, 1898, a tremendous explosion rocked the Capitol. Moments earlier, a Capitol policeman had detected a strong smell of gas, but that was not uncommon in the building, which was honeycombed with gas pipes. This time, however, the odor was the harbinger of disaster: gas was pouring out of an old pipe that had recently been capped during the electrification of the building. Within minutes, there was a huge blast and tongues of flame shot out of the east front windows of the Senate wing. Black smoke billowed up against the darkened sky.

The explosion occurred almost directly under the first floor crypt area in the center of the building. The blast blew out windows and doors in both the Senate and House wings, but the fire that followed spread mainly through the Senate side, filling this chamber and all the rooms around it with dense, dark smoke. Immediately in the conflagration's path on the first floor was a room used to store valuable old Supreme Court records, all of which were lost. Flames quickly engulfed that room; the floor buckled; stone pillars cracked; an elevator, only recently installed for the justices, melted into a twisted mass. One floor above was the Supreme Court chamber, now restored as the old Senate chamber. It too suffered serious damage.

By the orange glow of the flames, bystanders could see long ladders flung up along the east front and firemen climbing up toward the Supreme Court chamber's windows to direct water onto the flames. After nearly three exhausting hours, the flames were doused. The last wisps of smoke puffed out, and rivulets of water running down the Capitol's sides dried up. Guards were posted at all entrances to prevent souvenir hunters from entering the building, and everyone else went home, knowing the next day would bring the grim task of assessing the terrible damage.

Albert J. Beveridge Sworn In

On March 4, 1899, Albert J. Beveridge was sworn in as United States senator. His was one of those Horatio Alger stories that we Americans treasure so much. Born on a struggling small midwestern farm, Beveridge in his teens worked as a plowboy, railroad hand, logger, and teamster. All that time, he was saving money for his education, and in 1881 he was able to attend what is now DePauw University, from which he graduated with honors. After a career as a lawyer in Indiana, he was elected as a Republican member of the United States Senate in 1899. At thirty-six, he was the youngest senator at the turn of the century.

Beveridge was not just any senator. He was by far the most powerful and popular orator in the Senate of his time. He also became a leader in the progressive wing of the Republican party, during the period we call the Progressive Era. Beveridge was a strong supporter of President Theodore Roosevelt's "Square Deal" politics. In reaction to revelations about unsanitary conditions in the meat-packing industry, Beveridge drafted the Meat Inspection Act. He was also a leader in the movement to outlaw child labor and he fought against the rise of corporate monopolies.

In foreign affairs, Beveridge was equally outspoken. He endorsed American overseas expansion and even traveled to the Philippines to get a first-hand look at the territory the United States acquired as a result of the Spanish-American War. In the days before jet travel, such a journey meant a considerable commitment of time and energy.

Beveridge lost his bid for reelection to a third term. He retired to become an outstanding historian. Today, the American Historical Association names one of its most prestigious annual awards after Albert J. Beveridge.

Albert Beveridge of Indiana

HON. JOHN JAMES INGALLS, OF KANSAS, PRESIDENT OF THE SENATE OF THE UNITED STATES.—Drawn by Paul Renouard.—[See Page 498.]

John Ingalls of Kansas

1900
AUGUST 16

John J. Ingalls Dies

On August 16, 1900, John James Ingalls died. The son of a shoe manufacturer, Ingalls was born in Middleton, Massachusetts, and spent his early years in New England. He graduated from Williams College before joining so many of his generation in the great migration westward. In 1858 he arrived in the frontier territory of Kansas, which he made his home. From 1873 to 1891, he represented Kansas in the United States Senate.

From all accounts, Senator Ingalls was one of the sharpest-tongued debaters ever to serve in this institution. His biographer wrote that Ingalls seldom took the middle ground. "He was inclined to annihilate critics, whether friend or foe, and compromise in debate was to Ingalls a form of surrender." Once, he caught Senator Joseph E. Brown, a Georgia Democrat, changing the substance of the *Record* on a previous exchange between them. Ingalls denounced this "falsifying and forgery," compared Senator Brown to a "thug stabbing a sleeping enemy," and branded his opponent as the "Uriah Heep of the Senate . . . a sniveling political Pecksniff."

Senator Ingalls never hesitated to say what he thought. He decried British imperialism, calling that nation "a ruffian and coward, and the bully among the nations of the earth." He dismissed as political eunuchs those Republican reformers who supported the policies of Democratic President Grover Cleveland. Alluding to Cleveland, he charged that "there is no man in this country whose ignorance is so profound, whose obscurity is so impenetrable, and whose antecedents are so degraded that he may not justifiably aspire to a Presidential nomination—by the Democratic Party."

Kansans enjoyed John J. Ingalls' vivid style and elected him to three terms in the Senate, where he served for four years as president pro tempore. Today his statue stands in Statuary Hall, seemingly poised to do verbal battle with all foes.

Benjamin Tillman of South Carolina

168

1902
FEBRUARY 28

Senate Censures Members for Fist Fight

Under the Constitution the Senate retains the exclusive right to set standards for the conduct of its members. On seven occasions in its two hundred-year history, the Senate has found it necessary to censure members for inappropriate behavior. One of those occasions occurred on February 28, 1902.

On February 22, the Senate had debated a bill providing funding for the recently acquired Philippine Islands. At that time, a dispute arose between the two senators from South Carolina. Senator Benjamin Tillman charged that "improper influences" had been used to change the vote of his colleague John McLaurin on the Philippine treaty.

Word of Tillman's charges reached McLaurin at a committee session. He raced back to the Senate chamber and, pale with anger, branded the allegations "a willful, malicious, and deliberate lie." Upon hearing this, the fifty-four-year-old Tillman jumped forward and struck the forty-one-year-old McLaurin above the left eye. McLaurin returned a punch to his adversary's nose. Both men traded blows until separated by a doorkeeper and several senators. The presiding officer immediately ordered the doors closed and the galleries cleared. The Senate, by unanimous vote, found both members in contempt and referred the matter to a committee. On February 28, the Senate, after debating the relative guilt of the two, and its authority to suspend members, censured both men "for disorderly conduct and flagrant violation" of its rules. Each combatant was suspended for six days from the time of the fight.

As a consequence of this event, the Senate adopted the regulation we know today as Rule 19. That rule provides that "no Senator in debate shall, directly or indirectly, by any form of words impute to another Senator or to other Senators any conduct or motive unworthy or unbecoming a Senator."

1906
FEBRUARY 17

"Treason of the Senate" Series Begins

On February 17, 1906, the March issue of *Cosmopolitan* magazine arrived on the nation's newsstands, with the first in a series of nine articles entitled "The Treason of the Senate."

For several decades prior to the appearance of the series, the Senate had come into public disrepute through the intimate association of some of its members with large corporate interests. At a time when senators were still elected by state legislatures, there were ample grounds for concluding that the industrial capitalists who influenced the statehouses also exercised great power in the selection of some members. Only weeks before the *Cosmopolitan* series began, two senators had been convicted on charges of taking fees from corporate clients for interceding on their behalf with federal agencies.

Publisher William Randolph Hearst had hired popular novelist David Graham Phillips to prepare an investigative series. Employing the innuendo and overstatement typical of other so-called muckraking writers of the day, Phillips selected twenty-one senators for particular attention. His first installment included the following typical statement: "Treason is a strong word, but not too strong, rather too weak to characterize the situation in which the Senate is the eager, resourceful, indefatigable agent of interests as hostile to the American people as any invading army could be, and vastly more dangerous."

Phillips overplayed his hand. Although his series initially doubled the magazine's readership, it soon backfired. Genuine reformers feared that his carelessly researched articles would seriously harm their own efforts. When the series concluded in November, Phillips gladly returned to writing novels. In spite of its limitations, however, the series hastened adoption of a constitutional amendment providing for direct election of senators.

Cover of *Cosmopolitan,*
April, 1906

1906
JUNE 4

Arthur Pue Gorman Dies

On the wall outside the Senate chamber hangs an oil portrait of a person whose career in this institution is unique. Over a span of fifty-six years, Arthur Pue Gorman of Maryland served in positions ranging from Senate page to Democratic party leader. On June 4, 1906, Gorman died following a long illness.

Gorman began his Senate career in 1852 at the age of thirteen. Although he had ended his formal schooling to work here, his education in the ways of practical politics—and of human nature—was just beginning. As the nation raced toward the crisis of disunion, and the Senate chamber served as the major theater for that drama, Gorman had a front-row seat. One of the principal actors in that drama, Senator Stephen A. Douglas, hired him as a private secretary. In that capacity, Gorman accompanied the Illinois senator during the 1858 senatorial campaign tour which featured the now legendary series of debates between Douglas and Abraham Lincoln. After that campaign, Gorman moved up through the ranks of choice Senate patronage positions, first as messenger, then assistant doorkeeper, assistant postmaster, and finally as Senate postmaster during the Civil War. Gorman's political ties to President Andrew Johnson cost him his job in 1866, as Senate Republicans locked horns with this increasingly unpopular president.

In the 1870s Gorman served in the Maryland legislature, but by 1880 he had decided that the most interesting political arena in the nation was the United States Senate. When Maryland Senator William Whyte refused to support Gorman in his wish to be elected secretary of the Senate, Gorman put his political education to work. To Whyte's surprise, Gorman maneuvered within the state legislature and defeated him in the 1880 senatorial election. In 1893 he became the first official chairman of the Senate Democratic caucus. Although defeated for reelection in 1898, he returned to the Senate in 1903 and resumed his post as Democratic floor leader. He served in that capacity until his death in 1906.

1906
OCTOBER 14

"People's Lobby"

On October 14, 1906, there was talk of creating a "People's Lobby" in Congress. In the wake of the muckraking magazines' attacks on "the Treason of the Senate," prominent reformers called for the establishment of such a citizens' lobby, to scrutinize legislation, detect any "snakes," and warn the public about them.

Charles Thompson, a *New York Times* Washington correspondent, responded that in fact a "People's Lobby" already existed. It consisted of 150 trained professional observers, who were "weighing, doubting, scrutinizing, [and] suspecting" congressional behavior every day. He was referring to the Senate and House press galleries.

According to Thompson, "Not a week goes by that some bill is not killed or some departmental error corrected by the People's Lobby." He cited the example of the Hepburn railroad rate bill, which had recently been enacted after a long and bitter congressional debate, as follows:

> At every step of the way every proposition that was offered was scrutinized and its character shown up. Every attempt to hamstring the bill met instant and wide publicity. . . . When the bill came over from the House it was to be an easy matter to emasculate it and turn it back to the president in a harmless condition. That no such effort succeeded is due to the People's Lobby. So closely did it watch the game that day after day senators, red with indignation, were obliged to rise in their places and hurl back some new charge that had appeared in the morning's paper. The People's Lobby was unmoved by such spectacular denial; it went right on with its work.

Eighty-three years later, it is good to report that the "People's Lobby" is still on the job, keeping a watchful eye on the Senate's proceedings.

"The 'People's Lobby,'" *New York Times*, October 14, 1906

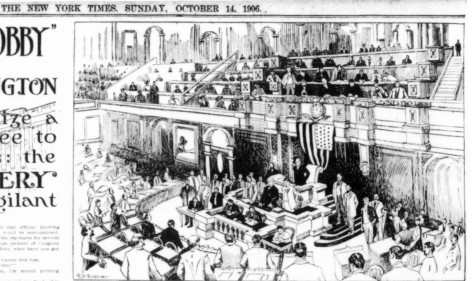

1907
DECEMBER 2

The "Cherokee Strip"

When the first session of the Sixtieth Congress convened on December 2, 1907, Republican senators found themselves in a pleasant quandary. Since the 1860s, Republicans had dominated almost every Congress, and since 1900 they had controlled the Senate by increasingly large majorities. The November 1906 elections had given the Republicans their most decisive victory ever. The Senate party composition in the new Congress would be a lopsided 61 Republicans to 31 Democrats. The immediate problem became how to find space for all of those Republicans on the east side of the center aisle, where party members had sat ever since the Civil War.

In the old Senate chamber, an equal number of desks had been placed on either side of the aisle, without regard to party size. There was no firm rule as to placement, and during the 1840s and 1850s some Democrats could be found sitting at random on the Whig side. The new chamber, however, was large enough to permit a more flexible seating arrangement; since the 1870s, desks had been moved back and forth across the aisle to permit all members of each party to sit together.

Party leaders finally decided that ten Republicans, all junior members, would have to sit with the Democrats in the rear row or on the end seats. Their new location became known as the "Cherokee Strip," meaning that the overflow majority party members were off their reservation. (The Cherokee Strip in Oklahoma referred to land belonging to neither the Indian Territory nor the states.) The "Cherokee Strip" has only been called into play one other time since 1907. In 1937, during the Seventy-fifth Congress, 13 of the 76 Democrats sat with the 16 Republicans and 4 independents.

1908
AUGUST 4

William B. Allison: Longest-Serving Standing Committee Chairman

When Senator William Boyd Allison of Iowa died in office on August 4, 1908, he established a Senate record as the longest-serving standing committee chairman. For twenty-four-and-a-half years, from 1881 to 1893 and from 1896 to 1908, Allison chaired the Committee on Appropriations, quietly shaping its character during those turbulent years of national growth.

As a young lawyer in the 1850s, Allison cast his lot with the newly established Republican party. After four terms in the House, Allison won election to the Senate in 1872. Given his choice of committee assignments, he selected Finance and Appropriations. Considered a "politician's politician," Allison rose quickly within the Senate's Republican hierarchy. After only eight years on the Appropriations Committee, he became its chairman. At the turn of the twentieth century, when the Republican party enjoyed overwhelming majorities in this body, Allison served for six years as chairman of the Senate Republican Conference.

William Allison established several other Senate records. In 1905, he became the first member of the Senate to serve more than thirty-two years.

His overall tenure of thirty-five years and five months stood until 1928 as the longest service of any senator.

Senator Allison's twenty-four-and-a-half-year record as a committee chairman is not likely to be broken soon. Senator John P. Jones of Nevada, who chaired the Committee to Audit and Control the Contingent Expenses of the Senate for all but two congresses between 1875 and 1903—a total of twenty-three years and two months—holds the record as second longest-serving standing committee chairman. Senator Warren G. Magnuson of Washington served twenty-three years as chairman of the Commerce Committee, from 1955 to 1978, the longest *unbroken* term for a standing committee chairman.

William Allison of Iowa

1909
MARCH 9

First Senate Subway Opens

On March 9, 1909, the Senate subway system opened.

As senators know all too well, our attendance may be required on the floor for a vote at all hours. This keeps members rushing between the Capitol and the Senate office buildings. Given only fifteen minutes to cast our votes, we rely heavily on the subway to facilitate passage back and forth.

The need for the first subway occurred as the Senate constructed its first office building, now known as the Richard Russell Building. When the building opened in March 1909, it provided at least two rooms for every senator, along with the small Senate staff. A tunnel, through which the first subway ran, connected the office building with the Capitol. This subway, however, was not a railroad but rather a pair of lemon-yellow, storage-battery-powered buses, made by Studebaker. These high, four-wheeled coaches carried eight passengers—whose heads bobbed just inches from the tunnel's ceiling. The old *Washington Evening Star* announced the first run with a headline: "All Aboard for the Capitol! Car Leaves at Once. Through Express." And the *New York Evening Journal* added a little doggerel:

> A subway for our Senators is running every day:
> There's no 'Step Lively!' 'Hurry Up!' and best of all, no pay.

The electric buses, however, proved too slow, and in 1912 they were replaced by electrically powered cars operating on a single-rail track. Our current subway system was installed in 1960 to extend to the Dirksen Building and more recently to the Hart Building. We salute the subways for the eighty years that they have kept the Senate on the move.

The first Senate subway car

VOL. XXXVII. No. 949.   PUCK BUILDING, New York, May 15th, 1895.   PRICE 10 CENTS.

Copyright, 1895, by Keppler & Schwarzmann.

"What fools these Mortals be."

Puck

Entered at N. Y. P. O. as Second-class Mail Matter.

WITHOUT A FRIEND.

Puck's reaction to the income tax of 1894

176

1909
JULY 5

Senate Adopts Income Tax Amendment

On July 5, 1909, the Senate unanimously approved a constitutional amendment that has had an impact on this nation's economic and social development far exceeding the expectations of those who voted for it. In February 1913, the thirty-word resolution became the Constitution's Sixteenth Amendment. The amendment states simply, "The Congress shall have the power to lay and collect taxes on incomes, from whatever source derived, without apportionment among the several states, and without regard to any census or enumeration."

The nation's first income tax—a 3-percent levy on incomes above $800—had been passed as an emergency measure during the first year of the Civil War. Its rates were increased during the war until incomes between $600 and $5,000 were taxed at 5 percent and those over $5,000 at 10 percent. The tax was abolished in 1872. In 1894, Congress added a 2-percent tax on incomes over $2,000 to a tariff reduction measure to offset its anticipated lower revenues. A year later, the Supreme Court declared this provision unconstitutional, ruling that taxes on personal property were direct taxes and, as provided in the Constitution, could only be levied by apportionment among the states.

In 1909, members of Congress removed an income tax provision from a pending tariff bill out of concern that it, too, would be ruled unconstitutional. This prompted them to pass the Sixteenth Amendment. The Underwood Tariff Act of 1913 contained the first regular income tax under the new amendment. It set a 1-percent tax on incomes from $3,000 to $20,000 and, at the upper end, a 6-percent levy on incomes over $500,000. By 1920, this tax was contributing ten times as much revenue as was received from customs duties—the previous major source of national funds. Since that time, income taxes, however unpleasant, have continued to be the prime means of funding America's domestic and defense programs.

1910
MARCH 6

Thomas Collier Platt Dies

On March 6, 1910, Thomas Collier Platt died. His career as a New York political boss and as a United States senator typifies the influence of political party machines at the turn of the twentieth century. Early in his life, Platt became a close ally of the powerful New York "stalwart" Republican Roscoe Conkling. Gaining influence in the party from his position as county clerk, Platt parlayed his skill in obtaining political favors for others into seats first in the House of Representatives in 1873, and then in the Senate in 1881.

Platt's Machiavellian political maneuvers backfired in early 1881 over a patronage dispute. In return for Conkling's support in the presidential campaign of 1880, President James Garfield had agreed to consult the senator on all New York appointments. When Garfield appointed William H. Robertson, a Conkling enemy, to the strategic post of collector of the port of

New York, Conkling was livid. He called the appointment "perfidy without parallel" and promised a bitter fight, from which he expected to emerge victorious. After a two-month struggle, however, it appeared that the Senate would back Garfield.

On May 16, 1881, only seventy-three days after taking his place in the Senate, Platt, along with Conkling, resigned from the Senate before the confirmation vote. Both men were confident that the New York legislature would quickly vindicate their opposition to the president by reelecting them to their Senate seats. To their consternation, the legislature selected two others. The episode ended Conkling's political career and began a period of seclusion for his protégé, Platt, Eventually, Platt recovered his power and inherited Conkling's organization. The New York Legislature elected him to the Senate in 1897 and again in 1903. Although virtually silent in the Senate, Platt would continue to orchestrate New York politics from Washington.

1911
MAY 11

Jacob Gallinger of New Hampshire

President Pro Tempore Election Deadlocked

On May 11, 1911, the Senate became entangled in a bitter deadlock over the election of a president pro tempore. This dispute demonstrated a significant change of political ideology within the early twentieth-century Congress.

In the 1910 midterm congressional elections, Democrats had gained a majority in the House of Representatives and had picked up ten Senate seats. This reduced the Republican margin of control to seven votes. The forty-nine Senate Republicans were split into progressive and conservative wings. Among the progressives were seven "insurgents" who hoped to topple the Senate's entrenched old-guard leadership. In this effort, they were inspired by the success of a recent major revolt in the House. There, insurgents had stripped Speaker Joseph Cannon of his power to appoint committees and their chairmen.

On April 27, 1911, shortly after the Senate of the Sixty-second Congress convened, Maine's William Frye resigned as president pro tempore due to illness. Frye had served in that post for fifteen years. A man of conservative personal and political temperament, he was considered one of the "wheel-horses" of the Senate and was deeply respected by senators of both parties.

On May 11, the Senate began balloting for Frye's replacement. Each party caucus nominated a senior member. Republican insurgents divided their votes among four lesser candidates. On each of the seven ballots, Georgia Democrat Augustus Bacon received a plurality but remained several votes short of the necessary majority. The other major candidate, New Hampshire Republican Jacob Gallinger, followed closely behind. After several days of rancorous debate, leaders of both parties reluctantly agreed to alternate the duties of president pro tempore between Bacon and Gallinger for the remainder of the Sixty-second Congress.

1911
JULY 30

New Senators Ignore Traditions

On July 30, 1911, the combination of an oppressive summer heat wave and a large new class of freshmen senators provoked the *Washington Sunday Star* to publish a feature article entitled "Smashing the Time-honored Precedents of the Senate." The article provided a tongue-in-cheek account of recent and alarmingly unsenatorial innovations. Accounting, in part, for this break with the past was the extraordinary statistic that 41 percent of the Senate's members had begun their service within the past four years. Among them, according to the article, were "a whole drove of unruly and upstart young men, who move, with a pitiful and openly admitted lack of knowledge of rules and precedents, and with a shameless disregard of their own ignorance, [to denounce] the time-honored precedent and courtesy of the Senate, and [to] bait the few survivors of the old dignity."

The results of this new attitude could be seen in the work of Utah's Reed Smoot, who arranged for the hanging of four "plebeian propeller-blade electric fans" from the ceiling of the Senate chamber. This followed Vice President James Sherman's earlier unprecedented action of installing a noiseless electric fan on the presiding officer's desk. The writer asked: "Has not the palm leaf fanned the Senate through untold summers? Is one heated spell more or less to induce the abandonment of honorable customs of a century or so, and the adoption of the vulgar attributes of the modern age?"

The sweltering July sessions prompted newer members to suggest that the Senate conclude its seemingly endless debate on pending legislation, vote, and go home. Despite the twin pressures of heat and indifference to tradition, the Senate of 1911 lumbered on for another two weeks into the dog days of August before adjourning.

1912
MAY 28

Senate Committee Reports on "Titanic" Disaster

On May 28, 1912, a special Senate subcommittee issued a dramatic report on its investigation into the sinking of the *Titanic*. Six weeks earlier, on April 15, 1912, the maiden voyage of the world's largest ship had ended in disaster, with the loss of fifteen hundred lives. Among the dead were many prominent Americans, including the brother of United States Senator Simon Guggenheim.

In the resulting wave of national anguish, Senator William Alden Smith of Michigan introduced a resolution authorizing a Senate investigation. His six-member subcommittee began its inquiry on April 18, as surviving passengers and crew sailed for New York City. When Chairman Smith learned that the *Titanic*'s owners intended to return the surviving crewmen to England to prevent them from giving potentially damaging testimony, he used the Senate's subpoena power to compel the presence of key witnesses.

Subcommittee hearings opened in New York City's Waldorf-Astoria Hotel and then moved to the newly opened Caucus Room in what is now called the Russell Senate Office Building. On April 22, senators, House members, diplomats, reporters, and hundreds of other spectators crowded into that room. When police blocked further entrance, many rushed to nearby rooms and climbed out onto balconies to watch the proceedings through the room's great French windows. Disconcerted by this raucous mob, the subcommittee held the remainder of its hearings in a much smaller room.

Although Senator Smith knew little about nautical matters, he proved to be a resourceful and tireless investigator. He contended that, in such calamities, "energy is often more desirable than learning." In this inquiry, Chairman Smith significantly broadened the precedents undergirding the Senate's investigative powers. The work of his subcommittee ultimately produced significant reforms in international maritime safety.

Senate subcommittee conducting hearings on the *Titanic* disaster, April 1912

1912
JULY 13

Senate Invalidates Lorimer Election

On July 13, 1912, the Senate invalidated the 1909 election of Senator William Lorimer of Illinois. This was not the first Senate election invalidated, but it was the last under the old system in which state legislatures elected senators.

The U.S. Constitution had left it entirely up to the state legislatures to decide the manner in which they would select senators. This created a chaotic situation in many states. Often the two houses of the legislature could not agree on how to proceed, and for whole congresses Senate seats remained vacant. In such an unsettled situation, corruption was inevitable, and reformers charged that some senators had bought their elections by bribing state legislators.

In 1909, a split within the Republican party divided the Illinois legislature. After ninety-four fruitless ballots, the legislature finally elected William Lorimer to the Senate. Known as the "blond boss," the former U.S. representative had been instrumental in selecting three Chicago mayors, two Illinois governors, and one U.S. senator. Immediately after Lorimer took his Senate oath in June 1909, opponents petitioned the Senate to deny him his seat because of his alleged efforts to bribe state legislators. Eighteen months later, a Senate committee recommended that Lorimer keep his seat, concluding that he had been unaware of his aides' corrupt actions.

That recommendation sparked an explosion of national indignation. In spite of this uproar, the Senate, in the final hours of the Sixty-first Congress, exonerated Lorimer. When the new Senate convened in April 1911, a greater number of progressive reformers had joined its ranks. Presented with additional evidence, the Senate renewed its investigation and, in July 1912, voted 55 to 28 that Lorimer was not entitled to his seat.

Shortly after the Lorimer case, the states ratified the Seventeenth Amendment to the Constitution which, by providing for direct popular election of U.S. senators, was designed to rid our political system of the type of behavior that Lorimer's election had symbolized.

William Lorimer of Illinois

1913
JANUARY 28

Senator Elected by 89-Vote Margin

On January 28, 1913, the Nevada state legislature elected Key Pittman to the United States Senate. This event—three-quarters of a century in the past—is worth noting for two reasons. It marked the passing of the system under which state legislatures elected senators, and it was based on the closest popular vote margin of victory for a senator in the history of this institution.

The Constitution gave to the individual state legislatures the power to elect U.S. senators. Beginning in the 1890s, reform advocates regularly introduced constitutional amendments to provide for the election of senators directly by the people. Although the House of Representatives routinely passed those amendments, the Senate routinely rejected them. In the early years of the twentieth century several states—particularly the newer western states—devised plans that essentially achieved such amendments' objectives. In those states, the legislatures made a commitment to follow the voters' will by electing the candidate who won a popular referendum. By 1910, Nevada had adopted this two-track plan.

In November of that year, Republican incumbent Senator George Nixon defeated Democrat Key Pittman in a referendum by 1,100 votes. Although control of the Nevada legislature shifted to the Democrats as a result of the 1910 election, its new majority agreed to follow the referendum, and Nixon was reelected.

In 1912, Key Pittman ran again. This time he succeeded, but by the narrowest electoral margin in Senate history. Pittman's election established two Senate records. He won his four-way race with the smallest total number of votes—7,942; and he won by the smallest margin ever—a mere 89 votes.

1913
APRIL 8

Woodrow Wilson Breaks a Tradition

These days, members of Congress expect as a matter of course that the president of the United States will travel to Capitol Hill near the beginning of each session to deliver his State of the Union message. After all, the Constitution mandates such regular reporting from the chief executive. For more than half of our history, however, presidents did not appear in person. On April 8, 1913, President Woodrow Wilson broke the 113-year-old tradition of written messages.

Presidents George Washington and John Adams did deliver their annual messages in person. But Thomas Jefferson discontinued the practice. Most likely, Jefferson acted out of both philosophical and personal considerations. As a staunch republican, he disliked all trappings of monarchy, and for him the annual appearance of the president in Congress too closely resembled the king's annual message to Parliament. Nor did Jefferson, who lisped slightly and spoke softly, particularly enjoy making public addresses. He preferred to send his messages to Congress and have them read by a clerk. Each of Jefferson's successors throughout the nineteenth century followed his precedent.

But Woodrow Wilson was a different breed. Although philosophically an admirer of Jefferson, Wilson nevertheless believed that presidents should take an active role in promoting their legislative proposals in Congress. In his many writings on American history and politics, he envisioned a role for the president closer to that of the British prime minister, and his election to the presidency gave him the opportunity to put his theories into practice. On April 8, 1913, Wilson stunned Congress by appearing in person at a joint session to deliver his message—a practice continued by each of Wilson's successors.

J. Hamilton Lewis of Illinois

J. Hamilton Lewis Becomes First Senate Party Whip

On May 28, 1913, James Hamilton Lewis, a Democratic senator from Illinois, became the first elected Senate party whip. The creation of that post, and Lewis' appointment to it, followed in the wake of the 1912 elections. Those contests had placed the Democratic party in control of the White House and the Senate for the first time in nearly twenty years. The Democratic victories were largely the result of a split between the Republican party's progressive and regular factions.

President Woodrow Wilson and Senate Majority Leader John Kern recognized that they had a limited time to demonstrate to the nation that their party could govern effectively. In the House, the Democrats enjoyed a huge majority. In the Senate, however, that party had a modest six-vote margin. This placed a great responsibility on Majority Leader Kern for the success of the president's legislative program. Accordingly, he and senior progressives within the Democratic caucus sought to impose rigorous party discipline on party members. This called for the establishment of a system that would ensure the necessary votes were available to support administration measures both in the caucus and on the Senate floor.

It is worth noting that both Majority Leader Kern and Whip Lewis were freshmen senators at the time of their leadership election. Kern had begun his service just two years earlier. Lewis had been a senator for only two months. J. Hamilton Lewis, whose portrait today hangs outside the Senate chamber, served as whip until his election defeat in 1918. He was reelected to the Senate in 1930. In 1933 he resumed the post of Democratic whip, which he held until his death six years later.

In 1915, Senate Republicans appointed New York's James Wadsworth as their first whip and conference secretary. A week later, they divided those positions and elected Charles Curtis of Kansas as whip.

1913
MAY 31

Direct Election of Senators

On May 31, 1913, the Seventeenth Amendment officially became a part of the United States Constitution. That amendment provided that U.S. senators would be elected directly by the people of each state, rather than by individual state legislatures.

Delegates to the 1787 Constitutional Convention spent relatively little time discussing the manner in which senators were to be elected. Selection by state legislatures worked reasonably well for the Senate's first fifty years, but as political parties began to play a greater role in the operation of those bodies, stalemates developed. This was particularly common when different parties controlled the two houses of a legislature, or when a party held only a slim margin in a single chamber. In 1857 the Democratic-controlled Indiana legislature named two Democrats—one to fill an unexpired vacancy and the other to a new term. The following year, Indiana's rapidly growing Republican party won majorities in both legislative chambers. That new majority promptly sent two Republican senators-elect to Washington. The Senate, under Democratic control, rejected the Republican challengers by a strict party-line vote.

In the remaining years of the nineteenth century, the number of deadlocks and contested election cases increased. In 1895 the Delaware legislature took 217 ballots over a period of 114 days without electing a senator. Several states went without full representation in the Senate for two years or more.

By the start of the twentieth century, direct popular election of senators had become a major objective of progressive reformers. Although the House of Representatives repeatedly adopted constitutional amendments, only in 1911 did the Senate finally act. Within a year, the necessary three-quarters of the states had ratified this amendment, the only substantive alteration in the Senate's structure under the Constitution during its first two centuries of existence.

1913
JUNE 2

Senators Disclose Financial Holdings

On June 2, 1913, senators for the first time publicly disclosed their financial holdings. The circuitous road that led to this unprecedented action had its beginning with a tariff bill and an angry president.

President Woodrow Wilson ranked tariff reduction at the top of his legislative agenda when he took office in March 1913. By May, the House of Representatives had passed just what he wanted—a bill that lowered the average tariff rate by 29 percent. That measure ran into trouble in the Senate, however, when large numbers of lobbyists, seeking to retain the protected status of the manufacturers they represented, descended upon members.

The resulting delay on his priority legislation infuriated President Wilson. In a strongly worded statement, he condemned the "industrious and insidious" lobby and accused lobbyists of trying to thwart the will of the people. The press took up the cry, demanding an investigation of the lobby and the legislators it might possibly control. Senators could hardly refuse to pursue the matter. To do so would only seem to give credence to the president's charges. When Republican Senator Robert La Follette suggested that all senators disclose any holdings that might be affected by tariff reductions, no senator dared publicly protest.

Beginning on June 2, each member of the Senate appeared before the newly created special committee to investigate the lobby and revealed how many shares of coal or steel stock, acres of sugar cane and citrus trees, and textile mills he owned. Amidst intense press coverage of each day's revelations, opposition to downward revision of the tariff quickly collapsed. Debate dragged on in the Senate throughout a suffocatingly hot summer, and in September President Wilson got his wish. By a vote of 44 to 37 the Senate passed the Underwood tariff.

1913
OCTOBER 3

Cartoons in the Congressional Record

Readers of the October 3, 1913, *Congressional Record* must have been surprised to discover two political cartoons illustrating a reprinted article by South Carolina Senator Benjamin Tillman. Since its establishment in 1873, the *Congressional Record* had maintained an austere and unillustrated format. In the early years of the twentieth century, an occasional chart or outline map would appear—but never a political cartoon.

Senator Tillman had drawn the cartoons in 1896 to accompany an article, entitled "The Money Power," in which he attacked Wall Street interests for preying on the nation's farmers. Tillman's purpose in reprinting the article was to demonstrate that many of the predictions he had made as a freshman senator had come true. Each of his drawings depicted an "Allegorical Cow," shown standing astride a map of the United States. As described in an accompanying caption, the first cow is shown facing west, "feeding on the produce of the farmers of the West and South, while her golden milk is drawn by the . . . speculators in Wall Street." A second drawing depicted an eastward-facing cow. Its caption explains: "In this cartoon Senator Tillman shows the result of the attempt of the farmers to turn the big cow around to let her feed on income tax in the East while they should milk her in the West and South. But the cow . . . was not a reversible cow. As soon as she tried to feed on income tax, the Supreme Court seized her by the throat as a reminder that she must do her eating exclusively in the agricultural regions."

Although Tillman had routinely obtained the Senate's unanimous consent for publication of these cartoons, several senators later announced they would have objected to his request had they known of it. Today, a statute forbids insertion in the *Record* of maps, diagrams, or illustrations without approval by the Joint Committee on Printing.

1913
OCTOBER 9

The Senate Makes a Movie

On October 9, 1913, a movie was filmed in the Senate chamber. Cameras recorded Vice President Thomas R. Marshall presiding and Majority Leader John Worth Kern and other senators at their desks. Various Senate clerks sat at senators' desks as well, to make the chamber seem a little more occupied. The film was being made to show at the upcoming exposition in San Francisco, to accompany a lecture on the working of the government of the United States.

The only problem was that it was against the rules of the Senate, even then, to take pictures inside the Senate chamber. A day after the filming, Senator Lee Overman, chairman of the Senate Rules Committee, reminded his colleagues of this prohibition, pointing out that the Rules Committee had not been consulted, and demanded to know under whose authority the motion pictures had been taken. The sergeant at arms claimed to have proceeded with the endorsement of the vice president's staff, but the vice president denied granting permission. It seems that everyone thought that someone else was in charge, not an unusual occurrence in government, to be sure.

Despite the violation of the Senate rules, we would all probably enjoy seeing the film of the Senate at work three-quarters of a century ago, with senators sitting at these very desks, in this chamber, gesticulating perhaps a little more grandiosely than usual for the silent film. All attempts to track down the film, however, have been unsuccessful. Most likely it was destroyed or discarded, or it may have simply deteriorated in the years after it was shown at the exposition. Not until 1986 did the Senate permit cameras into its chamber on a daily basis to record an audiovisual image of its debates for posterity.

SWIRLING, SHRIEKING SPECULATORS ON THE MAIN FLOOR. THE LINES IN HIS FACE DEEPENED.

"'I HAVE BEEN HERE BEFORE,' HE MUTTERED. 'I CAME AS GOVERNOR OF SOUTH CAROLINA TO SELL THE BONDS OF MY STATE. I KNOW WHAT A HORDE OF WOLVES THEY ARE. THESE ARE THE MEN WHO HAVE THE NATION BY THE THROAT.'

"SO FOR TWO DAYS SENATOR TILLMAN WENT ABOUT IN THE STRONGHOLDS OF THE MONEY KINGS OF AMERICA SEARCHING FOR FACTS.

"'THERE ISN'T A DROP OF PATRIOTIC BLOOD IN THIS CROWD,' HE SAID. 'AND YET IT WRITES THE LAWS AND CONTROLS THE POLICY OF THE COUNTRY. NOTHING BUT A REVOLUTION CAN OVERTHROW

SENATOR TILLMAN'S ALLEGORICAL COW.

This cartoon, designed by Senator Tillman, shows his idea of the present American situation. The cow, symbolical of national resources, is feeding on the produce of the farmers of the West and South, while her golden milk is all drawn by the "sharpers," gamblers, and speculators in Wall Street.

SENATOR TILLMAN'S ALLEGORICAL COW No. 2.

In this cartoon, Senator Tillman shows the result of the attempt of the farmers to milk the big cow while they should milk her in the West and South. But the cow, as Senator Tillman shows, feeds on income tax the Supreme Court refuses her by the throat as a revenue. The farmers in the West are disappointed and get no income-tax milk.

The cartoon that appeared in the *Congressional Record*, October 3, 1913

187

Blair Lee Becomes First Directly Elected Senator

On November 4, 1913, Blair Lee of Maryland became the first person to be elected to the United States Senate under the provisions of the then recently ratified Seventeenth Amendment to the Constitution.

The new amendment had taken effect five months earlier, on May 31, 1913. At that time, Maryland's Senator William Jackson was serving under a temporary appointment by that state's governor to fill a vacancy caused by the death of the previously elected incumbent. As soon as the Seventeenth Amendment was officially ratified, the governor, following its provisions, arranged for a special election to replace Senator Jackson. On November 4, 1913, Democrat Blair Lee defeated his Republican opponent by a 20-percent margin.

When Lee presented his credentials to the Senate a month later, Senator Jackson immediately challenged them on the grounds that, since he had been appointed under the Constitution's original provisions, he was entitled to be treated as if the Amendment had never been ratified. This would have extended his Senate tenure for several months until the state assembly adjourned, presumably increasing his political prospects within Maryland.

On January 19, 1914, the Senate Committee on Privileges and Elections issued a majority report favorable to Blair Lee. The committee stated that Jackson's tenure had always been uncertain because of the temporary nature of his appointment. The passage of the Seventeenth Amendment increased the instability of his term because it ended the state legislature's authority in the matter of senatorial selection.

On January 28, 1914, the Senate declared Blair Lee duly elected. He served the remaining three years of his term. Failing to be renominated in 1916, Lee retired to a successful law practice. He lived until 1944.

Blair Lee of Maryland

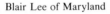

Shelby M. Cullom of Illinois

1914
JANUARY 28

Shelby M. Cullom Dies

On January 28, 1914, Senator Shelby M. Cullom died. Author of the Interstate Commerce Act, a landmark statute of the late nineteenth century, Cullom also served as chairman of the Senate Interstate Commerce and Foreign Relations committees, and as chairman of the Senate Republican caucus.

Although born in Kentucky, Shelby Cullom grew up on an Illinois prairie farm, where his antislavery father had moved in 1830. Unhappy with the hard life of a farmer, Cullom studied law and embraced a political career. An early member of the Republican party, he enthusiastically supported Abraham Lincoln's campaigns for United States senator in 1858 and president in 1860. Cullom served as speaker of the Illinois state legislature, as a member of the U.S. House of Representatives, and as governor, before he entered the Senate in 1883.

During the 1880s, anger built up in the Midwest against the high-handed business and political tactics of the railroads. In the state legislature and as governor, Cullom had strongly endorsed state regulation, but he had come to realize its inadequacy against an interstate enterprise. He used his position as chairman of the Senate Committee on Interstate Commerce to secure enactment of the first national regulatory legislation in 1887.

With all these accomplishments, why is Shelby Cullom so little known today? The *Dictionary of American Biography* blames his even temperament. "He was a man of facts; even-tempered, conservative 'regular,' conscientious . . . ; fairminded . . . ; thoroughly democratic. For these reasons and others (he did not, for example, drink or smoke) he was colorless." It is too bad that historians, like journalists, seem to prefer flashier, more eccentric politicians. They may make better stories; but we ought not to forget the contributions of diligent, hard-working senators like Shelby M. Cullom.

1914
OCTOBER 24

The Longest Continuous Session Ends

The Sixty-third Congress set the record of 567 days for the longest continuous session—actually two sessions which simply merged together without break.

The Sixty-third Congress met during the first two years of the administration of Woodrow Wilson, a president with an ambitious legislative program. It tackled successfully such significant issues as the creation of the Federal Reserve System, establishment of the Federal Trade Commission, passage of the Clayton Antitrust Act, and enactment of tariff and tax reform.

The first session of the Sixty-third Congress opened on April 7, 1913, and came to a close 239 days later at noon on December 1. Although the House took a day's rest, the Senate did not allow even a minute to elapse between its first and second sessions. Back to work again, it continued for another 328 days. By then, tired senators were ready to go home—particularly those scheduled to run in the first direct election of senators that November. The session might have ended even earlier, but, as often happens during the closing hours of a Congress, a filibuster had erupted, in this case over federal relief for southern cotton farmers. Not until those conducting the filibuster conceded defeat did the leadership of the Senate and House introduce resolutions that would end the second session at 4 p.m. on October 24, 1914.

Senators were debating nominations in closed session when word came that the House had adopted the adjournment resolution. Moving back into legislative session, the Senate threw open its doors at 3:15 p.m. An alert doorkeeper then leaned over the balcony and advanced the clock by forty-five minutes, allowing the presiding officer to declare the Senate of the Sixty-third Congress adjourned. Thus ended the Senate's longest continuous session.

1915
JULY 2

Bomb Explodes in Senate Wing of Capitol

On July 2, 1915, a bomb exploded behind a telephone switchboard in the Capitol's Senate Reception Room. Although no one was injured in the blast, it caused extensive damage.

Initially baffled by the explosion, local police soon developed a lead. A former German instructor at Cornell University, Frank Holt, was arrested in New York the day after the blast for attempting to murder financier J.P. Morgan, Jr. in his Long Island home. J.P. Morgan and Company was then Great Britain's chief purchasing agent in the United States for World War I munitions. Holt's written confession to this crime was strikingly similar to the phrasing found in four letters, claiming responsibility for the Capitol bombing, that were sent to the city's newspapers. At first, Holt denied involvement in the Capitol explosion, but he soon admitted his guilt.

Described as "decidedly pro-German" by colleagues, Holt explained his actions in a letter to President Wilson. He stated that he needed to "call attention to the murders being done in Europe by American ammunition." In a letter to a Washington newspaper he wrote, "This explosion is the exclamation point to my appeal for peace." Each of the four letters was typewritten, but each letter also contained the handwritten word "Senate." Investigators speculated that he wrote this word in only when he decided where the blast was to take place.

Holt claimed that he strolled the halls of the Capitol for half an hour before finding a spot where the bomb would not hurt anyone and where minimal damage would be sustained. As the investigators' probe deepened, Holt became implicated in various other explosions. It also turned out that Holt was actually Erich Muenter, a Harvard professor of German who had disappeared nine years earlier. He committed suicide less than a week after his arrest.

1916
JANUARY 28

Supreme Court Justice
Louis D. Brandeis

Supreme Court Nomination of Louis D. Brandeis

On January 28, 1916, the Senate received from President Woodrow Wilson the nomination of Louis D. Brandeis to be an associate justice of the United States Supreme Court. This nomination initiated a four-month confirmation battle that ranks as one of the most bitter in Senate history. Among those who opposed the nominee were seven previous heads of the American Bar Association, including former President William Howard Taft.

Louis Brandeis was born in 1856 of Jewish parents who had fled central Europe following the collapse of the 1848 liberal movement. A brilliant student, he graduated from Harvard Law School at twenty-one. Brandeis quickly made a fortune as a lawyer and turned his legal skills to the quest for social reform. He excelled in "translating parochial controversies into universal moral terms." In arguing cases before the Supreme Court, Brandeis emphasized social consequences and views of substantive experts rather than the applicable principles of law. He became known as "the people's lawyer."

In 1912 Brandeis served as a valued adviser in Wilson's presidential campaign. Many expected he would secure a cabinet position in the new Wilson administration. His Judaism and his attacks on powerful financial interests led opponents to brand him as a dangerous radical. In 1916, Wilson decided to name him to the Court, partly in recognition of his gifted legal mind and partly to curry favor with Brandeis' fellow progressives. Because tradition in those days dictated that Supreme Court nominees not appear before the Senate Judiciary Committee, Brandeis directed his campaign from Boston. A biographer recently concluded, "Perhaps no nominee, before or since, has been subjected to as searching an examination as he was, the target of such baseless charges and innuendoes." Ultimately, on June 1, 1916, the Senate confirmed the nominee on a straight party-line vote. Brandeis went on to become one of the Court's greatest justices, retiring in 1939.

1917
JANUARY 22

Wilson's "Peace Without Victory" Speech

At 1:00 p.m. on January 22, 1917, President Woodrow Wilson was escorted into the Senate chamber by a committee of senators and took a seat to the right of Vice President Thomas R. Marshall, the presiding officer.

At that time, the First World War was raging in Europe, with England, France, and Russia combatting Germany and Austria. The United States had maintained its neutrality—Wilson had just won reelection under the slogan: "He Kept Us Out Of War"—but German infringements upon United States neutrality rights were increasingly pressuring the nation into war. On this day, however, President Wilson addressed the Senate, "as the council associated with me in the final determination of our international obligations," in order to outline his vision for permanent peace in the future.

Pacifists opposed to U.S. entry into World War I gathered on the Capitol steps

Wilson took the bold step of calling for a "peace without victory." This was difficult to propose in wartime, but he argued that "victory would mean peace forced upon the loser. . . . It would be accepted in humiliation, under duress, at an intolerable sacrifice, and would leave a sting, resentment, a bitter memory upon which terms of peace would rest, not permanently, but only as upon quicksand. Only a peace between equals can last." The warring powers, of course, ignored and ridiculed Wilson's proposals, and even the United States forgot them as soon as this nation entered the war in April 1917. When World War I ended, not by "peace without victory" but with the total defeat of Germany, the resulting peace was built upon the quicksand that Wilson had predicted, leading to the Second World War just twenty years later.

1917
MARCH 8

Senate Adopts First Cloture Rule

On March 8, 1917, the Senate adopted its first cloture rule. This rule provided for the limitation of debate to one hour per member when two-thirds of the senators present and voting agreed to a cloture petition signed by at least sixteen members.

The Senate took this action as it debated entering World War I. Several weeks earlier, the House had readily approved President Woodrow Wilson's urgent plea for authority to arm U.S. merchant ships against German attack. In the Senate, however, the president's proposal ran into the determined opposition of a dozen members opposed to intervention in this European conflict. These opponents launched a historic filibuster on March 2, 1917, just hours before the arrival of the mandatory March 4 adjournment date. The filibusterers succeeded, and the session expired without action.

That same day, President Wilson took his oath of office for a second term and then angrily attacked the Senate dissidents as "a little group of willful men, representing no opinion but their own [who] have rendered the government of the United States helpless and contemptible." He called the Senate into special session on March 5 and demanded that it change its rules to permit cutting off debate. After decades of resisting similar provisions to limit its ancient tradition of unrestricted debate, the Senate quickly complied.

Over the half century that followed, the cloture rule proved very difficult to apply. Between 1917 and 1964, the Senate invoked cloture only five times in twenty-eight attempts, and no cloture effort was successful between 1927 and 1962. Today, Rule 22 provides that when three-fifths of all senators "duly chosen and sworn" agree to a cloture petition, no more than thirty hours of debate may be devoted to the pending matter on which cloture has been invoked.

1917
DECEMBER 18

The Senate Votes for Prohibition

On December 18, 1917, the Senate approved legislation that would become the Eighteenth Amendment to the Constitution. That resolution provided that "after one year from the ratification of this article the manufacture, sale, or transportation of intoxicating liquors within, the importation thereof into, or the exportation thereof from the United States and all territory subject to the jurisdiction thereof for beverage purposes is hereby prohibited."

Behind this amendment lay years of lobbying by those who believed that drinking, especially among the millions of newly arrived immigrants, posed a clear threat to the maintenance of national law and order. These advocates argued that working-class men were squandering money in local saloons, thus contributing to their families' poverty and social distress.

American entry into World War I earlier in 1917 paved the way for adoption of the Eighteenth Amendment. To preserve the morals of draftees, Congress had enacted legislation prohibiting the sale of alcoholic beverages in or near military camps. It also had banned the use of foodstuffs necessary to the war effort in the manufacture of distilled liquors. Ultimately, wartime hostility toward Germany fueled ill feelings against distillers and brewers of German descent, and the prohibition amendment passed as the nation became more deeply entangled in the European conflict.

Idaho Senator William Borah objected to the provisions of the amendment that provided seven years for ratification and a one-year delay before its implementation. With an eye to the forthcoming women's suffrage amendment, Borah saw no authority within the Constitution for Congress to impose such restrictions. Despite these objections, the Senate adopted the amendment by a 47 to 8 margin. But the "noble experiment," as Prohibition was called, was not successful, and the amendment was repealed in 1933.

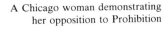
A Chicago woman demonstrating her opposition to Prohibition

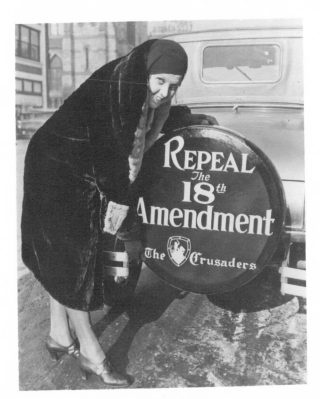

194

1918
SEPTEMBER 24

French Tribute to the Senate

This chamber has witnessed many dramatic events in the past 130 years. One of the most poignant of those events occurred on September 24, 1918, at a time of an intensifying United States role in World War I. As the Senate convened that day, the nation rejoiced at news from the Western Front that the first distinctively U.S. offensive of the war had resulted in a major victory, seriously weakening the position of German forces. Plans were then underway for a final major United States-French offensive that would ultimately bring victory.

Against this hopeful background, the government of France requested the opportunity to pay a special tribute to the United States Senate. In a

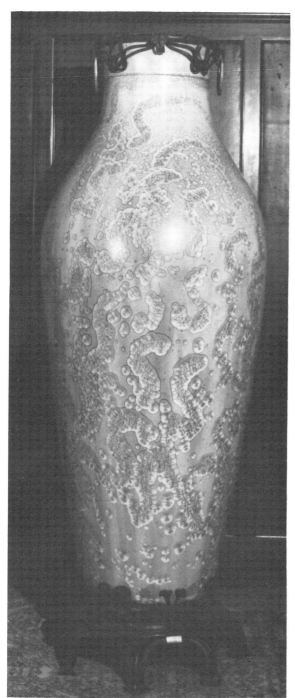

chamber packed to capacity, with the American and French flags brightly displayed behind the presiding officer's desk, French Ambassador Jules Jusserand addressed the Senate. He officially thanked members for the friendly reception accorded to the French prime minister when he had conveyed his nation's appreciation to the Senate in May 1917 for United States entry on the allied side of the war. Recalling that the decision had "sent a thrill of joy throughout France," the ambassador declared:

> Our Faith that our living and our dead have made their manifold sacrifices for a supremely great and just cause received its most telling confirmation when, from across the ocean, the voice of this great Nation was heard above the din of battle, saying from now on "until the last gun is fired," until right triumphs, not for a time, but for all times, we take our place by your side.

Following this moving address and a warm response from Vice President Thomas Marshall, the Senate received as a gift from France two magnificent, sixty-eight-inch tall Sèvres porcelain vases. Members of the Senate and the French delegation then posed for a photograph on the Senate steps outside the Capitol. Today, those vases are displayed in the lobby to the north of this chamber as a continuing reminder of the friendship between the United States and France.

One of the two Sèvres porcelain vases given to the Senate by France

1918
SEPTEMBER 30

President Wilson Speaks Out for Woman Suffrage

On the afternoon of September 30, 1918, President Woodrow Wilson made a surprise visit to Capitol Hill to address the Senate. The subject of the president's speech was votes for women, and, in a dramatic turnabout, he strongly urged the senators to approve the suffrage amendment then before them.

The president had inadvertently added impetus to the suffrage movement by casting World War I as a crusade for democracy. It was unconscionable, argued suffragists, for America to deny its female citizens the right to participate in government while at the same time fighting a war to "make the world safe for democracy." Wilson saw the issue differently. He opposed a constitutional amendment granting women the vote and favored state action instead. His opposition sparked stormy demonstrations by suffragists. Hundreds of women protesters, who chained themselves to the White House fence and blocked its entrances, were arrested and jailed at the direction of the Wilson administration.

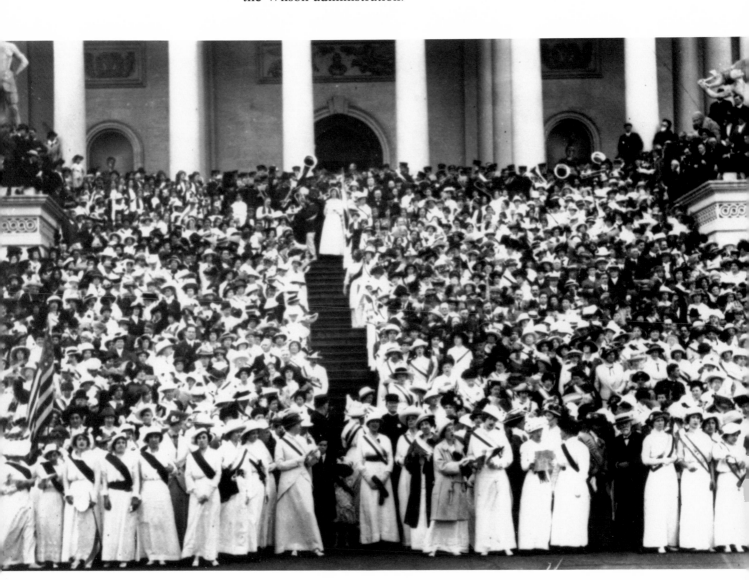

Woman suffragists at the Capitol, 1918

In January 1918, the president experienced a change of heart. He endorsed the suffrage amendment, explaining his conversion in terms of the war. The House quickly approved the amendment, but the Senate remained opposed. Its intransigence prompted the president's September 30 visit, on the eve of another vote. In his impassioned plea, Wilson urged adoption of the amendment as "virtually essential to the successful prosecution of the great war of humanity in which we are engaged." Yet, while the senators had cheered as Wilson entered their chamber, they voted down the amendment after he left and rejected it again in February 1919. It wasn't until a new Congress convened in the spring of 1919 that the House and Senate finally approved the suffrage amendment. In August 1920 the Nineteenth Amendment giving women the right to vote became a part of the Constitution of the United States.

1918
NOVEMBER 5

Jeannette Rankin Runs for Senate

In November 1918, Jeannette Rankin became one of the first women to run for a seat in the United States Senate. Although her 1918 Senate bid was unsuccessful, Rankin, a longtime spokeswoman for peace and women's rights, could still claim several congressional "firsts." Foremost among them was the fact that she was the first woman ever elected to the U.S. Congress.

Rankin was elected to the House in 1916, four years before the Nineteenth Amendment gave women the right to vote. Women in Montana and other western states had gained that right through state action before women in the East. Rankin had long been involved in suffrage and reform movements, and she campaigned across Montana for the state's at-large seat in the House on a platform of federal suffrage, an eight-hour day for women, tax law reform, legislation to protect children, and Prohibition.

Rankin was best known during her first term in Congress for her vote against U.S. entry into World War I, but she worked hardest at getting the suffrage amendment passed. In 1918, Rankin decided to run for the Senate. After losing the Republican primary, she ran as a candidate of the National Party, a coalition of Progressives, farmers and Prohibitionists. Her stand against the war led to her defeat, although she received 23 percent of the votes cast.

A quarter century later, Jeannette Rankin returned to Congress on the eve of the Second World War. Still an ardent pacifist, she was the only member of Congress to cast a dissenting vote against America's entry into World War II. After casting her vote, Rankin needed the protection of the Capitol Police to return to her office in the Cannon Building.

After this second term, Rankin retired from Congress to devote the rest of her life to working for peace. In 1968, at eighty-eight, she was back in Washington to lead several thousand women in a demonstration on the steps of the Capitol to protest the Vietnam War. Jeannette Rankin died in 1973 at the age of ninety-four.

1919
FEBRUARY 26

Foreign Relations Committee at White House

On February 26, 1919, members of the Senate Foreign Relations Committee attended an unusual dinner at the White House. President Woodrow Wilson, just back from negotiating the treaty ending World War I, invited members of the Senate Foreign Relations and House Foreign Affairs committees to dinner to answer their questions and to satisfy their concerns—especially about the proposed League of Nations. Thirty-four members attended, among them twenty-one Democrats and thirteen Republicans. Two key Republicans, Senators William E. Borah and Albert B. Fall, boycotted the dinner on the grounds that they would not be bound to silence on any point the president might raise.

President Wilson in fact placed no veil of secrecy on the discussions, which were reported in banner headlines the next morning. After a brief statement, the president offered to answer any and all questions as frankly as he could. As the *New York Times* later commented, "No man not entirely confident of the strength of his cause would have risked the chance of such a test." President Wilson had great confidence, as his performance that evening demonstrated. But he did not succeed in reducing members' fears that the United States would lose some of its sovereignty by joining the League.

Despite having gotten off to a strong start, President Wilson found himself locked in battle with a skeptical Senate. Neither the president nor his chief legislative opponents would compromise, and the Senate eventually defeated the Treaty of Versailles. The dinner at the White House had been a fine gesture, but only a gesture, and it failed to achieve its ultimate objectives.

The Senate Foreign Relations Committee, 1919

1919
MAY 27

First Open Party Conference

On May 27, 1919, Senate Republicans held the first open party conference in the history of this institution. Republican members who gathered for that meeting also reaffirmed their commitment to the seniority system for choosing committee chairmen.

For most of the half century after the Civil War, Republicans had held both the White House and majorities in Congress. During the Progressive Era at the beginning of this century, the party split between its progressive and conservative wings. The presidential race of Theodore Roosevelt against William Howard Taft in 1912 not only enabled Woodrow Wilson to win the presidency, but also gave both houses of Congress to the Democrats. In 1918, Republicans reunited and won back their congressional majorities.

But when the Republican Conference drew up its committee assignments, progressives objected to Pennsylvania Senator Boies Penrose becoming chairman of the Senate Finance Committee. For a while, a small band of progressive Republicans threatened to call for a separate vote for each committee chairman and to throw their support behind the ranking Democrat on the Finance Committee. To forestall such a possibility, Republican majority leader Henry Cabot Lodge, Sr., called an open party conference that the press could attend. This arrangement would give the progressives the chance publicly to voice their opposition to Penrose and to cast their votes against him, on the condition that all sides would abide by the conference decision. The open meeting was held, and the Republican Conference voted 34 to 8 to seat Senator Penrose as chair of the Finance Committee. One Republican senator could not resist the opportunity to quote from the incumbent Democratic President Woodrow Wilson's "Fourteen Points," describing the Republican Conference as "open covenants, openly arrived at."

1920
MARCH 19

Senate Rejects Treaty of Versailles

On March 19, 1920, the Senate chamber served as the setting for the final act of one of the greatest dramas in American political history. Several months earlier, President Woodrow Wilson had personally delivered to the Senate a bulky copy of the peace treaty ending World War I. On that occasion, he had been escorted by Henry Cabot Lodge, who, as a result of the return of the Senate to Republican control in the elections of 1918, served as both majority leader and chairman of the Foreign Relations Committee. In a dramatic speech to the Senate, the president urged quick consent to the treaty's ratification. He expected no changes and assumed that the Senate, which had never before rejected a treaty, would grant its approval.

Following protracted hearings, Lodge reported the treaty to the Senate with four so-called reservations, directed at provisions for a League of Nations, and forty-five specific amendments. Democratic supporters of the president and a number of Republican "mild reservationists" voted down the amendments and returned the treaty to the committee for further consideration. At that point, President Wilson set out on a 9,500-mile tour of the West to bring popular pressure on the Senate for approval without change. During that trip, he suffered a stroke. With a stricken president more determined than ever to hold out, Lodge brought the treaty before the Senate in November 1919. It contained fourteen reservations, but no specific amendments. The Senate decisively defeated the treaty.

As sympathy for the president faded, and with the 1920 elections on the horizon, loyal Democrats came under increasing pressure to support the treaty with its reservations. On March 19, as the final vote approached, two members of the president's cabinet worked the Senate floor to prevent defections. With the galleries jammed and the atmosphere electric with tension, the Senate failed to achieve the necessary two-thirds majority to approve the treaty. This action mortally wounded the League of Nations as a viable defense against a second world war.

Senators "Refusing to give the lady a seat"

REFUSING TO GIVE THE LADY A SEAT.

1920
MARCH 20

Senator Newberry Found Guilty

On March 20, 1920, Senator Truman H. Newberry and sixteen of his eighty-four codefendants were found guilty of criminal conspiracy growing out of his 1918 campaign for the Senate. This startling event in one of the most dramatic Senate elections in our history involved America's most famous automobile manufacturer.

The 1918 Michigan Senate race pitted against each other two industrialists of great personal wealth: Truman Newberry and Henry Ford. After a hard-fought campaign, Newberry won the election. But Ford and many newspapers assailed Newberry for excessive campaign spending and for intimidating voters. The Senate referred Ford's complaint to the Committee on Privileges and Elections. In the meantime, Newberry and 134 others were indicted for violating the Federal Corrupt Practices Act, which had set a $3,750 limit on campaign spending in Senate races. By contrast, it was estimated that Newberry had spent the then shocking amount of $195,000 on his election. In 1920 the senator was convicted.

Newberry appealed to the Supreme Court, arguing that the federal government had no authority to control state primaries. In 1921, the Supreme Court unanimously overturned Senator Newberry's conviction, on the grounds that the lower court judge had given erroneous instructions to the jury. But the justices were divided over the constitutionality of a federal statute controlling state elections.

In 1922 the Senate's Privileges and Elections Committee agreed that Newberry was the duly elected senator from Michigan but declared that his excessive campaign spending had harmed the honor and dignity of the Senate. Since Henry Ford gave no indication of abandoning his own crusade against the senator, Newberry decided to resign voluntarily from the United States Senate.

Henry Ford, *left*, ran against Truman Newberry, *right*, for the Senate in 1918.

1920
MAY 27

Senate Cuts Useless Committees

On May 27, 1920, the Senate abolished forty-two of its seventy-four standing committees. The Senate made this change in its rules without debate and in the face of calls for greater efficiency in the conduct of its business. As one newspaper reported, "Under present conditions with the senators serving on many important committees, it is difficult for them to keep up with the work of the committees or even to attend meetings."

Among the panels that would not be renewed in 1921 were the Committee on Revolutionary War Claims, the Committee to Investigate Trespassers upon Indian Lands, and the Committee on Pacific Railroads. Most of the committees to be abolished had not conducted business in at least ten years. They existed solely to provide office space and staff assistance to senators.

In addition to cutting the number of committees, the new rule placed limits on the number of members for each panel, reducing the maximum for major committees from twenty to fifteen. The average number of committee assignments per member would drop from nine to three. Presumably, smaller committees and fewer assignments per member would make it easier for each committee to obtain a quorum for business.

At the time the Senate agreed to this reform, the Republicans held a 49 to 47 majority in the chamber. In the election of 1920, a sitting senator won the presidency for the first time in the nation's history. Many Republican candidates for the Senate also experienced the sweep of victory that propelled Senator Warren Harding to the White House. At the start of the new Congress in 1921, the number of Republican senators would increase to 59. With only thirty-four chairmanships, it would no longer be possible for every member of the majority party to preside over a committee. Such was the price of senatorial efficiency sixty-nine years ago.

1920
JUNE 12

Warren G. Harding Nominated for President

On June 12, 1920, Senator Warren G. Harding of Ohio won the Republican presidential nomination. He went on to become the first sitting senator in the nation's history to be elected president. (The second was John F. Kennedy in 1960.) I am not certain there will ever be a third, but we will keep working on that.

Warren Harding was born in Ohio in 1865. Until the close of the century, the tall, handsome young man devoted himself wholly to his newspaper, the Marion *Star*. As that paper's circulation increased, however, so did Harding's influence, and he soon found his way into Republican politics. He served in the Ohio state senate from 1899 to 1903 and as lieutenant governor in 1904 and 1905. In 1910, he ran unsuccessfully for governor.

Four years later, Harding won a seat in the United States Senate. His dramatic victory by 102,000 votes attracted national attention. During his six years in the Senate, which he characterized as a "very pleasant place," Harding became known as a safe and conservative member.

In 1920, as the nation sought release from the tensions and hardships of World War I, Harding's limited range of ideas and amiable temperament made him an attractive presidential candidate. When the Republicans met in Chicago in June, Harding had the support of Senators Henry Cabot Lodge, Boies Penrose, and others of the senatorial oligarchy that dominated the gathering. He received the nomination on June 12, on the tenth ballot.

The Republican victory in November was staggering: 404 electoral votes for Harding compared to 127 for Democrat James M. Cox. Harding resigned from his Senate seat, effective January 13, and, on March 4, 1921, was inaugurated as the twenty-ninth president of the United States. Two and a half years later, on August 2, 1923, President Harding died in office.

Warren G. Harding of Ohio as president

Facing page, the east front of the Capitol
during Calvin Coolidge's inauguration, March 4, 1925

CHAPTER VII
Reorganizing
America
1921–1945

The Marble Room

1921
MARCH 6

The Marble Room

On March 6, 1921, the *Washington Evening Star* reported the establishment of a Senate perquisite that senators continue to enjoy today. "Famous Marble Room To Become Retreat for Senators" read the headline, and the accompanying story told of the decision reached the day before to close the Marble Room to all but senators. In explaining how the future policy would work, the *Star* also revealed how the Marble Room had been used in the past: "Hereafter visitors calling upon the senators while the Senate is sitting will send in their cards, as at present, from the [Reception] room adjoining the Senate. . . . But instead of being invited into the Marble Room, if the senators desire to see them, the visitors will wait in this anteroom until the senators come out to them." Senators gave two reasons for the change: first, the cloakrooms, where senators had retired with their colleagues, were getting too crowded and stuffy; and, second, so many lobbyists had begun to clog the Marble Room that senators could not make their way through the congestion.

The Marble Room is aptly named. Its ceiling, pilasters, and columns are of veined Italian marble, and the walls and wainscoting are of dark brown Tennessee marble. Huge mirrors reflect and re-reflect the magnificent crystal chandelier to give the illusion of endless halls and fireplaces. This room and those fireplaces have a colorful history. Not long after this chamber and the Marble Room were completed in 1859, the Civil War broke out. Union troops were actually quartered here in this chamber and in the surrounding rooms. In 1869, *Harper's* magazine reported that the soldiers who called the Marble Room home, "hung this white place full of flitches of bacon, slices of which our hungry sentinels toasted on their jack-knives at roaring fires in the chimney-place."

1922
OCTOBER 3

First Woman Senator Appointed

October 3, 1922, witnessed an important "first" in the Senate's history. On that day, Rebecca Latimer Felton of Georgia became the first woman appointed to the United States Senate. When she was sworn in seven weeks later, Mrs. Felton claimed three Senate "firsts." The first woman senator, she was also entitled to the record for the shortest Senate service. One day after she took her oath, her Senate career ended. This occurred with the arrival of Walter George, who had been elected to fill the vacancy to which she had been temporarily appointed. Mrs. Felton also set the record for being the oldest person ever sworn in as a senator for the first time—she was eighty-seven years old.

Rebecca Latimer was born in Georgia in 1835, during Andrew Jackson's second administration. She graduated with honors from Madison Female College in 1852 and fifteen months later married the commencement speaker, William Felton, a Methodist minister and physician. Both husband and wife shared a strong commitment to women's rights.

The Feltons lost their sons, their farm, and their fortune during the Civil War. In 1874, Dr. Felton, running as an Independent, was elected to the House of Representatives and the couple moved to Washington, where Mrs. Felton served as her husband's secretary and wrote a weekly column for her hometown newspaper. When Dr. Felton was defeated in 1880, they returned to Georgia and began their own newspaper to push the reform measures they held dear. When William Felton died in 1909, Rebecca traveled the reformer's route alone.

As Rebecca Felton, white haired and bespectacled, entered the Senate chamber on November 21 to take her oath, she found it overflowing with cheering women. Two years after ratification of the Nineteenth Amendment guaranteeing all women the right to vote, the nation had its first woman senator.

1924
NOVEMBER 4

Reelection of Senator Thomas du Pont

On November 4, 1924, the voters of Delaware returned Republican Senator Thomas C. du Pont to the United States Senate. This made du Pont the first person since the 1913 constitutional provision for direct election of senators to be elected to the Senate after having previously served and been defeated.

Du Pont, a Wilmington businessman, had been appointed in 1921 to fill a Senate vacancy. The following year, Democratic candidate Thomas Bayard defeated du Pont in a special election by only 60 votes. Du Pont ran again that year for the full term, this time losing by only 325 votes. He ran once more in 1924. On that occasion, he won by over 16,000 votes, or 59 percent of the total.

Since Senator du Pont's time, fourteen other defeated senators were subsequently reelected. The list includes such colorful members as Thomas P. Gore, the blind senator from Oklahoma; James Hamilton Lewis of Illinois, the Senate's first party whip; and Iowa's Guy Gillette, who was regularly cited as the "best dressed Senator."

The record for sheer persistence was clearly established by Kentucky's John Sherman Cooper. He was first elected in 1946 to fill a vacant seat in the Senate, then defeated when he ran in 1948. Although he was elected to fill another vacancy in 1952, he was defeated when he ran again in 1954. Once more, in 1956, he won election to fill yet another vacancy, and this time it stuck. The voters continued to send John Sherman Cooper to the Senate until he retired in 1973.

A more recent case of a defeated senator being reelected was our colleague Howard Metzenbaum, who was appointed to the Senate in 1974 but defeated by John Glenn in the Democratic primary that same year. Two years later, Senator Metzenbaum returned by winning election to Ohio's other Senate seat. And in 1988, in the state of Washington, former Senator Slade Gorton followed the precedent set by Thomas du Pont back in 1924.

1925
MARCH 10

Charles Warren

Senate Rejects an Attorney General

In March 1925, the Senate rejected the nomination of Charles Beecher Warren to serve as attorney general in the cabinet of President Calvin Coolidge.

The Senate had not voted down a cabinet nominee since 1868, fifty-seven years earlier. President Coolidge submitted the name of Charles Warren, a Michigan lawyer, to succeed Attorney General Harlan Fiske Stone, who had just gone to the Supreme Court. During the 1920s, however, the Republican members of the Senate were sharply divided between the conservative and progressive wings of their party. Warren met the approval of conservatives, but his ties to the "Sugar Trust" upset progressives. They charged that he would not pursue a vigorous antitrust policy in the Justice Department.

On March 10, 1925, progressive Republicans joined with Democrats to block Warren's nomination by a 40 to 40 vote. Normally, Vice President Charles Dawes could have cast the deciding vote, but the vice president was absent, taking his regular noontime nap at his suite in the Willard Hotel. Frantic calls finally aroused the sleeping statesman, who rushed to the Capitol. A Republican senator changed his vote in order to move for reconsideration and allow Dawes to cast the tie-breaker, but now the lone Democratic senator who had voted for Warren changed his vote, and the nomination failed, 39 to 41.

President Coolidge quickly sent Warren's nomination back to the Senate and intimated that if the Senate failed to act he would make Warren a recess appointment. Angered by this strategy, the Senate rejected Warren once again, by the even wider margin of 39 to 46. Finally, the president nominated as attorney general an obscure Vermont lawyer, whom the Senate promptly and overwhelmingly approved.

1928
JUNE 15

Charles Curtis Nominated for Vice President

On June 15, 1928, the Republican majority leader of the Senate, Charles Curtis, was nominated to run for vice president on the Republican party ticket headed by Herbert Hoover. Curtis went on to become the only native Kansan elected vice president of the United States.

Curtis' selection represented some "ticket balancing" by the Republican convention, for he was considered a more conservative and more traditional Republican than Herbert Hoover. This may seem odd today, since we tend to think of Hoover as a conservative president. But in fact, Hoover had first entered government service during the Democratic administration of Woodrow Wilson, and in 1920 he was mentioned as a possible candidate for the Democratic nomination. Hoover also had roots in the progressive movement, leading one of his biographers to call him the "Forgotten Progressive."

When President Harding nominated Hoover to be secretary of commerce in 1921, Senator Charles Curtis joined those conservative members of the Senate who objected. They viewed Hoover with suspicion as a progressive and an internationalist. In 1928, Curtis was one of several senators who ran favorite-son candidacies to stop the frontrunner Hoover. Thus, when Hoover won the nomination, Curtis was brought on board to achieve party unity.

The Hoover-Curtis ticket won a landslide victory over the Democratic ticket of Alfred E. Smith and Joseph T. Robinson. Robinson, by the way, was Curtis' counterpart in the Senate, as Democratic minority leader. Charles Curtis served four years as vice president and ran for reelection in 1932. By then, however, the depression had struck, political fortunes had reversed, and the Hoover-Curtis ticket went down to defeat.

Charles Curtis of Kansas

appreciative of the
Guardian Angel
of the
Press Gallery.

FELLOWSHIP

INFORMATION

SKETCHES

Sara Moore
The Detroit News.
April, 1911.

Sketch of Jim Preston from
his scrapbook

1928
OCTOBER 28

Jim Preston, Press Gallery Czar

On October 28, 1928, the *Washington Evening Star* paid special tribute to the "Czar of the Senate Press Gallery," James S. Preston. Old newspapermen in Washington said Preston knew more and told less than any other living person. "If only he could write what he knows," said journalists, he would scoop them all. But, they concluded, "He never will write it. He can't even tell it."

Jim Preston was one of those remarkable Senate employees who devote their entire lives to this institution. Born in Washington in 1876, the son of a Washington correspondent, he became the unofficial superintendent of the Senate press gallery in 1897—the post had not yet been established. As superintendent, he was supposed to keep the reporters' inkwells filled and supply them with writing paper. But Preston began gathering copies of bills and committee reports and finding bits and pieces of information to help the reporters cover the Senate. He also began coaxing the senators to make copies of their speeches available in advance.

After thirty-four years as czar of the press gallery, Preston became Senate librarian. To mark the occasion, reporters held a mock impeachment trial, finding their former superintendent "guilty of devotion, friendship, and service." In later years he transferred to the National Archives, where he helped to process the Senate's historical records, and then returned again to the Senate. In the mid-1950s, the Senate paid tribute to Preston in honor of his sixty years on the Senate staff.

The reporters were correct in predicting that Preston would never write nor tell the secrets he knew. As an elderly man he burned his diaries and correspondence. It was a sad loss for the Senate's recorded history but an understandable act for a man who spent his lifetime keeping secrets.

Opening the Senate's Executive Sessions

On May 21, 1929, the Senate adopted a resolution to investigate how a United Press reporter learned the vote on a nomination taken in closed session. This was not the first time that the Senate sought to uncover leaks from its executive sessions, but it proved to be the last time that this chamber would routinely close its doors for all debates on treaties and nominations.

President Herbert Hoover had nominated former Senator Irvine L. Lenroot of Wisconsin to become a judge on the U.S. Court of Customs and Patent Appeals. As was its tradition, the Senate approved the nomination in secret session. Several days later, reporter Paul Mallon published a list of senators voting for Lenroot. Incensed at this breach of confidence, Senator David A. Reed of Pennsylvania demanded an investigation. When Mallon refused to divulge his source, Reed moved to cite him for contempt of the Senate.

Senator Robert La Follette, Jr., rose in Mallon's defense. The reporter had actually performed a valuable public service, La Follette claimed, because voters must be able to hold elected officials accountable for all their actions. Any attempt to punish Mallon for his supposed offense would suppress the freedom of the press and violate the First Amendment.

Senator La Follette then quoted from a newspaper article written by Theodore Huntley, which not only divulged a secret session but contained a direct quote from Senator Reed. La Follette observed that, instead of citing Huntley for contempt, Reed had hired him as his personal secretary. This news convulsed the entire Senate chamber with laughter, including the red-faced Senator Reed. La Follette had deftly made his point. Thus, we now cast our votes on nominations and treaties in sessions open to the public and the press.

Robert La Follette, Jr. of Wisconsin

1929
JUNE 20

Majority and Minority Secretaries Established

On June 20, 1929, the Senate offices of secretary for the majority and secretary for the minority were established. Carl A. Loeffler became the first Republican secretary and Edwin A. Halsey the first Democratic secretary. They filled the posts that are currently held by Howard O. Greene and C. Abbott Saffold.

The two party secretaries aid the majority and minority leaders, and all other senators, in a profusion of activities on the Senate floor and in the cloakrooms. They serve as the principal staff members of the party conferences and attend party steering committee and policy committee meetings. The party secretaries spend much of their time in the Senate chamber, where they assist the leadership in counting heads before a vote; and they advise party members on the nature of bills under consideration. They keep the leadership informed of any members of their party who will be absent from town, to help in scheduling votes, and arrange "pairs" for members who will miss votes. In short, they are expected to know all that there is to know about what is happening on their side of the aisle—and a good deal about the other side as well—and to assist their party in whatever ways may be required.

Considering this wide range of responsibilities, it is surprising that the positions were established so recently in the Senate's history. But in fact, even before there were officially designated party secretaries, there were staff members performing the roles. Between the 1890s and 1929, the Senate provided for two assistant sergeants at arms to be appointed by each party and to serve the parties directly. The last two men to hold these posts were Carl Loeffler and Edwin Halsey. By 1929, their positions had grown so essential that the formal titles of majority and minority secretary were adopted.

1929
OCTOBER 7

British Prime Minister Ramsay MacDonald Addresses the Senate

On October 7, 1929, British Labour party Prime Minister Ramsay MacDonald delivered a major address before the Senate. He spoke warmly of British-American friendship and advocated making the Kellogg-Briand peace pact, ratified earlier that year, a living principle. While MacDonald's was one of the more substantive addresses by a visiting dignitary to be given before the Senate, it was not the first. Ever since 1852, when Governor Louis Kossuth of Hungary addressed the Senate, foreign leaders occasionally have sought the Senate chamber as the site of major speeches. Prior to MacDonald, the only Englishman to address the Senate had been Prime Minister Arthur James Balfour, whose grim mission in May 1917 was to brief the senators on the terrible war in Europe that the United States had just voted to enter.

The purpose of MacDonald's 1929 visit to America was to invite the United States to join England, France, Italy, and Japan for a naval conference in London, designed to avert future wars. The prime minister arrived at the Senate trailing clouds of good will and hope for a safer world, and he made his way into the Capitol through the cheering crowds of well-wishers lining the stairs. Nearly every senator was present, and the galleries were packed with notables eager to hear more about the conference he proposed. The Labour party leader was roundly applauded when he declared that "There can be no war—nay, it is absolutely impossible, if you and we do our duty in making the peace pact effective, that any section of our arms, whether land, or sea, or air, can ever again come into hostile conflict."

The conference MacDonald espoused did take place and in April 1930 the London Naval Treaty was signed by the United States, Great Britain, and Japan. The next Englishman to address the Senate was King George VI in June 1942. Like Balfour before him, the king came in the midst of a devastating war, which had not been averted as MacDonald had hoped in 1929.

1929
OCTOBER 29

State Funeral for a Senator

On October 29, 1929, the Senate met for three minutes and adjourned out of respect for the memory of Senator Theodore Burton, who had died the previous day. On the following day, the Senate chamber was filled to capacity for Burton's memorial service, the first to be held here in fifteen years. Among the attendees were President Hoover, who had been Burton's close friend, the chief justice of the United States, members of both houses, and representatives of the diplomatic corps.

Burton was the only man in American history to have the distinction of serving first in the U.S. House of Representatives, then in the Senate, returning to the House, and again moving back to the Senate. Beyond this footnote to history, the Ohio Republican senator, acquainted with twelve presidents from Cleveland to Hoover, was respected as a brilliant and independent legislator who had written extensively on governmental finance. He was best remembered as a leader in the cause of international peace.

Theodore Burton first came to the Senate in 1909, following sixteen years of service in the House. He decided not to seek reelection in 1914, the first direct popular election of senators under the Seventeenth Amendment, partly because he feared he might lose. He also believed that service in the House offered more flexibility and that the Senate had become populated with men who "said one thing in the cloakroom and voted another way on the floor." Burton was succeeded in the Senate by Warren Harding, who used his Senate seat as a springboard to the White House. Burton later regretted his decision to leave the Senate, believing that if he had remained he might have been the Republican party's logical presidential nominee in 1916. He returned to the House in 1921, and in 1928, at the age of seventy-six, he was elected to the Senate by a record-breaking majority. Within weeks, the pressures of Senate service began to take their toll, and he died within a year.

Senate Telephone Controversy Ends

On June 25, 1930, the Senate resolved a month-long controversy over the installation of dial-operated telephones. Earlier, the Chesapeake and Potomac Telephone Company had installed 450 dial phones on the Senate side of the Capitol and in the Senate office building. Many members immediately took a dislike to these instruments, which had been frustrating users since their invention several decades earlier. President Herbert Hoover had banned them from the White House after he took office in 1929.

Senatorial opponents of dial phones, often veiling their arguments in humor, charged that they were mechanically unreliable, that they "required Senators to perform the duties of telephone operators in order to enjoy the benefits of telephone service," that they contributed to the national unemployment rate by throwing telephone operators out of work, and that they required a good deal of light to see how to operate.

On May 22, Virginia's Senator Carter Glass called up his resolution to "have these abominable dial telephones taken out of use on the Senate side." Arizona's Henry Fountain Ashurst thanked Glass for his moderate language. The *Congressional Record*, he observed, "would not be mailable if it contained in print what Senators think of the dial-telephone system." Senator Clarence Dill of Washington state suggested that Glass expand his measure to outlaw dial phones from the District of Columbia as well.

The Senate quickly adopted the Glass resolution, which provided for restoration of operator-assisted phones within thirty days. Over the next several weeks, representatives of the telephone company vigorously lobbied senators and staff to reverse this decision. Finally, on June 25, the Senate accepted a compromise measure that permitted members to choose the type of instrument that best suited them.

Vice President Charles Curtis'
secretarial staff

1931
FEBRUARY 14

Completing the Russell Building

On February 14, 1931, the Senate voted to spend three million dollars to complete the office building that we know today as the Richard Russell Building. This first Senate office building was begun in 1906 and completed in 1909. The structure's architectural plans mirrored the Cannon House Office Building in most respects, except that it was originally C shaped, with the east end open along First Street. The 1931 plan called for closing in the east end and creating a quadrangular building.

The growing size of the Senate staff and senators' need for more space provided the rationale for this expansion. In supporting the funding request, Appropriations Committee Chairman Wesley Jones pointed out that about twenty senators had only two rooms apiece. "I know that the work of Senators is increasing every year," said Senator Jones. "I know that a Senator with four or more clerks—and there are none with fewer—cannot get along very well with only two rooms. He must have some privacy. He must have some means of meeting the people from his State in a private sort of way."

Senator David Walsh of Massachusetts objected that the new wing to the office building would curtail ventilation and light to inside rooms and would cause "a mad scramble for outside rooms." He added, "I come from a large State; I have a fairly large mail and a fairly large number of callers. I occupied two rooms for three years. It was unpleasant and there was some discomfort, but what harm is there in having fifteen or twenty new senators for a year or two being content with two rooms, with the assurance that finally they will get three good rooms." But in the end, the need for more space prevailed over these arguments, and the new wing was completed in 1933.

The Russell Senate Office Building in the 1930s

1931
DECEMBER 7

President Hoover and the Senate

Before the Twentieth Amendment was added to the Constitution in 1933, new sessions of Congress traditionally began on the first Monday in December. Thus, the first session of the Seventy-second Congress met on Monday, December 7, 1931.

The Democrats had won the majority in the House, but Senate Republicans—who had held the majority in the Senate since 1919—claimed a one-vote margin (48 to 47, with one independent). This statistic would not be worth commemorating had it not been for President Herbert Hoover's recommendation that the Republicans step aside and allow the Democrats to organize the Senate. This was remarkable and certainly unprecedented advice from a Republican president to the members of his party in Congress.

In 1931 the United States was mired in a terrible economic depression, and Herbert Hoover was directing all of his considerable energy toward finding some way out. Historians credit Hoover with being the first president to accept national economic recovery as a responsibility of the federal government. While Hoover's programs were more restrained than those that followed during the New Deal, they were far more ambitious than anything that had preceded him.

Because he had an ambitious program, President Hoover believed that the opposition party might cooperate with him if they held the majority in both houses. For this reason, he suggested that Republicans allow the Democrats to organize the Senate. Senate Republicans, however, saw matters quite differently. They knew the importance of committee chairmanships for setting the Senate's agenda and were not about to abandon their majority, no matter how slim. Thus Republicans rejected Hoover's advice and continued their majority throughout the Seventy-second Congress.

1932
JUNE 17

Senate Defeats Bonus Bill

On June 17, 1932, United States senators voted to defeat a "bonus bill" for veterans of the First World War. A difficult vote to cast under any circumstances, it was made even more ominous by the twelve thousand marchers waiting outside the Capitol Building.

The time was the Great Depression. Among the millions of unemployed Americans were thousands of veterans of the First World War. Some of these veterans proposed that the bonus scheduled to be paid to them in 1945 be made payable immediately in 1932. From all over the country, veterans converged on Washington in what became known as the bonus march. They camped at various sites near the Capitol, where they lobbied for the bill's passage.

On the evening of June 17, the bonus marchers congregated on the Capitol Plaza, silently awaiting the outcome of the Senate vote. Inside the building, Capitol policemen armed with rifles guarded the doors. There was an unsettling sense of trouble brewing, for no one knew how the marchers would react if the bill did not pass.

At 9 p.m., one of their leaders emerged and announced that the Senate had rejected the bonus bill by a vote of 62 to 18. Promising to continue their fight, the veterans stood facing the Capitol and sang "America." Then they peacefully departed for their camps.

One month later, the bonus army was violently dispersed. Nervous government officials ordered the U.S. Army to clear the veterans out of their camps. Soon, tanks were rumbling down Pennsylvania Avenue, mounted cavalrymen were charging the crowd, and tear gas was tossed. The situation got completely out of hand. Thus, the bonus march on Washington ended with the former American servicemen and their families suffering more than a hundred casualties.

Bonus Marchers in front of the Capitol, 1932

The Senate Removes Its Sergeant At Arms

On February 7, 1933, the Senate voted 53 to 17 to fire its sergeant at arms, David S. Barry. Now, it was certainly rare for the Senate to dismiss one of its high-ranking, elected staff members and to call the individual to the Senate floor to answer charges. David Barry, at seventy-two years of age, had spent almost his entire life around the Senate, first as a page, as secretary to various senators, as a newspaper correspondent, and finally, for fourteen years as sergeant at arms. Why did the Senate fire him?

It appears that David Barry was a victim of bad timing and bad editing. The Republicans had lost control of the Senate in the 1932 election, and Barry knew he would not be reelected sergeant at arms when the next Congress met in March 1933. As a former journalist, he expected to write occasional pieces for publication during his retirement. He had already submitted an article entitled "Over the Hill to Demagoguery" to the *New Outlook* magazine. It was scheduled for publication in March.

Unfortunately for David Barry, the editor moved the article's publication up to February and edited out an unexceptional first paragraph. When the magazine appeared at the newsstands, it began with these words:

> Contrary, perhaps, to the popular belief, there are not many crooks in Congress; that is out-and-out grafters, or those who are willing to be such. There are not many Senators or Representatives who sell their votes for money, and it is pretty well known who those few are; but there are many demagogues.

Although these were strong words, they probably would have received little attention if some reporter had written them. For the Senate's sergeant at arms, however, it was an entirely different matter, and the Senate voted him out of office, less than a month before his term would have ended.

David S. Barry, sergeant at arms

1933
MARCH 9

First Hundred Days of the New Deal

On March 9, 1933, the first session of the Seventy-third Congress convened for a legislative period that lasted one hundred days. This was the first Hundred Days of Franklin D. Roosevelt's New Deal, one of the most productive congressional sessions in our history.

Roosevelt took office at the nadir of the Great Depression. Millions of Americans were unemployed. Factories were closed, and banks had failed. It was vital that the government respond quickly and positively. Members of Congress closed ranks to enact Roosevelt's sweeping program of recovery, relief, and reform. Attesting to the bipartisan nature of the response to the national economic crisis—although the Democrats were the majority party—Republican Senator George Norris fathered the Tennessee Valley Authority Act and Arthur Vandenberg proposed federal deposit insurance for bank accounts.

In addition to TVA and FDIC, the first Hundred Days saw enactment of major banking and securities reforms to stabilize the nation's precarious banking system and prevent fraud in the stock markets. The Agricultural Adjustment Act aimed at reducing vast farm surpluses by paying farmers to take land out of cultivation. The National Industrial Recovery Act set up the NRA, which attempted to increase production while holding the line on wages and prices. The Federal Emergency Relief Act provided the first direct federal aid to the unemployed. And the Home Owners Loan Corporation helped families refinance their mortgages and save their homes.

By June 16, Congress had passed fifteen major laws recommended by the president. Never had a chief executive enjoyed more support. As Will Rogers observed: "The whole country is with him. Even if what he does is wrong, they are with him. Just so he does something. If he burned down the Capitol, we would cheer and say, 'Well, at least we got a fire started, anyhow!' "

1933
JUNE 1

J. P. Morgan and the Pecora Committee

During the depths of the Depression, the Senate Banking and Currency Committee conducted illuminating investigations into Wall Street banking and stock exchange practices. The Banking Committee hearings, which began in 1932, became popularly known as the Pecora investigation when the energetic Ferdinand Pecora became chief counsel in 1933 and reinvigorated the Senate inquiry. In late May 1933, Pecora called the nation's most powerful banker, J.P. Morgan, Jr., to the witness stand.

Depression-weary reporters and curiosity seekers filled the corridors of the Senate office building to view the spectacle. Pecora unveiled evidence that the extremely wealthy Morgan had not paid income taxes during the years 1931 and 1932 and had been distributing stock and financial favors to influential individuals for some time. These disclosures seriously undermined Morgan's power.

J.P. Morgan and circus midget

Symbolizing the fall of the Olympian banker was a photograph which appeared on June 2, 1933, in newspapers across the nation. During a break in the hearings, an enterprising press agent slipped into the Senate Caucus Room and placed a circus midget in the lap of the unsuspecting J.P. Morgan. Believing she was a child, Morgan put his arm protectively around her. "I've got a grandson bigger than you," he said. "But I'm older," replied the midget. "She's thirty-two," the press agent informed him, whereupon Morgan slid the woman off his lap, but not before press photographers managed to snap pictures of the embarrassing incident.

Through his investigations, Pecora succeeded in diminishing the power of many of Wall Street's bankers and investors. By the time he had concluded his inquiries, the Securities Act of 1933, the Banking Act of 1933, and the Securities Exchange Act of 1934 had become law.

1935
MAY 6

Senator Cutting Killed in Plane Crash

On May 6, 1935, New Mexico Republican Bronson Cutting earned the tragic distinction of becoming the first sitting senator to die in an airplane crash. Cutting had been appointed to the Senate in 1928 to fill the vacancy caused by the death of Andrieus Jones. He won election in his own right later that year and again in 1934.

Senator Cutting was born in New York in 1888 into a distinguished old-line family. Suffering from tuberculosis, he was forced to drop out of Harvard University after two years. Cutting's doctors ordered him west for recovery. Settling in New Mexico, he became one of the new state's commercial, cultural, and political leaders via the newspapers he published. During World War I, he volunteered for military intelligence work in London. Upon his return, he became active in the newly founded American Legion, whose members became his most ardent supporters.

For many years, members of New Mexico's political establishment smiled at Cutting's scholarly reserve, cultured manners, and progressive views. But, in recognition of his large following among voters of Mexican descent and members of the American Legion, the governor appointed him to the vacant Senate seat in 1927. In the Senate, Cutting identified himself with the most progressive senators and became a vigorous critic of President Hoover's administration.

Cutting's reelection campaign in 1934, decided by only 1,261 votes, was a bitter, hard-won fight against Democrat Dennis Chavez. Chavez contested the election, alleging that illegal votes had been counted in Cutting's favor. Cutting, who had already been sworn in, flew home to New Mexico to direct an investigation into the charges. It was on his return trip to Washington, armed with documents he believed exonerated him, that Cutting lost his life when his plane went down near Atlanta, Missouri. Ironically, Dennis Chavez was appointed to Cutting's vacant seat, and he served New Mexico in the Senate for nearly thirty years.

Youngest Constitutionally Eligible Senator Sworn In

On June 21, 1935, Rush Holt of West Virginia became the youngest person in history to take the oath of office as a United States senator in accordance with the provisions of the Constitution. Holt had been elected the previous November at the age of twenty-nine. The Constitution provides that "no person shall be a Senator who shall not have attained the age of thirty years." Although Holt, a Democrat, filed his election credentials with the Senate on January 3, 1935, the so-called Boy Senator did not attempt to claim his seat until his thirtieth birthday in June.

Holt's defeated Republican opponent, former Senator Henry Hatfield, petitioned the Senate to invalidate Holt's election. He argued that Holt failed to meet the constitutional age requirement, both at the time of his election and at the start of the term to which he was elected. Hatfield sought to be seated as the recipient of the second highest number of votes.

The Senate Committee on Privileges and Elections disagreed and recommended that Holt be sworn in. The committee observed that Holt's age had been well known to the voters of West Virginia and that the date on which the senator-elect presented himself in the Senate to take the oath was the only date of consequence. The committee also reaffirmed the principle that the voiding of an election does not confer the office on the candidate receiving the second highest number of votes. On June 21, by a vote of 62 to 17, the Senate agreed to seat Holt.

During the early nineteenth century, three senators who had not yet reached the constitutionally mandated age of thirty were nevertheless seated without challenge by their colleagues. In 1806 Henry Clay took his oath at the age of 29 years and 8 months. A decade later, the Senate admitted Armistead Mason at the age of 28 years, 5 months and 18 days. John Henry Eaton became the youngest senator in history when he took his oath in November 1818 at the age of 28 years, 4 months, and 29 days.

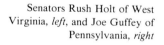

Senators Rush Holt of West Virginia, *left*, and Joe Guffey of Pennsylvania, *right*

1935
JULY 1

Senate Parliamentarian Established

On July 1, 1935, the Senate officially established the post of parliamentarian. Today, the parliamentarian has become such an integral part of the functioning of this chamber that it is hard to believe that the Senate went so long without one.

In the nineteenth century the average session of Congress lasted perhaps six months of the year, and the volume of legislation handled was minuscule by current standards. Vice presidents presided daily in the Senate chamber and took pride in knowing the Senate rules. (In fact, Thomas Jefferson wrote a rules manual while he presided as vice president.) The senators also had the time to debate the fine points of parliamentary procedures and tended to be far better versed in the rules and precedents than today's busy legislators. Under these circumstances, the function of the parliamentarian could be carried on sporadically and unofficially by various clerks at the front desk.

While it is surprising that none of these clerks was designated as parliamentarian before 1935, it is not surprising that the office was created in the middle of the New Deal, at a time when the Senate's legislative load had increased dramatically. On July 1, 1935, the Senate promoted its journal clerk, Charles Watkins, to the new combined post of parliamentarian and journal clerk. Two years later, the titles were divided and Watkins, on July 1, 1937 became solely the parliamentarian. He held the position until his retirement in 1964.

Under Charles Watkins and his successors, Floyd Riddick, Murray Zweben, Robert Dove, and Alan Frumin, the Senate parliamentarians have played an ever expanding and essential role, advising the presiding officers, the leadership, committee chairmen and other senators, and helping us all to operate within the rules and precedents of this institution.

1935
SEPTEMBER 10

Senator Huey Long Dies

On September 10, 1935, Louisiana Senator Huey Long died in Baton Rouge, the victim of an assassin's bullet two days earlier. The senator's shocking demise cut short one of the most dramatic political careers of the twentieth century, just as it was reaching its apex.

Born in Louisiana in 1893, Huey Long worked as a traveling salesman to earn money for law school. The canvassing experience he gained on Louisiana's back roads later proved politically advantageous. The young attorney began his career by attacking the enemy he would grapple with so flamboyantly all his life—the concentration of wealth.

In 1918, Long, a Democrat, was elected public service commissioner and enhanced his reputation as a foe of corporate interests. From a power base anchored in the rural poor, he was elected governor in 1928. As governor, he sponsored "the people's" reforms—free textbooks for schoolchildren and the repeal of the poll tax—all the while creating a powerful political machine.

Huey Long entered the United States Senate in 1932. An expert at courting the press, he quickly gained a national following by his advocacy of the "share-our-wealth" plan, which promised every American family a five-thousand-dollar "homestead allowance" and a guaranteed annual income of at least two thousand dollars. By 1935, the Kingfish, as he was called, had become a vitriolic critic of the New Deal, and he was considered a possible third-party candidate for the 1936 presidential election.

Senator Long's widow, Rose McConnell Long, briefly succeeded him. In 1948, Senator Long's son, Russell Long, with whom many of us had the privilege of serving, was elected to the Senate and served for thirty-eight distinguished years. The Long family is the only one that can claim the distinction of having father, mother, and son serve in the Senate.

Huey Long of Louisiana

1936
NOVEMBER 4

Claude Pepper Becomes a Senator

On November 4, 1936, Claude Pepper took his oath as a United States senator. Born on an Alabama farm in 1900, he moved to Florida after graduating from Harvard Law School. As a young boy he once got into difficulty when he carved on the back of a closet door the statement that "one day Claude Pepper will be a United States Senator." From that time on, he was known as "Senator Pepper." He fulfilled that dream in 1936 by being elected to serve the remaining two years of an unexpired Senate term.

Claude Pepper emerged as the Senate's most outspoken supporter of President Franklin Roosevelt. In his 1938 primary campaign for election to a full term, he vigorously supported the president's minimum wage bill, which had been bottled up in Congress because it was considered unpopular in the South. His impressive victory demonstrated to the nation the strength of the New Deal in the South and sparked passage of the Fair Labor Standards Act. Claude Pepper remained in the Senate until 1951. In 1962 he was elected to the House of Representatives, where he served with great distinction until his death in 1989.

In 1939, on the occasion of the Senate's 150th anniversary, Claude Pepper penned the following classic description of the Senate's constitutional role:

The varied and extraordinary functions and powers of the Senate make it, according to one's point of view, a hydra-headed monster or the citadel of constitutional and democratic liberties. Like democracy itself, the Senate is inefficient, unwieldy, inconsistent; it has its foibles, its vanities, its members who are great, the near great, and those who think they are great. But like democracy also, it is strong, it is sound at the core, it has survived many changes, it has saved the country many catastrophes, it is a safeguard against any form of tyranny, good or bad, which consciously or unconsciously might tend to remove the course of government from persistent public scrutiny.

"In the last analysis," he concluded, "it is probably the price we in America have to pay for liberty."

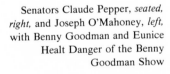

Senators Claude Pepper, *seated, right,* and Joseph O'Mahoney, *left,* with Benny Goodman and Eunice Healt Danger of the Benny Goodman Show

Republican Leader Occupies Front-Row Desk

Most senators are aware that they are members of a continuous body that began in 1789; that they sit in this chamber at desks once used by Henry Clay, Daniel Webster, and John C. Calhoun; that they occupy offices in the Senate office building once used by Robert Taft, Harry Truman, and Everett Dirksen; and that they serve on committees which were created in the early nineteenth century.

For instance, I am standing at a desk that traditionally is assigned to the Republican floor leader. It would be a mistake to think that Republican leaders have always sat here, but this tradition is now fifty years old. On January 5, 1937, Charles McNary of Oregon became the first Republican leader to sit at this desk. Previously, it was occupied by a senior Republican, Arthur Capper of Kansas, while Republican Leader McNary sat several seats down on the front row. By contrast, Democratic leaders had been seated front and center on their side of the aisle since 1927. Out of a sense of symmetry, and in recognition of the growing role of the floor leader, Republican Leader McNary moved to the aisle desk at the beginning of the Seventy-fifth Congress, and Senator Capper took the desk at his side. Here, over the next fifty years, have sat each of the Republican floor leaders: Wallace White, Kenneth Wherry, Robert Taft, William Knowland, Everett Dirksen, Hugh Scott, Howard Baker, and myself. I am proud to stand in that company and to continue that tradition.

FDR Submits His "Court Packing Plan"

On February 5, 1937, one of America's most skillful politicians made his greatest political mistake. Franklin D. Roosevelt, fresh from his landslide re-election as president in 1936, and buoyed by unprecedented margins of 76 Democrats to 16 Republicans in the Senate, and 331 to 89 in the House, took a gamble that he eventually lost. He submitted to Congress a plan to reorganize the Supreme Court.

The president suggested that when a federal judge reached the age of seventy, an additional judge be appointed to help carry the increasingly complex case load. In 1937, most of the "Nine Old Men" of the Supreme Court were over seventy. Roosevelt's plan would have permitted him to name up to six new justices to the Supreme Court. During his first term, FDR had not made a single appointment to the Court, which had struck down several major New Deal laws as unconstitutional. Too impatient to wait for the Court to change through retirements, and fearful for the rest of his program, Roosevelt seized the initiative.

But the president had not anticipated the reaction within his own party. Many conservative Democrats, who had supported the New Deal because of the economic emergency of the depression, bolted against this assault on the Supreme Court. Even some progressive Democrats, notably Montana's Burton K. Wheeler, came to the Court's defense. The tiny Republican minority had only to sit back and watch Democrats war against each other. The Court packing plan eventually died in the Judiciary Committee. In a sense, FDR won, for within the next four years he had named seven of the nine justices. In another sense, he lost badly: the rifts within his party did not heal. Few New Deal initiatives were enacted during the remainder of his administration, despite the overwhelming Democratic margins.

1937
MARCH 25

Senate Agrees to Preserve Historical Records

On March 25, 1937, the Senate agreed to transfer its historical records to the newly opened National Archives.

Ever since Congress moved to Washington in 1800, Senate clerks had followed the practice of sending noncurrent records to the Capitol's attic and basement storerooms and promptly forgetting about them. Over the years war, vermin, moisture, and souvenir hunters ravaged these documents. In 1927, Harold Hufford, a young file clerk in the office of the secretary of the Senate, went to a storeroom to locate some older documents. As he cautiously opened the door, he saw papers stacked in boxes and strewn on the floor. He looked down to see that he was standing on an official-looking document. He later recounted that the document bore two important markings: "the print of my rubber heel, and the signature of Vice President John C. Calhoun."

During the following decade, Hufford diligently searched the Capitol and the Senate office building. He found records dating from the First Congress in more than fifty locations. With great care, he moved most of them to a dry storage area in the Capitol attic.

Early in 1937, an appraiser from the National Archives examined the collection and found that most records were dirty, water-damaged and brittle. In spite of their poor condition, the examiner concluded: "From the standpoint of historical, as well as intrinsic interest, this is perhaps the most valuable collection of records in the entire Government. It touches all phases of governmental activity and contains a vast amount of research material that has never been used." On the strength of that report, the Senate agreed to send the documents to the National Archives for proper care and public access.

1940
JANUARY 19

William E. Borah Dies

On January 19, 1940, Senator William Borah, "the Lion of Idaho," died here in Washington. Each day as I walk between the Republican leader's office and the Senate chamber, I pass Senator Borah's statue, looking as resolute as he did during his entire thirty-three years in the Senate.

William Borah began his Senate career during the presidency of Theodore Roosevelt and died while Franklin Roosevelt was contemplating a third term. Because of his reputation as a successful prosecutor of labor radicals in Idaho, Borah was named chairman of the Senate Committee on Education and Labor during his freshman term. But those who expected him to take an antilabor stance were sorely disappointed.

Senator Borah sponsored legislation to create the Department of Labor and the Children's Bureau. He led the fight for the eight-hour work day for projects done on government contract. He encouraged an investigation of working conditions in the steel industry. As a reformer, he also promoted establishment of the federal income tax and of direct election of senators.

In international affairs, Borah took a consistently nationalist approach. He only reluctantly supported American entry into the First World War and was a leader of the Senate forces that defeated the Treaty of Versailles, which contained President Wilson's internationalist League of Nations. In 1924, Borah became chairman of the Senate Foreign Relations Committee, where he resolutely opposed "entangling alliances" of any kind. Throughout the 1930s, he was the Senate's staunchest advocate of neutrality legislation aimed at keeping the United States out of the next world war. But one man cannot hold back world events. Borah died in 1940, the year after World War II erupted in Europe and the year before Pearl Harbor.

William Borah of Idaho

1940

DECEMBER 13

Prospective Chairmen With Equal Seniority

On December 13, 1940, two senators conducted a quiet struggle for the soon-to-be-vacant position as chair of the Senate Judiciary Committee. Never before had two men with exactly equal seniority contended for a committee chairmanship.

Incumbent chairman Henry F. Ashurst had been defeated for reelection to the Senate. The next most senior majority member of the committee, Matthew Neely, had been elected governor of West Virginia and planned to resign from the Senate early in January.

The *Congressional Directory* of 1940 listed Senator Patrick McCarran of Nevada as the next ranking majority member of the committee. His name was followed by Senator Frederick Van Nuys of Indiana. Both men had entered the Senate on March 3, 1933. At that time, McCarran, whose name came earlier in the alphabet, took his Senate oath several minutes ahead of Van Nuys. Both men were appointed to the Judiciary Committee on the same day, although Van Nuys' name appeared before that of McCarran on the list of recommended new members. From 1933 until 1937, the Indiana senator was listed ahead of McCarran on the *Congressional Directory*'s roster of committee members. Then, in 1938, the order of their names was mysteriously reversed.

As 1940 drew to a close, Majority Leader Alben Barkley privately urged both men to settle the contest informally. Neither chose to do so. Consequently, the Democratic Steering Committee was obliged to make the choice. The committee selected Van Nuys, presumably because his state of Indiana entered the Union before Nevada. Van Nuys chaired the Judiciary Committee for three years, until his death in 1944. Then McCarran got his turn and served for most of the following decade.

1941

JUNE 2

Senator Andrew Jackson Houston is Sworn In

On June 2, 1941, an elderly mustachioed gentleman was sworn in as a United States senator from Texas. At eighty-seven years of age, he was the oldest man ever to enter the Senate. This man bore another distinction as well. His name was Andrew Jackson Houston. He was the son of Sam Houston, who 118 years earlier had been sworn in as a young representative from Tennessee and went on to become a legendary general, president of the Republic of Texas, and a colorful senator from Texas. Together the father's and the son's lives spanned the history of the nation. The father had been born in 1793. He vividly remembered George Washington's death in 1799 and often described it to his little boy, Andrew, born in 1854, late in the general's life.

Andrew Jackson Houston, named for his family's great friend, Old Hickory, grew up in the shadow of his famous father. The younger Houston attended several colleges, including West Point, and studied law. He held various government posts, and, in 1902, President Theodore Roosevelt made him a federal marshal. In 1941, when he was appointed to the Senate to fill the vacancy caused by the death of Senator Morris Sheppard, he was living in a wooden cabin he had built himself, writing books on Texas history and serving as superintendent of the San Jacinto battleground park, the site of his father's greatest military campaign. His Senate appointment was announced on April 21, 1941, exactly 105 years after the Battle of San Jacinto.

Andrew Jackson Houston told friends that the supreme joy of his long, long life was occupying the same Senate seat to which his father had been elected when Texas joined the Union. He did not live long enough, however, to fully savor the honor. Just twenty-four days after he entered the Senate, Andrew Jackson Houston died in office. His passing ended the remarkable continuum that stretched back to the nation's earliest days.

Pat Harrison of Mississippi

1941
JUNE 22

The Death of Pat Harrison

On June 22, 1941, a distinguished chairman of the Senate Finance Committee died. Pat Harrison of Mississippi, who was just fifty-nine years old at his death, had been judged by Washington newspaper correspondents as the "most influential" member of the United States Senate, despite his one-vote loss of the majority leadership four years earlier.

Elected to the Senate in 1918—the year that the Democrats lost their majority in the upper house—Harrison became chairman of the Finance Committee when the Democrats returned to the majority in 1933. Far more conservative than President Franklin D. Roosevelt, Harrison nevertheless ushered through his committee several key New Deal bills, most notably the Social Security Act of 1935 and early New Deal tax legislation.

Although Harrison supported the president's policies, he could not obtain Roosevelt's endorsement when he ran for majority leader in 1937. Instead, the president wrote his famous "Dear Alben" letter, implicitly supporting Senator Alben Barkley. While Roosevelt pretended to remain neutral in the race, Harrison angrily told reporters, "He's into it up to here," drawing his index finger across his throat.

Eventually, Barkley won the hard-fought contest by a single vote. But defeat freed Pat Harrison to take a more independent course from the Roosevelt administration. He took the lead in repealing a tax on undistributed profits that Roosevelt had strongly supported, fought with the president over the Revenue Act of 1938, and deflected White House efforts for a new tax bill in 1939. By then, Washington newspaper correspondents came to recognize Harrison as the real leader of Senate Democrats, even though Senator Barkley held the official title.

1943
SEPTEMBER 14

Supply of Senate Bean Soup Dries Up

Whatever uncertainties may exist within the Senate of the United States, one thing is certain: bean soup is available in the Senate's restaurants every day. Bean soup has been featured on the Senate menu for at least eighty-five years. On only one occasion did the kettles stop bubbling. That landmark event occurred on September 14, 1943. The *Washington Times Herald* reported that, even though bean soup was on the menu that day at ten cents a cup, fifteen cents a bowl, it wasn't cooking on the stove, because wartime rationing had slashed the Senate's supply of white Michigan beans. Somehow, by the next day, more beans were found, and bowls of bean soup have been ladled up without interruption ever since.

It is often stated that bean soup is served in the Senate restaurants every single day by decree. The origins of that culinary edict have been lost in antiquity, but there are several oft-told legends. One story has it that Senator Fred Thomas DuBois of Idaho, while presiding over the Rules Committee that supervised the Senate restaurant at the turn of the century, gaveled through a resolution requiring that bean soup, his personal favorite, be on the menu every day. Another account attributes the bean soup mandate to Senator Knute Nelson of Minnesota, who expressed his fondness for bean soup in 1903 and asked that it be served each day. In the House of Representatives, the ubiquitous presence of beans in the restaurants is linked with Speaker Joe Cannon. One hot Washington day in 1904, finding no bean soup on the menu, the speaker is said to have roared, "Thunderation, I had my mouth set for bean soup. From now on, hot or cold, rain, snow, or shine, I want it on the menu every day."

Between the Senate and the House there are many differences. The chief difference between their bean soups is an onion. The Senate recipe calls for onions braised in butter; the House recipe omits them.

1943
OCTOBER 19

First Woman Presides over Senate

On October 19, 1943, Senator Hattie Caraway, a Democrat from Arkansas, approached the presiding officer's chair, took her seat, and made history. When she assumed the chair in the absence of Vice President Henry Wallace and the president pro tempore, Senator Carter Glass of Virginia, Mrs. Caraway became the first woman to preside over this body.

Senator Caraway holds other important Senate distinctions as well. She was the first woman ever elected to the Senate and the first to chair a committee. How she arrived at these historic firsts was due to an unlikely twist of fate, all the more ironic because of her traditional background and beliefs. The first elected woman senator was not a feminist. As a Senate wife, spouse of Arkansas Senator Thaddeus Caraway, she had adhered closely to the belief that a woman's place was in the home, and she rarely made public appearances.

When the governor of Arkansas suggested Mrs. Caraway as a compromise candidate to fill the vacancy created by her husband's death in 1931, he never dreamed that she would decide to run for a full term in the regular election the next year. In fact, she had promised him she would not. But Mrs. Caraway had enjoyed her brief tenure as senator and wished to continue. She won in 1932 with a vote that equaled the combined total of her six opponents, and she won reelection in 1938.

In her two terms in the Senate, Mrs. Caraway served on the Agriculture and Forestry Committee and the Commerce Committee. She exhibited strong interest in farm relief, flood control, and commercial aviation safety. In 1944, Mrs. Caraway was defeated in her bid for a third full term by J. William Fulbright.

Hattie Caraway of Arkansas

1943
NOVEMBER 18

A Report from the Secretary of State

On November 18, 1943, the Senate proceeded to the House chamber to witness a unique event. For the first time in history, a member of the president's cabinet addressed a joint meeting of Congress. The speaker was Secretary of State Cordell Hull.

Secretary Hull had just returned from a major conference of foreign ministers in Moscow. The first Allied three-power meeting of World War II, that conference brought together representatives of the United States, Great Britain, and the Soviet Union to plan military and diplomatic strategy. Soviet leader Joseph Stalin pledged that after Germany's defeat, Russia would enter the war against Japan. Secretary Hull reported that the conference had established a European Advisory Commission to develop a postwar policy for Germany. Most significantly, the secretary noted, the conference recognized the "necessity of establishing at the earliest practicable date a general international organization, based on the principle of the sovereign equality of all peace-loving states, and open to membership by all such states, large and small, for the maintenance of international peace and security."

Members, happily receiving this optimistic message, repeatedly interrupted the secretary with cheers and shouts. He assured his audience that Stalin would not deal separately with the Germans and would not abstain from an Allied peace-keeping coalition. Secretary Hull's assessment of Stalin as "one of the great statesmen and leaders of this age" triggered prolonged applause. Following this address, Senate Republican leaders, in a spirit of bipartisan foreign policy cooperation, agreed that the forthcoming 1944 election campaigns should be confined to domestic policy issues. As senators left the chamber, some speculated that this address by a cabinet secretary heralded a new era of legislative-executive consultation and harmony.

1944
FEBRUARY 4

Henry Cabot Lodge Resigns from Senate to Join Army

On February 4, 1944, the Senate heard its legislative clerk read the following message: "The fact that the United States is entering the period of large scale ground fighting has, after grave thought, brought me to the definite conclusion that, given my age and military training, I must henceforth serve my country as a combat soldier in the Army overseas. In order to serve in combat I hereby resign from the United States Senate." The letter was signed: Henry Cabot Lodge, Jr.

By the time that letter was read in the Senate chamber, former Senator Lodge was flying to England. Then forty-two years old, Lodge had long been a member of the army reserves and as a senator had seen previous service with American tank crews in Libya in 1942. Then the War Department issued orders requiring that members of Congress choose to be either legislators or military men and prohibiting short-term service during congressional recesses. Faced with the choice, Lodge resigned from the Senate.

As he flew to England, Lodge thought his political career was over. He was wrong. After his tour of duty in Europe during World War II, he was reelected to the Senate in 1946. Six years later, he lost his bid for reelection to John F. Kennedy. For the next eight years, Lodge served as ambassador to the United Nations; he then ran unsuccessfully for vice president on the ticket headed by Richard Nixon. Both Presidents Kennedy and Johnson later sent Lodge to South Vietnam as ambassador. President Nixon appointed him as his representative to the Paris peace talks and as special envoy to the Vatican. Henry Cabot Lodge died in 1985. His was a life of public service to his country, for which he was willing to sacrifice anything, including his seat in the United States Senate.

Henry Cabot Lodge, Jr. of Massachusetts

1944
FEBRUARY 23

The Majority Leader Resigns

A majority leader of the United States Senate dramatically resigned on February 23, 1944. Senator Alben Barkley of Kentucky had been Democratic leader of the Senate since 1937 and a loyalist for the administration of Franklin D. Roosevelt, but he was outraged over the harsh language in the president's veto of a tax bill he supported.

Journalist Allen Drury recorded in his journal the scene as rumors spread and the Senate gallery and floor began to fill: "For almost 45 minutes, point by point, [the majority leader] denounced the veto message and the man who sent it to the Hill. In a speech that very evidently came from the heart and at times rose to heights of moving passion and sincerity, he repudiated the President whose errand boy in the upper house he had been for seven years." Barkley announced that he intended to resign as majority leader and then urged Congress to override the president's veto "if it has any self-respect yet left."

Senators from both sides of the aisle stood to applaud and rushed to gather around Barkley to congratulate him. Not only did the Senate and House overwhelmingly vote to override the veto, but the next day the Democratic conference voted unanimously to reelect Barkley as majority leader. Utah Senator Elbert Thomas told reporter Drury that for years Barkley had given the impression that he spoke to the Senate for the president, but that now that he had been unanimously reelected, "he speaks for us to the President."

There is, however, a historical coda to this story. In July 1944, when the Democrats met in convention, they sought a vice presidential candidate to run with Roosevelt for his fourth term. Many believed that Alben Barkley would have been the odds-on favorite had he not broken with Roosevelt just five months earlier. The convention chose Senator Harry Truman instead, and within a year Truman, not Alben Barkley, was president of the United States.

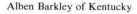

Alben Barkley of Kentucky

1944
SEPTEMBER 2

Death of George Norris

On September 2, 1944, one of the most effective United States senators, George Norris, died.

George Norris spent forty years in Congress. He served in the House of Representatives from 1903 to 1913, then in the Senate from 1913 to 1943. Those years were jammed with activity and accomplishment. As a progressive Republican, Norris led the forces of reform that reduced the power of "Uncle Joe" Cannon, the dictatorial speaker of the House. In the Senate he fought for the rights of farmers and workers. During the 1920s, he was the prime mover behind legislation enabling the federal government to buy American farm products and sell them abroad.

Norris' thirty-year Senate career affected many aspects of American society. He was the author of the Tennessee Valley Authority Act. He put his efforts and his name on the Norris-La Guardia Act of 1932 to restrict the power of courts to break labor strikes through injunctions. He was a chief supporter of the Rural Electrification Administration or the "electrical revolution" as some called it. Norris added his mark to the U.S. Constitution by sponsoring what became its Twentieth Amendment, which set new dates for presidential inaugurations and the beginning of new sessions of Congress, thus eliminating the need for most lame-duck sessions. He also held the respect of his colleagues and the press for his "100-percent integrity."

Norris' opposition to American involvement in international affairs prior to the Second World War finally led to his defeat for reelection in 1942. The next year, listening over the radio to the president's message to Congress, Norris imagined himself back at the Capitol, until his own applause made him recall that he was "just a private citizen, sitting in my home at McCook, Nebraska." He died there in 1944, but his contributions to the Senate, the Constitution, and the federal government survive him today.

George Norris of Nebraska

237

1944
OCTOBER 22

War Movies in the Senate Chamber

On October 22, 1944, the United Press uncovered a secret plan, hatched in the Senate Military Affairs Committee, to show war movies in the Senate chamber. When confronted with this intelligence, an army colonel on detail to the committee admitted that he had been involved in covert planning to place a screen in the chamber and to test the best projection angles. He explained that committee leaders hoped that the regular showing of battle films would allow the Senate to keep better informed about current World War II developments.

Up to that point, the experiment had been kept quiet, for it was rightly seen as a radical encroachment on senatorial dignity and tradition. Earlier, when committee staff had quietly set up a screen in the empty chamber, a representative of the Senate sergeant at arms raced into the chamber shouting: "Take that thing down. Nothing like that has been in the chamber for 100 years, and isn't going to be."

Sergeant at Arms Wall Doxey attempted to defuse this controversy in comments to a reporter. "I just told them I hoped they would get through with the experiment as quickly as possible, because that's a very expensive screen and if anything happened to it while it was hanging there, I would be responsible." Military Affairs Committee Chairman Robert Reynolds helpfully added, "The Senate could find out as much about a matter of legislation in a minute through pictures as it could in an hour of talk."

The last that was heard of this innovative proposal, as the 1944 session drew to a close, was that it remained securely in the custody of the Senate Rules Committee.

1945
JANUARY 18

Harry Truman Resigns from Senate

In January 1945, Harry S. Truman resigned from the United States Senate shortly before being inaugurated as vice president of the United States. From humble origins as a farmer and a haberdasher, he rose to become president of the United States. There he was called upon to make some of the most difficult and significant presidential decisions in our history, determining this nation's role in world affairs.

We remember Harry Truman for many things, but we should not forget that before becoming vice president and president, he spent what he called "the happiest ten years" of his life as a U.S. senator. Truman was elected senator from Missouri in 1934. When he arrived as a freshman, somewhat intimidated by the famous names around him, he received some good advice from the Democratic whip, J. Hamilton Lewis: "Don't start out with an inferiority complex. For the first six months you'll wonder how you got here, and after that you'll wonder how the rest of us got here."

Harry Truman quickly learned that the real work of a senator was done in committee, and he worked hard at his committee assignments. Later he wrote: "I made it my business to master all of the details of any project

Harry S. Truman of Missouri as a senator

confronting a committee of which I was a member." Such dedication and hard work made Truman "a senator's senator," well-liked and respected by his colleagues in this chamber.

It further aided him in 1941 when he became chairman of the Special Committee to Investigate the National Defense Program. His hard-hitting, uncompromising investigation into defense contracting saved the nation millions of dollars, protected servicemen from shoddy equipment, won Truman bipartisan praise, and propelled him into the vice presidency—which within months placed him in the White House. In Truman's case, good work had its reward. I am pleased to be able to honor his memory today.

1945
FEBRUARY 19

Night School for Senators

In February 1945, headlines carried stirring news of Iwo Jima, Generals MacArthur and Patton, and Yalta. Those of us who lived through those harrowing, momentous days and weeks had the sense that the world was rapidly changing as events in Europe and the Pacific built to a climax.

Beneath the headlines in February 1945 there appeared a small item captioned "Night School for Senators." It told of a proposed innovation by Senate Republicans to keep abreast of the fast-changing issues confronting them. The idea was to have a series of evening meetings, featuring outside experts, to discuss the complexities of matters before the Senate. The decision to begin such a "night school" sprang specifically from the need to understand the implications of the Bretton Woods Monetary and Financial Conference of the previous summer. Attended by representatives of forty-four countries, the conference had established the International Monetary Fund and the International Bank for Reconstruction and Development.

While a laudable idea, the night school was apparently short-lived. The pace of world events quickened still further as the next two months brought the American victories on the Rhine and in Okinawa, the sudden death of President Roosevelt, and the drafting of the United Nations Charter in San Francisco. The work of the Senate accelerated, leaving little time for leisurely evenings of study and reflection.

I might add a personal note. We do have a few night schools around here, but they are always on the record, of course, doing business.

1945

Vacant Seat from Virginia

On November 19, 1945, a Virginia Republican official petitioned the Supreme Court to review the status of one of the state's seats in the United States Senate. At that time, eighty-seven-year-old Democratic Senator Carter Glass, president pro tempore and chairman of the Appropriations Committee, was ill and had not attended the Senate since June 20, 1942—a period of more than three years. The Supreme Court declined to consider the matter, since constitutionally only the Senate could expel or otherwise declare vacant the seat of any senator.

During his long career in Congress, Carter Glass had had a powerful impact, particularly on economic issues. A Lynchburg, Virginia newspaper publisher, Glass entered politics in the 1890s when he advocated the free coinage of silver and attacked the gold standard policies of President Grover Cleveland. He was elected to the House of Representatives in 1902 and assigned to the House Banking Committee. As chairman of the Banking Committee in 1913, he was one of the principal authors of the Federal Reserve Act and thereafter became the Federal Reserve Board's chief advocate in Congress.

From 1919 to 1920, Glass served as Woodrow Wilson's secretary of the treasury, and in 1920 he was appointed to fill a vacancy in the U.S. Senate. In the Senate he served on the Banking Committee and the Appropriations Committee, giving his name to the landmark Glass-Steagall Act of 1933, which established the Federal Deposit Insurance Corporation. The staunchly conservative Glass broke with the administration of Franklin D. Roosevelt over its New Deal domestic policies but gave strong support to Roosevelt's internationalist foreign policies.

An active and effective senator until confined by illness in 1942, Carter Glass tenaciously held his Senate seat until he died in 1946.

Facing page, the Capitol photographed during renovation of the east front, 1958

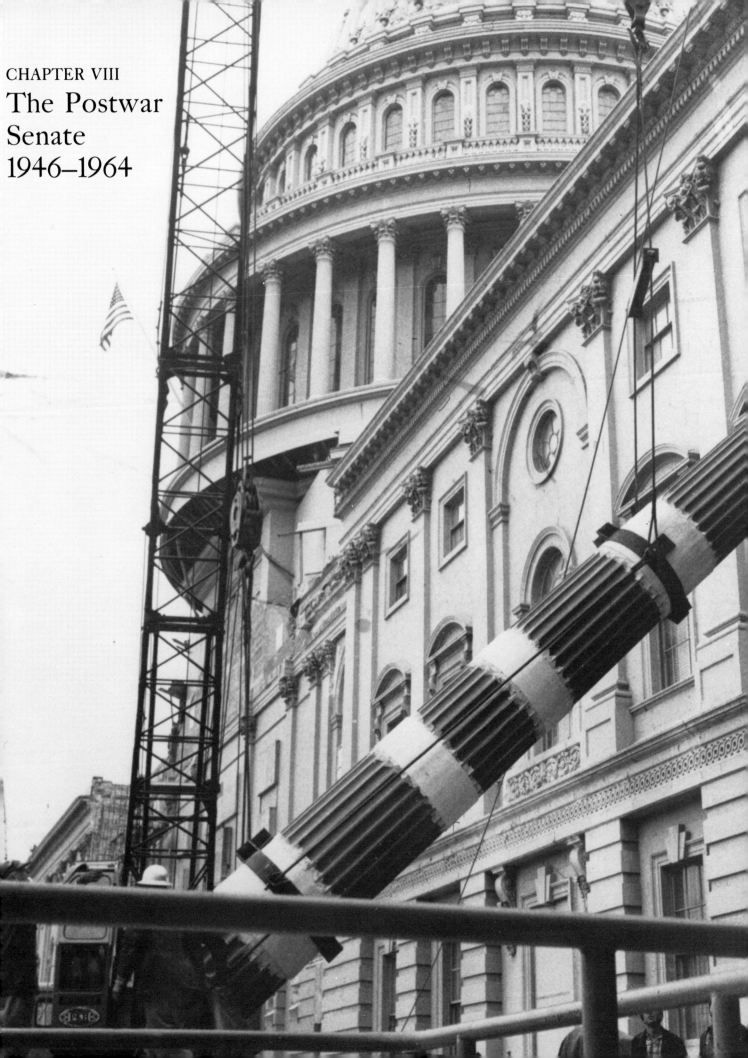

1946
AUGUST 2

Legislative Reorganization Act

On August 2, 1946, President Harry S. Truman signed the Legislative Reorganization Act.

In the aftermath of the Second World War, as America assumed vast new responsibilities of world leadership and the activities of the federal government expanded both at home and abroad, it became clear that Congress needed to modernize its machinery, particularly to keep pace with the growth of the executive branch. A joint committee, headed by Wisconsin Senator Robert La Follette, Jr. and Oklahoma Representative—later Senator—Mike Monroney, investigated the congressional workload. The joint committee determined that there was an overabundance of committees and insufficient staff to enable members of Congress to function effectively. It recommended that the then eighty-one standing committees in the Senate and House be reduced to thirty-four, with more carefully defined jurisdictions and more specific areas of executive oversight. It urged a major expansion of the Legislative Reference Service—now known as the Congressional Research Service. And it promoted the creation of a professional, nonpartisan staff for committees, as well as increased staff for individual members.

Although the House watered down the stronger Senate version of the bill, the final product was a major step forward for the national legislature. Obsolete committees were swept away. Duplication of effort was reduced, and for the first time the Congress began to establish an effective staff system to decrease its dependence on executive agencies for information. On August 2, 1946, President Truman signed the measure, noting that it was truly one of the most significant advances in the organization of Congress since its inception.

1947
MARCH 17

First Issue of the Congressional Record's "Daily Digest"

On March 17, 1947, the "Daily Digest" section of the *Congressional Record* was born.

As the *Congressional Record* expanded during the years of the New Deal and World War II, its readers found it increasingly difficult to use. Several commercial firms set out to provide legislative monitoring services. As early as 1926, David Lawrence, who later founded *U.S. News and World Report*, established the *United States Daily* "to inform the public about its government and what it is doing." In 1943, the United States Chamber of Commerce hired a young political scientist named Floyd Riddick to edit its new publication, the *Legislative Daily*. Distributed to every member of Congress, this service quickly became an indispensable source.

Three years later, Congress included in the Legislative Reorganization Act of 1946 a provision for publication within the *Congressional Record* of a daily digest of legislative activities. Not surprisingly, the secretary of the Senate hired Dr. Riddick to edit the Senate edition of the "Daily Digest." Based on his eight years of experience with similar publications, Riddick established a format that remains virtually intact today. He later recalled that

Floyd Riddick

the most difficult part of setting up the Digest was obtaining cooperation from committee clerks, the only source for consistent reports of committee activity. Most of those clerks initially did not want to be bothered with keeping notes for the Digest staff.

Dr. Riddick remained as Digest editor until 1951, when he became the Senate's assistant parliamentarian. To him, and to the fine staffs that labored on this publication during the past forty years, we owe a special tribute for its usefulness and its reliability.

1947
MARCH 18

Senate Admits Black Reporter to Press Gallery

The press frequently calls on Congress to reform, but Congress has also prompted some reforms in the press. On March 18, 1947, the Senate Rules Committee overruled the Standing Committee of Correspondents and gave press gallery accreditation to Louis R. Lautier, the first black reporter to sit there in seventy years.

The story goes back to 1879 when the Washington press corps was troubled over the number of lobbyists masquerading as reporters. Washington correspondents proposed to the Senate and House a system of journalistic self-policing of the press galleries. They established a Standing Committee of Correspondents to evaluate all requests for press gallery admission. One major criterion was that the individual devote the largest share of his working time to filing reports to a daily newspaper. This rule, in addition to eliminating lobbyists, also excluded reporters for weekly papers, which at that time included most of the black press. Before the rule went into effect, the prominent black editor Frederick Douglass enjoyed press gallery accreditation. After the rule, no black reporters were admitted.

In 1947, at the start of the Republican Eightieth Congress, Louis Lautier petitioned the Rules Committee for help. He had been turned down by a vote of 4 to 1 by the Standing Committee of Correspondents, even though he reported for the *Atlanta Daily World*, a black newspaper. The Committee of Correspondents responded that Lautier devoted more of his time to reporting for a group of black weekly papers. Nevertheless, the Senate believed it was time the color barrier came down within its own chamber and ordered that Louis Lautier be admitted to the press gallery.

1947
JULY 12

Former Capitol Policeman Shoots at Senator

On July 12, 1947, a former Capitol policeman attempted to assassinate Senator John W. Bricker of Ohio. The assailant fired twice at Bricker, who was on his way to the Senate chamber to answer a quorum call. The first shot just missed his head as he was making his way toward the old monorail subway in what is now known as the Russell Building. As Bricker crouched under the car's front seat and called to the operator to "step on it," the second shot whistled above his head. When he arrived at the Capitol, he coolly phoned his secretary on another matter and forgot to mention the incident. When the operator returned the car to the office building end of the line, he found the gunman waiting. The assailant then exited and took a cab to his wife's home, where he was apprehended.

Asked why he attempted to shoot Bricker, the assailant observed that he was "trying to refresh [his] memory." Senator Bricker interpreted this to be a reference to his role, as attorney general of Ohio, in liquidating a savings and loan association fifteen years earlier, an action from which the assailant had suffered financially. Later, as a Capitol policeman, the man had once accosted Bricker outside the Senate chamber to air this grievance. Bricker had also been responsible for removing him from the Capitol police force in favor of his own patronage appointee.

After his scare, Senator Bricker urged increased security measures and an end to the practice of selecting police on a patronage basis. He also called for an increase in the size of the police force on Capitol Hill. The Senate sergeant at arms, in defense of his men, accurately explained that his force was "spread pretty thin." At that time, police rolls carried the names of 157 men. Of that number, several dozen were allegedly not required to report for duty. One member of the 1947 force later recalled: "There were only about 100 of them working. About 50 never came to town."

1948
JUNE 11

Vandenberg Resolution Passes

On June 11, 1948, the United States Senate passed the Vandenberg Resolution, thereby paving the way for American participation in the North Atlantic Treaty Organization.

NATO has become such an integral part of our international defense network that we might forget what a controversial issue it had once been. Immediately after World War II, Western European nations formed an economic alliance to rebuild their continent, but by 1948 Soviet activities in Poland, Czechoslovakia, and Berlin raised the need for a military alliance. The Truman administration believed that no such western alliance could succeed without American participation, but in Congress there were still those who disapproved of "entangling alliances." Some worried that joining NATO would violate the spirit of the United Nations, that it would be seen as a provocative act against the Soviet Union, and that it would stimulate an arms race. Others argued that the United States was dangerously overextending its resources.

Arthur Vandenberg of Michigan

The pivotal person in forming a bipartisan foreign policy between the Republican-controlled Congress and the Democratic administration was Michigan's Arthur H. Vandenberg, chairman of the Senate Foreign Relations Committee. Working closely with Under Secretary of State Robert Lovett, Vandenberg drafted a resolution calling for a security pact between the United States and Western Europe that would be consistent with American participation in the United Nations—since the U.N. Charter permitted regional alliances—but outside the reach of the Soviet veto in the United Nations.

Vandenberg successfully steered his resolution through the Foreign Relations Committee and onto the Senate floor, where it was approved by an overwhelming vote of 64 to 6. One year later, by an equally wide margin, the Senate consented to ratify the NATO treaty.

1948
JULY 26

Senate "Turnip Day" Session Begins

Article II, section 3 of the Constitution provides that the president of the United States may "on extraordinary occasions, convene both Houses, or either of them," by proclamation. On July 26, 1948, President Harry Truman called the Senate and House of the Eightieth Congress into extraordinary session.

Only twenty-seven such sessions have convened in the past two hundred years, and none has occurred since 1948. President John Adams summoned the first such session in 1797 on the issue of suspension of relations with France. President Lincoln called the Congress into extraordinary session in the summer of 1861 as the enormity of the unfolding Civil War became clear. On April 2, 1917, President Woodrow Wilson convened an extraordinary session to ask for the declaration of war that signaled American's entry into the First World War.

Extraordinary sessions have also been called to discuss domestic issues. President Truman called for the 1948 session during his acceptance speech at the Democratic National Convention. He set it to convene on July 26, "Turnip Day" in his home state of Missouri. Truman conceived of the session as a political ploy to challenge the Republican majorities in both houses of Congress to enact the domestic policy platform pledges of their recently concluded national convention. He realized that time and tempers were short and that little was likely to be accomplished.

Lasting for two sweltering mid-summer weeks, the "Turnip Day" session met the president's expectations. This allowed Truman to campaign vigorously against the "do-nothing 80th Congress" throughout the fall, a strategy that contributed to his upset victory in November.

Arthur Capper of Kansas

1949
JANUARY 3

Arthur Capper Retires

On January 3, 1949, Arthur Capper retired from the Senate. Capper, who served for nearly thirty years as a member of the United States Senate, is best remembered for the significant gains he achieved for American farmers. After working for several years as a newspaper reporter and publisher, Capper in 1914 became the first native-born Kansan to be elected governor of the state. At the end of his second term as governor, Capper was elected as a Republican to the Senate and began his service on March 4, 1919.

In the Senate, Capper led the farm bloc. During the New Deal, he defended the Agricultural Adjustment Act as well as other legislation providing aid to farmers. He was a prime sponsor of the Capper-Volstead cooperative marketing act and the Capper-Ketcham Act, which expanded agricultural extension work to include youth clubs.

Arthur Capper also gained national prominence during the debate over the League of Nations, as President Woodrow Wilson frequently consulted him on the issue. Although he opposed the League and was known as an isolationist, Capper supported the 1943 Connally Resolution, which provided for U.S. participation in the international postwar organization for maintaining world peace that eventually became the United Nations.

At the time of his retirement from the Senate in 1949, Capper at eighty-four was the oldest member of the Senate and had served longer than all but one of his colleagues. Capper's retirement marked the end of a distinguished political career that benefitted both the state of Kansas and the entire nation. In a speech given upon his retirement, Capper indicated that he had achieved his goals, declaring that "if I had my life to live over again, I imagine it would be much the same kind of life. I think I have got a lot out of life."

1949
JULY 7

John Foster Dulles Becomes a Senator

On July 7, 1949, the Senate gained a new member with the appointment of John Foster Dulles as senator from New York. While everyone identifies John Foster Dulles as one of the most respected and influential secretaries of state in this century, he was a most unlikely senator, and I suspect that there are very few who know that he ever served in this body.

There are some who feel that John Foster Dulles was born to be secretary of state. As a young man he accompanied his grandfather, former Secretary of State John W. Foster, to the Hague Peace Conference of 1907, and his uncle, Secretary of State Robert Lansing, to the Versailles Peace Conference of 1919. In the 1920s and 1930s he was a successful lawyer dealing in international trade and investments. By the 1940s, John Foster Dulles had become a leading Republican spokesman for an internationalist foreign policy. He was a close adviser of New York Governor Thomas E. Dewey, and it was generally assumed that if Dewey won the presidency, he would appoint Dulles as secretary of state. When Harry Truman upset Dewey in the 1948 election, it appeared that Dulles had lost his chance to head the State Department.

In June 1949, New York's longtime senator, Robert F. Wagner, resigned for reasons of ill health. On July 7, Governor Dewey appointed John Foster Dulles to fill the vacancy. Dulles hoped to use the Senate as a platform for his foreign policy views during that critical period in the cold war. Unfortunately, his tenure in the Senate was a short one. Dulles was defeated in a special November 1949 election.

His few months in the Senate were valuable, however. Dulles became more aware of the Senate's role in foreign policy and took care to consult with Senate leaders after he became secretary of state in 1953 under President Eisenhower.

John Foster Dulles' campaign for the Senate in 1949

1950
SEPTEMBER 22

The Vice President's Desk

On September 22, 1950, the Senate gave one of its most historic pieces of furniture, the vice president's desk in the chamber, to Vice President Alben Barkley.

The Senate chamber was remodeled in 1950. The glass ceiling and elaborate wall panels were removed to improve acoustics in the chamber, and the wooden desks that served the vice president and clerks of the Senate were replaced by the current desks. At that time, Emory Frazier served as the chief clerk. Today that position has become the assistant secretary of the Senate, but back then the chief clerk sat at the front desk to call the roll and handle paperwork. A native Kentuckian and a Senate history buff, Frazier knew that the first vice president to sit at the desk in 1859, John C. Breckinridge, was a Kentuckian. The desk's last occupant in 1950, Alben Barkley, also hailed from Kentucky. Frazier lobbied the committee overseeing the remodeling of the chamber to present the desk to Vice President Barkley.

On September 22, 1950, Senator Dennis Chavez introduced a resolution offering the desk as "an expression of high appreciation" for Barkley's long service as a senator, Senate majority leader, and vice president. Republican leader Kenneth Wherry asked that all senators be permitted to join as cosponsors, and the motion passed without objection. Vice President Barkley took the occasion to express his gratitude to the Senate for the old desk, which had graced the Senate chamber for nearly a century, and extended the thanks of the people of Kentucky for this tribute to two of their native sons.

Today the mahogany vice president's desk is displayed in the modern political collection of the University of Kentucky Library in Lexington, Kentucky, along with a statue of Alben Barkley and photographs of numerous Kentucky senators whose papers are deposited there.

1950
SEPTEMBER 23

McCarran Act Becomes Law

On September 23, 1950, the Senate, by a vote of 57 to 10, overrode President Harry Truman's veto of the Internal Security Act. This act was more popularly known as the McCarran Act after Nevada Senator Pat McCarran, chairman of the Senate Internal Security Subcommittee. Since the House had already overridden the president's veto by a similarly large margin, the McCarran Act became law.

Stimulated by the outbreak of the Korean War and rising fears of internal subversion, this highly controversial measure was an outgrowth of an earlier Communist registration bill that Congressmen Karl Mundt and Richard Nixon had introduced in 1948. Employing exposure as a weapon against the threat of Communist infiltration, the Act provided for registration of Communist and Communist-front organizations, and for detention during national emergencies of persons likely to commit espionage or sabotage. The McCarran Act also prohibited employment of Communists in national defense work, denied them passports, and refused entry into the United States of anyone who had ever been a member of a Communist organization.

Senator McCarran and other supporters of the Act argued that it addressed the peculiar nature of the Communist threat in the United States. McCarran dismissed arguments that the Act might be unconstitutional, pointing out that it neither outlawed the Communist party nor made communism a crime. Nevertheless, in later years the Supreme Court substantially dismantled the McCarran Act, declaring unconstitutional its provisions for registration of Communists and for denial of passports. In 1971 Congress also repealed the McCarran Act's internment authority, which in fact had never been used.

1951
FEBRUARY 3

Physician of Congress

In February 1951, the *New York Times Magazine* featured a story entitled "Doctor of Law Makers." The article was about Dr. George W. Calver, the Capitol physician, and his program to indoctrinate freshmen members of the Eighty-second Congress on the health dangers that lay in wait for them as they began their new careers.

Dr. Calver spoke from first-hand knowledge. He had been the attending physician of Congress for twenty-three years. The office of attending physician was established in 1928, at a time when members were dying at the appalling rate of almost twenty a year. The office was then, and is still, staffed by navy physicians detailed to the Capitol.

Among Dr. Calver's tips to the new legislators were these: "Don't let yourself get off-balance, nervous, and disturbed over things," and "stay out of the Washington social whirl—go out at night twice a week at the most." Dr. Calver also drew up the "nine commandments of health," which he had printed on large placards and displayed in cloakrooms, on elevators, and in other conspicuous places about the Capitol. The placards read:
  I. Eat wisely.
  II. Drink plentifully (of water).
  III. Eliminate thoroughly.
  IV. Exercise rationally.
  V. Accept inevitables (don't worry).
  VI. Play enthusiastically.
  VII. Relax completely.
VIII. Sleep sufficiently.
  IX. Check up occasionally.

Although issued more than three decades ago, this advice for senators is indeed timeless.

1951
MAY 3

Senate Begins Inquiry into MacArthur Dismissal

On May 3, 1951, the Senate began an extraordinary series of hearings into President Truman's dismissal of General of the Army Douglas MacArthur from his Far Eastern command. This highly charged issue began, in the midst of the Korean War, with the general's firing on April 11, 1951 for insubordination. On April 14, the enormously popular general, returning to Washington following a fourteen-year absence, addressed a joint meeting of Congress.

A cartoonist's view of Richard Russell's 1951 inquiry into the MacArthur dismissal

In this superheated atmosphere, the Senate Committees on Armed Services and Foreign Relations announced hearings into the events that led to MacArthur's ouster. Under the leadership of Armed Services Chairman Richard Russell, the majority of both committees established ground rules that barred the public and other senators from these sessions. In response, the Senate's Republican leadership urged open sessions.

By the time the hearings began on the morning of May 3, the committees had agreed to allow the seventy senators who did not belong to either panel to attend as observers. Such senators were not permitted to participate in the questioning of either MacArthur or the many witnesses who followed him, but they were allowed to submit their questions to a committee member, who could then decide whether to pose the question. Although the press was barred, the joint committee released copies of the hearing transcript to reporters waiting outside the caucus room during the sessions, as soon as each page had been reviewed by a Defense Department censor.

The hearings lasted for seven weeks with a witness list that included the secretaries of state and defense, and the joint chiefs of staff. In August, the joint committee put the matter to rest by deciding not to issue a formal report.

1951
SEPTEMBER 14

Senator Douglas Fights Free Haircuts

On September 14, 1951, the United States Senate debated the weighty issue of whether to eliminate the free shaves and haircuts provided to members by the Senate barbershop. Senator Paul Douglas of Illinois, a vigilant watchdog over the public treasury, had gone down to the barbershop for a much-needed haircut. After the barber had done his work, Douglas began to think that his income was ample enough to pay for his own haircut—which then cost a dollar and a quarter—and not charge it to the taxpayers. So he introduced an amendment to that year's legislative appropriation to cut off funds for the barbershop unless it began charging its senatorial customers.

Speaking for the Legislative Appropriations Subcommittee, Senator Carl Hayden of Arizona began by complimenting Senator Douglas on his excellent haircut. He then recounted this story: "I can very well recall that when I first came to the Senate, a very active reporter in the Press Gallery decided that senators must pay for their haircuts. He wrote article after article on that subject for the newspapers. At that time, being a new senator, I was somewhat disturbed by the publicity and inquired of some of the other senators to see what might be done about it. I went to the honorable William Edgar Borah, a late senator from Idaho, who then had been in the Senate a long time and was very highly respected. I asked him what we should do. Senator Borah said, 'You tell that reporter to go to the devil. I want the same service that was received here by Henry Clay and John C. Calhoun.' "

After a good laugh, the Senate shouted down Senator Douglas' amendment, and the free haircut survived. I want to assure taxpayers, however, that today senators pay their own way when they have their hair cut, as Senator Douglas urged in 1951.

1952
JULY 28

Brien McMahon Dies

On July 28, 1952, Connecticut's delegates to the Democratic National Convention, meeting in Chicago, cast their sixteen ballots for their favorite-son candidate, Senator Brien McMahon. On that same day, Senator McMahon died at a Washington hospital after a battle with cancer.

By the time of his death, Senator McMahon had earned a world-wide reputation as an authority on atomic energy and nuclear weapons. As a freshman senator, he had been deeply moved by the destruction of Hiroshima by an atomic bomb in 1945. While he saw the military purposes of nuclear weapons, he also believed that atomic energy must be harnessed for peaceful purposes. In 1945, Senator McMahon introduced a resolution to create a special Senate Committee on Atomic Energy, of which he became chairman. This was a forerunner of the Joint Committee on Atomic Energy, which McMahon chaired starting in 1949.

In these posts, McMahon allied himself with nuclear scientists who opposed the exclusive military control of atomic energy and helped create a civilian agency, the Atomic Energy Commission, to oversee nuclear power development. As chairman of the joint committee, McMahon exercised a tight congressional oversight over the AEC and became one of its strongest advocates on Capitol Hill. Senator McMahon supported research into new nuclear weapons and was a leader in the fight to develop the hydrogen bomb. At the same time, he advocated a number of disarmament and arms reduction proposals. In 1951, despite the intense cold war atmosphere, McMahon won passage of a congressional resolution declaring America's desire for peace and friendship with all people. His death the following year deprived the Senate of its leading authority on atomic energy.

Brien McMahon of Connecticut

1953
JANUARY 3

John F. Kennedy Sworn In

John F. Kennedy was sworn in as a senator on January 3, 1953. While best remembered as the thirty-fifth president of the United States, John Kennedy was also a member of Congress for thirteen years. During that time, he demonstrated great affection for and interest in congressional history.

After a distinguished career in the navy during World War II, Kennedy was elected to the House in 1946 for the first of three terms. He represented the same district that his maternal grandfather, John F. Fitzgerald, had served a half-century before. In 1952, he successfully ran for the Senate and he was reelected in 1958.

In 1954, Kennedy underwent a serious operation to relieve terrible pain in his back. During the long convalescence, he began work on a series of sketches of American politicians who had risked their careers in the cause of principle. The result was the book *Profiles in Courage*, which won the 1957 Pulitzer Prize for biography. Each of the eight courageous men profiled in the book—John Quincy Adams, Daniel Webster, Thomas Hart Benton, Sam Houston, Edmund Ross, Lucius Quintus Cincinnatus Lamar, George Norris, and Robert Taft—had been a senator at some point in his career.

John Kennedy also left behind, in the Capitol itself, a mark of his esteem for the Senate's history. In 1955 the Senate established a special commemorative committee to identify "five outstanding persons from among all persons . . . who have served as members of the Senate. . . ." Senator Kennedy was named chairman of that committee and he directed its difficult task with great skill. Today, we remember him with many memorials. We should include among them the five medallion portraits of outstanding members that, thanks to his direction, now grace the walls of the Senate Reception Room.

John F. Kennedy of Massachusetts playing softball with Henry M. Jackson of Washington, *at bat*, and Mike Mansfield of Montana

Lyndon Baines Johnson of Texas

1953
FEBRUARY 13

LBJ Becomes Youngest Floor Leader

On February 13, 1953, Senate Democrats chose the youngest floor leader in the history of this institution. He was forty-four years old and still serving in his first term. His name was Lyndon Baines Johnson.

Johnson's quick rise to leadership in the Senate resulted from a series of events. In 1950, both the Democratic majority leader, Scott Lucas, and the Democratic whip, Francis Myers, were defeated in their races for reelection. Democrats then chose Ernest MacFarland as majority leader and Lyndon Johnson as whip. But two years later, an Arizona businessman named Barry Goldwater defeated MacFarland for his Senate seat and once again opened up the top post in the Democratic leadership. In addition, Dwight Eisenhower's candidacy in 1952 helped the Republicans win back the majority in the Senate. Senate Democrats now needed to elect a minority leader.

Based on seniority and respect, the post should have gone to Georgia's Senator Richard B. Russell, by all accounts the de facto leader of his party in the Senate. Yet Russell preferred to exercise his power and influence behind the scenes, within the party machinery, rather than at the leader's desk in the chamber. The young and ambitious Lyndon Johnson first ascertained Russell's decision not to run and then gained his endorsement. A challenge from a small group of liberal Democrats proved ineffective, and Johnson swept to an easy victory.

Two years later, with a shift in party control, Lyndon Johnson became majority leader and was viewed as the universally recognized master of the Senate. In another six years he was elected vice president and within three years had become president following the assassination of John F. Kennedy. Then, in 1964, he won a landslide election over Barry Goldwater, the man who just a dozen years earlier had opened the way for Johnson to become the Senate's youngest floor leader.

1953
JULY 31

Robert Taft Dies in Office

On July 31, 1953, the Senate mourned the death of one of its great leaders, Ohio's Senator Robert A. Taft. Senate Minority Leader Lyndon Johnson wrote that Taft, known to his contemporaries as Mr. Republican, "was characterized by a rocklike integrity, unconquerable common sense at all times, and an unswerving devotion to the principles in which he believed." In 1957, a special Senate committee chaired by Senator John F. Kennedy chose Taft as one of the five most significant senators in the institution's history, and his portrait is one of the five to grace the Senate Reception Room.

Coming from a long family tradition of public service, Taft served in both houses of the Ohio legislature before winning election to the Senate in 1938. Here, he vigorously opposed the foreign and domestic policies of the New Deal, believing instead in decentralization at home and nonintervention abroad. He sponsored the Taft-Hartley Act, designed to limit the

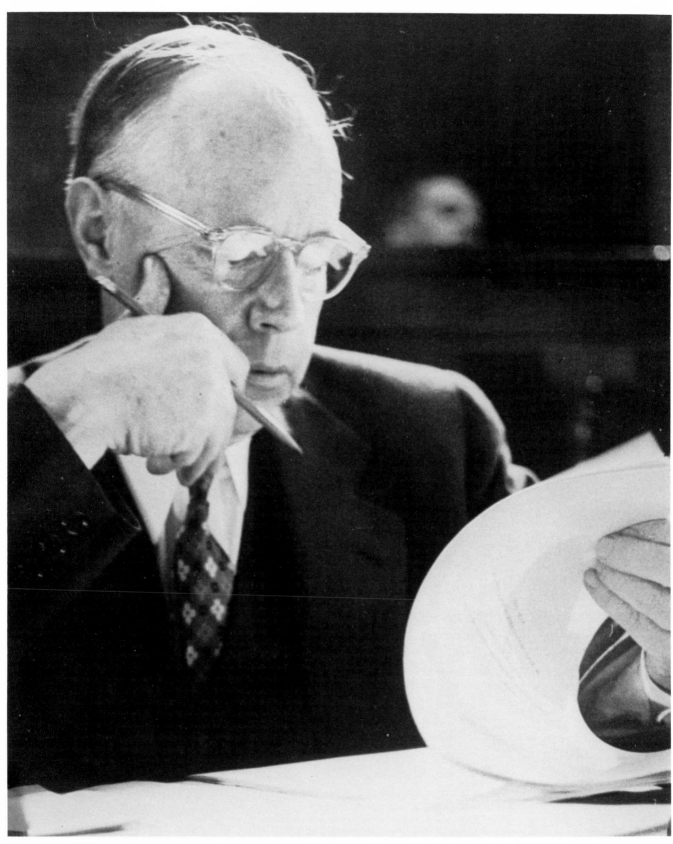

Robert Taft of Ohio

powers of labor unions, which became law in 1947 over President Truman's veto. He also persuaded his colleagues to create the Republican Steering Committee—later the Republican Policy Committee—which he chaired.

Robert Taft tried three times, unsuccessfully, to win the Republican presidential nomination, losing the last and closest contest in 1952 to Dwight Eisenhower. With his hopes for the presidency behind him, Taft seemed more conciliatory. He and Eisenhower agreed to an agenda for foreign and domestic policies. When Taft became majority leader in January 1953, he was Eisenhower's strongest Senate supporter. Four months later, at the height of his power, Taft learned that he had cancer. During his last months, he walked the Capitol's halls with the aid of crutches. After his death on July 31, a memorial service was held in the Capitol Rotunda, where thirty thousand people filed by to pay tribute to this extraordinary senator.

1953
NOVEMBER 10

See-Saw in Senate Majority

On November 10, 1953, Thomas Burke, Democratic mayor of Cleveland, was sworn in as United States senator from Ohio. Since the Senate had adjourned for the year and would not reconvene until the following January, Burke's appointment to the Senate had no immediate effect. But symbolically, it meant that the Senate majority had shifted in mid-Congress from the Republicans to the Democrats.

Ironically, the vacancy that Burke filled had been caused by the death of Senate Republican Majority Leader Robert Taft, Sr. At the time of Taft's death, the Senate was split between 48 Republicans, 47 Democrats, and 1 independent, Wayne Morse. When Ohio's governor, Frank Lausche, appointed Burke to Taft's unexpired term, he gave the Democrats a 48-to-47 edge. Would this mean that the Senate would be reorganized and committee chairs shifted between parties? No, because Senator Morse announced that he would vote with the Republicans on organizational matters. This would divide the parties evenly, allowing Vice President Richard Nixon to cast the tie-breaking vote.

During the course of the Eighty-third Congress, other deaths caused the majority to shift this way and that, but Republicans retained the majority status, on paper if not in reality. This led to a famous exchange between Republican Leader William Knowland, who complained about the difficulties in being a majority leader without a majority, and Democratic Leader Lyndon Johnson, who observed, "If anyone has more problems than a majority leader with a minority, it is a minority leader with a majority."

As for Senator Burke, in 1954 Republican George H. Bender defeated him for election to the remaining two years of the term. But, in 1956, Senator Bender lost his bid for reelection to a full term to Frank Lausche, the man who, as governor, had started it all.

1954
FEBRUARY 26

Senate Rejects the Bricker Amendment

On February 26, 1954, the Senate defeated what was known as the Bricker amendment to the Constitution.

The impetus for the amendment came from Ohio Senator John W. Bricker's fears that international agreements such as the United Nations' human rights agreement would supersede American laws and even the Constitution. Section one of the Bricker amendment provided that "a provision of a treaty which conflicts with this Constitution shall not be of any force or effect," and section two stipulated that "a treaty shall become effective as internal law in the United States only through legislation which would be valid in the absence of a treaty." It was section three, however, that most disturbed the Eisenhower administration, which considered the language that "Congress shall have power to regulate all executive agreements" as binding the president's hands in making foreign policy.

President Dwight Eisenhower and Secretary of State John Foster Dulles strenuously opposed the Bricker amendment. Since sixty-three senators had already endorsed the measure, the administration decided against trying to defeat it outright, and instead sought a more tolerable substitute. Thus, the Senate voted first on the Bricker amendment in full, and then on a revised version submitted by Senator Walter George of Georgia that embraced only the first two sections of the amendment. Senator Bricker's amendment was defeated on February 25 by a vote of 50 to 42. The next day, Senator George's amendment came up for a vote—but the administration, after having encouraged Senator George, now withdrew its support on the grounds that even this compromise measure would seriously weaken the presidency. On February 26, the substitute amendment fell just one vote short of passage.

1954
MAY 12

Clyde Hoey Dies

On the afternoon of May 12, 1954, senators on the floor were shocked and saddened by the announcement that one of their number, Senator Clyde Hoey of North Carolina, had died at his desk in the Senate office building across the street. He had just been on the floor among them that morning. The Senate immediately adjourned until noon the next day, as did the House, where Hoey had once been a member. The seventy-six-year-old Democrat had come to the Senate in 1945 and made a name for himself as head of the subcommittee on investigations, a position he held until 1953.

Clyde Hoey was born in 1877 in the North Carolina foothills, the son of a Confederate army captain. To help pay off family debts, he quit school at the age of twelve and became a printer's devil at the local newspaper. His education came chiefly from the dictionary he always carried and from the stories he set in type. Hoey studied law on his own and at the age of twenty was elected to the North Carolina House of Representatives. He turned twenty-one, the legal age for service, just before it was time to be sworn in.

For the next fifty-five years, Hoey's life was one of public service, as state legislator, governor, member of the U.S. House of Representatives, and finally as senator.

Hoey's death marked the passing of an era in the Senate. In both appearance and manner, he recalled an earlier age. The tall, white-maned senator, a slightly stooped man with sharp features, was always a conspicuous figure on the floor in his cutaway morning coat of Confederate gray, his high stiff collar, high-topped shoes, old-fashioned string ties, and red carnation in his lapel. Those privileged to witness his old-time courtliness, and flavorful, flowery oratory never forgot the experience.

1954
NOVEMBER 3

Strom Thurmond Elected as Write-In Candidate

On November 3, 1954, our colleague, Senator Strom Thurmond, accomplished a remarkable feat. On that day, he became the first senator in history to be elected to this body as a write-in candidate. It is an accomplishment that remains unequaled to this day.

Senator Thurmond, who was then a Democrat and who had already been a state senator, a judge, governor of South Carolina, and States' Rights candidate for president of the United States in 1948, won this unusual election in a campaign based on a wave of protest against the methods by which his Democratic opponent had been nominated. In September of that year, South Carolina Senator Burnet Maybank had died two days before the deadline for certifying candidates. The state Democratic executive committee decided to bypass a primary and nominated State Senator Edgar Brown for the full term to which Maybank had been renominated that summer. Dismayed at tactics that denied the people a voice in selecting their candidate, Strom Thurmond entered the race as a write-in candidate. Not only did he win, but he was elected by a margin of nearly 2 to 1.

In his victory statement, Senator Thurmond reiterated his promise to resign in 1956 so that voters could choose their senator for the remaining four years of the term in the next electoral primary to be held. He resigned in April 1956 and that fall was elected to fill the vacancy his resignation had created. Reelected in every race since then, Senator Thurmond was, at the start of the 101st Congress, the longest-serving member among us, having served a total of thirty-three years and five months. At the end of his current term in January 1991, Senator Thurmond will have served longer than all but eleven of the 1,792 persons who have been United States senators. Those of us privileged to serve with him expect that he will continue on to exceed even that estimable record.

1954
NOVEMBER 17

Old Senate Gavel Replaced

On November 17, 1954, one of the Senate's oldest relics was retired and replaced with a new artifact that continues in use today. I refer to the Senate gavel.

The old ivory gavel was one of the most revered articles in this chamber. According to tradition, it was the same small, handleless piece of ivory with which the nation's first vice president, John Adams, called to order the first Senate session in New York City in the spring of 1789.

In 1947, the old gavel began to splinter. Silver disks were added to each face to try to preserve it, but during a late night session in 1954, while the Senate was engaged in a heated discussion on atomic energy, the yellowed ivory began to disintegrate. The old gavel had made its last demand for order. When no commercial source of ivory for a new gavel could be found in the United States, the sergeant at arms turned to the Indian embassy for assistance. The government of India not only furnished a piece of ivory but had a new gavel carved from a model of the old one. The vice president of India even came to the United States to present it in person to the Senate.

On November 17, 1954, the formal presentation was made in this chamber. Vice President Richard Nixon accepted the gift on behalf of the Senate and promised: "We shall place the old gavel in a box which will be kept on the Senate rostrum, while the Senate is in session. We shall use in its place the gavel of solid ivory, which has been presented to us, it seems to me quite significantly and appropriately, by the largest democracy in the world." Before each Senate session, a page secures from the sergeant at arms the gavel case, which contains both gavels, carries it into the chamber, and places it on the rostrum. At the close of the session, the new gavel is returned to its place beside the old and entrusted to the sergeant at arms for safekeeping.

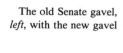

The old Senate gavel, *left*, with the new gavel

Joseph McCarthy of Wisconsin

1954
DECEMBER 2

The Senate Censures Joe McCarthy

On December 2, 1954, the Senate voted 67 to 22 to censure Joseph R. McCarthy of Wisconsin. This vote marked the end of a long, emotional, and painful period in the history of this institution, as well as the end of Senator McCarthy's political effectiveness.

McCarthy had entered the Senate in 1947, after defeating the formidable Robert La Follette, Jr., in the Republican primary. A colorful and unpredictable junior member of the Senate, he did not attract much national attention until 1950 when, in a speech at Wheeling, West Virginia, he claimed to hold in his hand evidence of Communists operating within the State Department. That charge catapulted McCarthy to the leadership of an anti-communist crusade that gained much public support during those troublesome early days of the cold war.

By 1953, Senator McCarthy had become chairman of the Permanent Subcommittee on Investigations, the platform from which he directed inquiries into the activities of various government agencies. His supporters saw him as protecting the country against internal subversion. His opponents accused him of smearing innocent people through bullying tactics.

The televised Army-McCarthy hearings during the summer of 1954 proved to be Senator McCarthy's undoing. Watching the hearings in their homes, many Americans formed negative opinions of McCarthy and his tactics, and his standing in opinion polls fell. Moreover, McCarthy's attack on loyalty in the army alienated the administration of President Dwight D. Eisenhower, along with a considerable number of his own party in the Senate. Thus, Senate Democrats and Republicans joined together on December 2, 1954, to condemn the conduct of Joe McCarthy.

1957
AUGUST 28

Senator William Proxmire's Voting Record

As the One-hundredth Congress drew to a close, so too did the remarkable career of the senior senator from Wisconsin, William Proxmire.

Bill Proxmire came to the Senate on August 28, 1957, after winning a special election following the death of Senator Joseph R. McCarthy. He left the Senate as the third most senior member. Senator Proxmire was the chairman of the Banking, Housing, and Urban Affairs Committee, the author of the Truth-in-Lending Act and the Competitive Banking Act, the chief promoter of the Genocide Treaty, and the presenter of many "Golden Fleece" awards that directed national attention to the unnecessary waste of taxpayers' money.

In addition to these remarkable accomplishments, the senior Wisconsin senator established two extraordinary Senate voting records. First, in his thirty-one years, he cast nearly 12,000 recorded votes—more than any other senator in history. Second, Bill Proxmire did not miss a single roll-call vote after April 20, 1966. This amounts to approximately 10,150 consecutive ayes and noes, covering every issue imaginable on the American political scene.

A record such as this depends upon great physical stamina—no illnesses to keep him from casting a vote. It demands political courage—no issues to be ducked. And it requires considerable force of will—no campaign appearances or other events too important to keep him from appearing on the Senate floor when the ringing bells summon us for a vote.

Bill Proxmire's phenomenal voting record will stand in our books the way the records of Babe Ruth, Ty Cobb, and Hank Aaron have dominated baseball statistics. It is a record we can all applaud, and do our best to emulate.

Robert C. Byrd Enters the Senate

On January 3, 1959, a new senator began what was to become a distinguished career in this chamber. He rose to become the majority leader and now serves as president pro tempore.

Robert C. Byrd came to the Senate from the coal mining regions of West Virginia. His early life was one of unremitting labor, as a butcher and as a shipyard worker. His education came simultaneously with his political career. He attended college while a member of the West Virginia legislature and law school while a member of the United States Congress.

Robert Byrd has achieved a remarkable record for winning elections and has held more elective offices than any other person in the history of his state. He won election to the West Virginia house of delegates in 1946, to the West Virginia senate in 1950, to the U.S. House of Representatives in 1952, and to the U.S. Senate in 1958. In the Senate he was elected secretary of the Democratic Conference in 1967. In 1971 he upset Senator Edward M. Kennedy to become Democratic whip. In 1977 his party elected him majority leader, and he continued to lead Senate Democrats as minority leader and once again as majority leader.

The secret of his success, any member of the Senate will testify, has been his infinite capacity for hard work. During his first years in the Senate, Robert Byrd could often be found in the parliamentarian's office, studying the rules. Three decades later, he is still a regular reader of the rules and precedents—and knows them as well as if he wrote them. On the floor he has applied those rules, sometimes gently, sometimes firmly, but always fairly, with a gentlemanly aplomb, and even with an appropriate verse.

He devotes similar time and care to studying the Senate's history, in which he has earned his own major place over the past thirty years.

Robert C. Byrd of West Virginia

1959
MARCH 12

Paintings of the Five Greatest Senators

On March 12, 1959, the Senate honored its five "most outstanding" former members by unveiling paintings of those senators in the Reception Room outside this chamber.

In part we have a nineteenth-century painter, Constantino Brumidi, to thank for this more recent addition to the Capitol's artwork. Brumidi painted many of our rooms, particularly in the Rotunda and in the Senate wing, but because he did not want to monopolize the history portrayed in the Capitol, he left spaces to be filled in later. For instance, in the Brumidi Corridor that runs below this chamber are recent medallion portraits of the landing of the first Americans on the moon, and a tribute to the crew of the space shuttle *Challenger*.

When senators meet their visitors in the Senate Reception Room, they can view one of Brumidi's more elaborate efforts in decorating the walls and ceiling. In that room, Brumidi left twelve vacant "portholes," oval-shaped areas, for future additions. In 1955, the Senate appointed a committee chaired by Senator John F. Kennedy, who had recently published his book *Profiles in Courage* about courageous senators in our history. Kennedy's committee was assigned to choose the five greatest United States senators to fill the lower five portholes.

Kennedy's committee had little trouble selecting the first three senators. Both the senators and their historical advisory committee unanimously chose the "great triumvirate," Henry Clay, Daniel Webster, and John C. Calhoun. They had far greater trouble selecting the final two. The historians they polled selected George Norris, a Nebraska Republican, but Norris was still too controversial a figure to satisfy everyone on the committee. After much deliberation, the committee chose Robert M. La Follette, Sr. and Robert A. Taft, Sr., both Republicans, for the remaining paintings.

Murals of the senators in the Senate Reception Room, *from top*: Calhoun, Clay, Webster, La Follette, and Taft

Facing page: The Senate Reception Room

1959
APRIL 10

Staff Salary Disclosure

On April 10, 1959, Senator Wayne Morse introduced a resolution to provide for public disclosure of Senate staff salaries. He took this step amid a brewing controversy concerning the extent to which members of Congress had placed relatives on their office payrolls. Although there was nothing illegal about hiring family members as legitimate employees, rumors of abuses triggered press curiosity. Weeks earlier it had been disclosed that a House member, whose wife was on his staff payroll, was billing the government a hundred dollars per month in rent charges for his front porch, which served as her office.

Until 1948, the secretary of the Senate had routinely issued semi-annual reports detailing all Senate expenses, including staff salaries. Beginning in that year, the reporting method changed. While the Senate continued to publish committee staff salaries, it simply listed a lump-sum figure for the personal staff of each senator. A Scripps-Howard Newspaper Alliance suit against the secretary of the Senate for disclosure of the Senate's ten-million-dollar personal staff payroll triggered a spirited debate. Senators opposing disclosure argued that the Senate is not a factory in which its employees receive uniform salaries. In the absence of uniform salaries for comparable work, they reasoned, the publication of salary information would only sow "discord among employees." While a few senators responded by immediately publishing their payrolls, others said they would do so only if it were required of all members.

Finally, on June 26, 1959, the Senate agreed to publish quarterly reports containing the salary of each personal staff member. When the first listing appeared in November, it revealed that at least nineteen senators employed relatives at annual salaries ranging from three thousand dollars for a messenger to sixteen thousand dollars for a top administrative assistant. Today, a federal statute and rulings by the Senate Ethics Committee regulate this practice.

1959
JUNE 19

Senate Rejects Cabinet Nominee

On June 19, 1959, the United States Senate rejected President Dwight Eisenhower's appointment of Lewis L. Strauss as secretary of commerce. In its entire history, the Senate had formally denied only eight cabinet nominations—with Strauss being the sole nominee rejected since 1925. President Eisenhower later deemed this extraordinary incident "one of the most depressing official disappointments I experienced during my eight years in the White House."

Lewis Strauss had made a number of well-placed enemies in Congress during his earlier tenure as chairman of the Atomic Energy Commission. His campaign to declare Dr. J. Robert Oppenheimer a security risk and his active support of the Dixon-Yates contract for private financing of nuclear power plants had disenchanted many senators.

His confirmation hearings quickly took on decidedly partisan overtones. They occurred in the wake of the 1958 elections in which the Democrats had picked up thirteen Senate seats—the largest single transfer of seats between parties in Senate history. A routine nomination evolved into a test of wills between an increasingly beleaguered Republican administration and a revived Senate Democratic majority. During the hearings, Strauss, a hard-line cold warrior, took what many perceived as an arrogant attitude toward senatorial prerogatives, needlessly alienating nominally supportive senators, who might otherwise have been expected to let the president have his own man in his cabinet.

Shortly after midnight on June 19, in a chamber jammed to capacity, the votes were cast: 49 senators opposed Strauss, while 46 approved. To the chagrin of the White House and party leaders, the margin of defeat was provided by two Republicans voting in opposition. This defeat marked the onset of a virtual legislative stalemate between Congress and the White House for the final year and a half of the Eisenhower administration.

Lewis L. Strauss, *left*, with Clinton P. Anderson of New Mexico

1960
APRIL 11

One Family's Century of Service to the Senate

On April 11, 1960, one of the most remarkable dynasties in the Senate's history came to an end. On that day, eighty-three-year-old James W. Murphy died. Murphy had been an official reporter of Senate debates for nearly 65 years. For 112 years, from 1848 until 1960, one or more members of the Murphy family had served as Senate reporters.

In 1848, on the recommendation of Senator John C. Calhoun, fourteen-year-old Dennis F. Murphy, James Murphy's uncle, was hired by the private *Congressional Globe* as a member of its Senate corps of verbatim shorthand reporters. Dennis served for forty-eight years, until his death in 1896. His brother Edward, who was James' father, began as a Senate reporter in 1860 and served fifty-nine years. Another brother served the Senate for twenty years.

James W. Murphy joined the corps of Senate reporters in 1896. While working here, he earned a law degree from Georgetown University and in 1934 he advanced to the post of chief Senate reporter. Murphy's skill came not only from his own diligence and the influence of his distinguished family, but also from the tradition of excellence set in place by other long-serving Senate reporters. They included Theodore F. Shuey, considered one of the world's preeminent shorthand reporters, and John Rhodes. Shuey's Senate career spanned sixty-five years, from 1868 to 1933. Rhodes, whom several of my colleagues will remember, began during the 1919 Versailles Treaty debate and retired in 1963.

Today, our own distinguished corps of official reporters carries on this tradition, as we are reminded by the 1988 retirement of Chief Official Reporter G. Russell Walker. In 1956, Majority Leader Lyndon Johnson described James Murphy in words that applied equally to Mr. Walker: "Under his deft touch the technicalities, the contradictions, the subtle nuances, and the bewildering phrases arrange themselves in a neat and orderly fashion. They fall into place in such a way that they have coherence and logic and reason."

1963
SEPTEMBER 24

First Official Senate Photograph

On September 24, 1963, the Senate sat for its first official photograph. I say "official" because although there had long been a rule against photographs in the Senate chamber, from time to time enterprising photographers had taken some illicit shots. But in 1963, when the Capitol Historical Society first prepared for publication of its guidebook to the Capitol, *We The People*, it convinced the Senate to pass a special resolution permitting it to arrange for an official photo of the Senate.

Not everyone liked the idea. "Vanity, vanity, all is vanity," said Senator Richard Russell, who worried that the photo session was setting an unhealthy precedent. Republican Leader Everett Dirksen warned that the photographer would like to have senators in their seats, not walking around. Senator Russell added that if that were the case they should add a footnote to the photograph that "this is the only time in the session of 1963 that every senator was in his own seat."

The photographic session was scheduled for September 24, at the same time that the Senate was to vote on the Nuclear Test Ban Treaty. I suppose it is debatable whether the leadership arranged to take the picture then because so many senators would be in the chamber for this important vote, or if they scheduled the photograph to *insure* that senators would be there.

The photograph appears on pages 108 and 109 of the 1963 edition of *We The People*, which is still in print. One can compare the 1963 picture to those the Senate has sat for in recent years. Back then, members did not turn to face the camera. Many appear to be writing at their desks. Senator Jacob Javits has a copy of the *New York Times* tossed on the floor beside his desk. A weary-looking Mike Mansfield, then the Democratic leader, is rubbing his eyes. All in all, it is a marvelous historical document.

First official photograph of the Senate, September 24, 1963

1963
OCTOBER 1

Senate Floor Privileges for Former Presidents

On October 1, 1963, the rules of the Senate were revised to extend floor privileges to former presidents of the United States. It was an idea that had been proposed from time to time by many members, as far back as 1944, but it was not adopted until 1963.

Senator Claiborne Pell introduced the rules change, arguing that it would add luster to the Senate to encourage the occasional participation of former presidents in significant debates. "To be specific," said Senator Pell, "I think it would have been useful indeed if former Presidents Hoover, Truman, and Eisenhower had given their views to the Senate relative to the test ban treaty right here on the Senate floor." Senator Pell also suggested that this rules change would be "a step in the direction of bridging the schism between our legislative and executive branches."

Despite the change in the rules, however, no former president has formally requested permission to deliver an address on the Senate floor. Former Presidents Truman and Ford did make brief remarks in this chamber, in connection with their visits to the Capitol, but neither made any reference to policy matters then before the Senate.

One can speculate on the reasons why former presidents have not taken advantage of this offer. There is no tradition of presidential speeches in the Senate but instead a strong history of separation of the branches. Former presidents generally have had little trouble finding forums elsewhere for airing their views on current issues. And, until recently, an address in the Senate chamber would be limited to an audience in the galleries. Televising of Senate proceedings may make this option more attractive for former chief executives, as Senator Pell and others hoped in 1963.

1964
JUNE 10

Dramatic Vote on Civil Rights Bill

On June 10, 1964, there took place in this chamber one of the most dramatic votes in Senate history. From his wheelchair, Democratic Senator Clair Engle of California cast a key vote which led to the passage of the Civil Rights Act of 1964, the most comprehensive civil rights measure since Reconstruction. Although terminally ill and unable to speak, Engle managed to vote for cloture to end a seventy-five-day filibuster by opponents of the civil rights legislation. During a tense ten-minute vote, Engle failed to speak when his name was called, but he raised his left arm as if attempting to point to his eyes and then nodded his head to indicate an "aye" vote. Nine days later, on June 19, 1964, the Senate passed the final version of the Civil Rights Act by a 73 to 27 margin, again with the help of Engle's vote.

Engle, who also served in the House of Representatives, was once called "Congressman Fireball," "a wildcat in Washington," and "the only active volcano in the House." His illness drastically changed the course of his life. On August 23, 1963, Engle had undergone surgery for a brain tumor, and eight months later he had a second operation which left him partially paralyzed. Engle's vote for the Civil Rights Act was a fitting end to his career. Earlier, on April 13, 1964, he had attempted to introduce a resolution for the bill. Senator Spessard Holland of Florida, who had the floor, yielded to Engle so that he could introduce the resolution. Two aides helped Engle to his feet, but he was unable to speak and nodded assent to Michigan Senator Pat McNamara's offer to introduce the resolution for him. A few minutes later, Engle was "virtually carried from the floor by his aides."

On July 30, 1964, just over a month after his Civil Rights Act vote, Engle died at the age of fifty-two.

Facing page, the east front of the Capitol during the 1970s

CHAPTER IX
The Modern
Senate

1965
JULY 9

The "Stennis Committee" Created

On July 9, 1965, the Senate created the Select Committee on Standards and Conduct and named Senator John C. Stennis to be its chairman. This forerunner of our current Select Committee on Ethics was the Senate's first internal disciplinary committee to operate on a permanent basis.

Discipline has always been a painful problem in as collegial an institution as the United States Senate. Historically, senators have preferred to let the voters decide whether a senator's behavior has been improper and to exert discipline via the ballot box. But from time to time the Senate has been called upon to examine serious charges of impropriety leveled against individual members. Traditionally, the Senate Committee on Rules and Administration dealt with such internal investigations, but Senator Hugh Scott and others argued that it was difficult for the Rules Committee, whose members included the Senate party leadership, to be able to assume a sufficiently independent stance to conduct an impartial investigation. After much criticism of these proceedings in the early 1960s, the Senate responded by creating the select committee.

On July 9, 1965, Vice President Hubert Humphrey announced that Senator John Stennis would chair the committee. Other members included Senators Mike Monroney, Eugene McCarthy, Wallace Bennett, John Sherman Cooper, and James Pearson. The "Stennis Committee" won excellent reviews from members of the Senate and the press, due in part to the great respect felt on both sides of the aisle for its chairman, who served in that post until 1974. He showed, as one senator said at the time, "great courage and fortitude in discharging the unpleasant responsibility that was pressed upon him by the Senate." The assignment was just one of the numerous services performed for this body during the forty-one-year career of our esteemed colleague, Senator Stennis.

John C. Stennis of Mississippi

President Johnson Signs Voting Rights Act in President's Room

On August 5, 1965, President Lyndon Johnson signed into law the Voting Rights Act. This landmark legislation provided an effective means for federal enforcement of the Fifteenth Amendment's bar against racial discrimination affecting the right to vote. It served as a cornerstone for Johnson's Great Society program, redressing with action injustices at the ballot boxes that the constitutional amendment had unsuccessfully addressed with words ninety-five years earlier.

The signing of that significant measure took place in the President's Room just outside the Senate chamber. Located at the west end of the Senators' Lobby, the President's Room is one of the most grandly embellished rooms in the Capitol. Its walls and ceiling display magnificent frescoes by Constantino Brumidi. First opened in 1859, the room was designed to provide a private office for the president in the Capitol.

Over the past century and a quarter, chief executives have used the President's Room on various substantive and ceremonial occasions. Until 1937, the president's term expired every fourth year on March 3, the final day of the congressional session. This made it necessary for the chief executive to come to the President's Room in the session's final hours to sign newly passed legislation. It was on such an occasion in March 1865 that Abraham Lincoln received word that Confederate General Robert E. Lee desired a meeting with Union General Ulysses S. Grant. Lincoln responded that Grant was to hold no meeting except for the purpose of accepting the surrender of Lee's army.

President Woodrow Wilson regularly used the President's Room to confer with senators and to lobby for his legislative programs. President Reagan, who visited that chamber immediately following his 1981 swearing-in ceremony, used it more than any chief executive since Franklin Roosevelt.

The Voting Rights Act of 1965

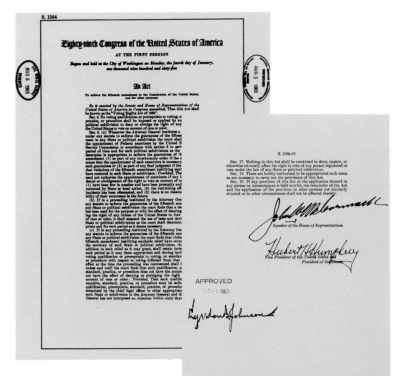

President Johnson signing the Voting Rights Act in the President's Room

Margaret Chase Smith of Maine

1968
SEPTEMBER 6

Senator Smith Misses Roll-Call Vote

On September 7, 1968, the *New York Times* ran a story under the headline "Mrs. Smith Misses a Vote." The fact that the "Mrs. Smith" was Senator Margaret Chase Smith of Maine and that the second line of the headline read, "First Time in Thirteen Years," makes this small, inside story one of historical interest. Senator Smith had indeed not missed a roll-call vote since 1955. During the intervening thirteen years, she had cast 2,941 consecutive roll-call votes, a record at the time.

Senator Smith missed the vote on September 6, 1968 because, as the Senate voted on amendments to an appropriations bill, she was in a New York hospital recuperating from an operation for an arthritic condition. That, she conceded, was a good excuse. But the fact still rankled that, back in 1955 when she was aiming at a record, she had missed one vote. On that occasion, assured that there would be no roll-call votes, she had gone to New York to accept an honorary degree from Columbia University. She returned that same afternoon, only to find she had missed a vote by thirty minutes.

Margaret Chase Smith began her political career in 1937 as an aide to her husband, Representative Clyde Smith. In 1940, upon his death in office, Mrs. Smith was elected to complete his term and won reelection to the House three times. When she was elected to the Senate in 1948, Mrs. Smith, a Republican, became the first woman ever elected to both houses of Congress. Her twenty-four years of Senate service from 1949 to 1973 is a record among women senators.

Throughout Senator Smith's political career, her major interest was military affairs. She was best known, however, as a consistent critic of bigotry and injustice. Her courageous 1950 "Declaration of Conscience" Senate floor speech condemning McCarthyism remains a classic today. Leaving the Senate in 1973, Senator Smith began her current career as educator and writer.

1969
SEPTEMBER 7

Everett Dirksen

On September 7, 1969, Senate Republican Leader Everett McKinley Dirksen died in Washington at the age of seventy-three. The following day, Congress honored the Illinois statesman by arranging for his body to lie in state in the Capitol's Rotunda, an honor accorded to only five other Americans on the basis of their service as United States senators.

Everett Dirksen began his long congressional career in 1933, representing central Illinois for eight terms in the House of Representatives. In 1950 he moved to the Senate by defeating Scott Lucas, who was then the Senate's Democratic majority leader. In 1957, Senate Republicans selected Dirksen as their party whip, and in 1959 he became Republican leader.

Dirksen excelled at both tough bargaining and at compromise, equally essential components of our legislative system. His ability to change a strongly held position was legendary. A resolute isolationist in the 1930s, Dirksen was actively supporting United States aid to Great Britain in the weeks before the attack on Pearl Harbor. In the 1960s, after first opposing the Nuclear Test Ban Treaty, he worked to ensure its ratification. In a memorable address, he recalled the bombing of Hiroshima, when, "for the first time the whole bosom of God's earth was ruptured by a man-made contrivance that we call a nuclear weapon." He determined that he would not go to his grave without doing what he could to end the threat of nuclear holocaust. Similarly, in 1964, he persuaded other opponents to support the Civil Rights Act, providing the votes essential for its passage. Explaining his change of heart, Dirksen quoted Victor Hugo, declaring, "Stronger than all the armies is an idea whose time has come."

In his last decade, Everett Dirksen became, in the eyes of many Americans, almost the personification of the Senate. His golden oratory, his theatrical presence, and his campaign to make the marigold the national flower endeared him to millions. In 1972, the Senate paid him a high tribute by naming one of its office buildings in his honor.

Everett Dirksen of Illinois

Richard Russell

On January 21, 1971, Senator Richard B. Russell died. To some people today, he may be just a name on a brass plate identifying the Russell Senate Office Building, but those who served with him remember him as the pre-eminently influential senator of his era.

When Lyndon Johnson served as majority leader, he used to divide the Senate into "minnows" and "whales" and to label Richard Russell as "the principal whale." The chief attributes that made Russell "the principal whale" were his seniority and committee chairmanships, his mastery of the Senate rules, and his unwavering assurance about exactly where he stood on the issues. Russell embodied the struggle of states' rights against civil rights. He was the South's chief legislative strategist from the 1940s through the 1960s—the last general of the "Lost Cause."

But Richard Russell also pursued other causes and interests during his Senate career. In the critical post-World War II era in American history, he was the Senate's leading authority on military matters, the chief advocate of the strongest possible national defense. From his dual positions on the Armed Services and Appropriations committees, he controlled the Pentagon's purse strings as did no other member of Congress. For many years, he was among the few members on Capitol Hill to receive regular briefings from the Central Intelligence Agency. Although Russell often expressed misgivings about American foreign policy, particularly in Vietnam, he steadfastly supported his commander in chief, whether a Democrat or a Republican.

Henry Jackson spoke of his admiration for Russell's "genius for cutting through confusion to get the facts and the truth." Milton Young credited him with always using "good judgment when we have faced difficult problems." Others simply called Richard Russell "the senator's senator."

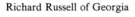

Richard Russell of Georgia

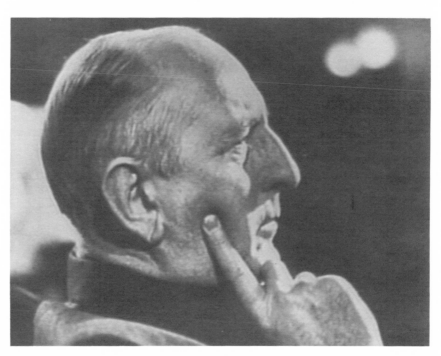

1971
MAY 14

Senate Appoints First Female Page

On May 14, 1971, sixteen-year-old Paulette Desell became the Senate's first female page. Five months earlier, Senator Jacob Javits named Miss Desell to the position upon learning that there were no restrictions against appointment of female pages. The Senate sergeant at arms, however, refused to accept her appointment until he received authorization from the Rules Committee. The committee subsequently agreed to allow female pages despite objections concerning "their safety, their ability to carry out the more arduous tasks, and what they would wear."

The issue of what pages would wear had surfaced previously in the mid-1940s. Near the end of World War II, pages in the House of Representatives had abandoned their knickers in favor of long pants, a dark blue jacket and tie. The Senate pages continued to wear the customary scratchy knickers. In 1946, when Senate Republicans won a majority for the first time in many years, they set about putting their own stamp on the era. To the great relief of the Senate pages, who had to endure merciless teasing from their House counterparts, the Senate adopted the more modern and stylish attire. In 1971 the female pages quickly adjusted to this style and proved themselves the equal of their male counterparts.

The history of Senate pages extends back to 1829. In that year Senator Daniel Webster arranged for the appointment of nine-year-old Grafton Hanson, the grandson of the Senate sergeant at arms, as this body's first page. Two years later, the Senate agreed to a second Webster appointment and twelve-year-old Isaac Bassett began a Senate career that would extend sixty-four years until his death in 1895. Throughout the Senate's history, pages have played an important role in this chamber, and in the process hundreds of young men and women have had a ringside seat on American history.

1972
OCTOBER 11

Senate Names Office Buildings

On October 11, 1972, the Senate officially named its two office buildings, the newest of which had already stood on Constitution Avenue for more than fifteen years. For many years, the buildings had simply been called the Old Senate Office Building and the New Senate Office Building. I remember when I first came to Congress as a Representative in 1961 wondering about the Old S.O.B. and the New S.O.B. across Capitol Hill! In October 1972, the two buildings finally were named for two of the Senate's most distinguished leaders. They were Richard Brevard Russell, a Georgia Democrat and president pro tempore who had served the Senate for almost forty years from 1933 until his death the year before in 1971, and Everett McKinley Dirksen, a Republican from Illinois and minority leader who served from 1951 until his death in office in 1969.

In 1904 the Senate authorized construction of a fireproof office building to meet its pressing need for working space. Along with the House, the

Senate awarded a contract to a prominent New York architectural firm, which designed buildings for both bodies as identical four-sided structures, although the First Street side of the Senate's building wasn't completed until 1933. The Russell Building encloses 315,000 square feet of floor space and cost $8.4 million.

Congress authorized the Senate's second building, the Dirksen Building, in 1948. The site was purchased and cleared, but the Korean War delayed ground breaking until 1955. Ready for use in 1958, the Dirksen Building has 419,000 square feet of floor space and cost $24 million. The third and newest of the Senate's three buildings, occupied in 1982, was dedicated in June 1987 to the memory of Michigan Democrat Philip A. Hart. The Hart Building has nearly 1,000,000 square feet of floor space and cost $138 million.

The Russell, *left*, the Dirksen, and the Hart Senate Office Buildings

1973
JANUARY 2

Clinton P. Anderson Retires

On January 2, 1973, Clinton P. Anderson, a distinguished United States senator and former secretary of agriculture, retired from the Senate. Born in Centerville, South Dakota in 1895, Anderson entered a sanatorium in New Mexico in 1917 when he was gravely ill with tuberculosis. His health restored, Anderson succumbed to the attractions of New Mexico's turbulent political and business climate and made that state his home until his death in 1975.

In 1940, following service as a regional New Deal agency administrator, Anderson won a seat in the U.S. House of Representatives. Several years later, his effective House committee investigation of wartime food shortages led President Truman to appoint him secretary of agriculture. In that position, he directed post-World War II programs to deal with national commodity shortages and European famine.

In 1949, Anderson began his twenty-four-year Senate career. During those years, he served at various times as chairman of the Interior Committee, the Committee on Aeronautical and Space Sciences, and the Joint Committee on Atomic Energy. Always in fragile health, Anderson co-founded Medicare. He was also a vigorous advocate of the peaceful uses of atomic energy. The landmark 1964 Wilderness Act, of which he was a principal author, represented the culmination of his career-long interest in resources conservation.

Senate historian Richard Baker concludes in his biography of Anderson that the New Mexico senator: "served at a time when issues that traditionally had been associated with the West—those involving management of energy, land, and water resources—rapidly evolved into national issues. Anderson's distinction as a legislator came because he was able to reconcile and balance the interests of his state and region with those of the country at large. When he advocated legislation of obvious value to his state, he did so in terms that colleagues from other regions found difficult to deny."

1973
JULY 23

Watergate Committee Subpoenas Nixon Tapes

On July 23, 1973, the Senate Select Committee on Presidential Campaign Activities, known as the Watergate Committee, subpoenaed audio tapes of Oval Office conversations that President Richard Nixon had previously refused to release. This action set up a constitutional confrontation over separation of powers between the executive and legislative branches that was ultimately resolved only after the Supreme Court ordered the president to turn the tapes over to the Watergate special prosecutor.

President Nixon cited executive privilege as his legal justification for withholding the evidence. Committee Chairman Sam Ervin countered that executive privilege could not be invoked when dealing with possible criminal activities. Nixon claimed that "inseparably interspersed in the tapes are a great many very frank and very private comments wholly extraneous to the committee's inquiry." He also stated that nothing on the tapes would indicate his complicity in the coverup.

Considering it a most logical and necessary step, the committee wasted no time in issuing the subpoena, which was served by six o'clock that evening. Even the staunchest defenders of the White House agreed with the action taken. Senator Howard Baker, committee vice chairman, contended that the tapes contained material "essential, if not vital, to the full inquiry mandated and required to this committee," though he did try unsuccessfully to suggest an alternate route for obtaining the evidence.

That afternoon, in an impassioned address, Senator Ervin told the Senate, "the Watergate tragedy is the greatest tragedy this country has ever suffered." And the drama continued to unfold. The months to come would bring the resignation of an attorney general, a vice president, and—for the only time in American history—a president of the United States.

The Watergate Committee: *left to right*, Senators Lowell Weicker, Howard Baker, Daniel Inouye, Sam Ervin, Herman Talmadge, and Edward Gurney.

1974
DECEMBER 19

Vice President Rockefeller Sworn In

On December 19, 1974, the Senate added two "firsts" to its extensive catalog of historic events. That day marked the first time that television cameras were allowed in the Senate chamber to record floor proceedings. Also, for the first time under the new Twenty-fifth Amendment to the Constitution, an appointed vice president took his oath here in the Senate chamber.

The chain of events that led to this occasion began in 1963 with the assassination of President John F. Kennedy. Under the Constitution, when Vice President Johnson became president, the vice presidency remained vacant. Fearing a repeat of this tragedy, Congress within four years had approved, and the necessary number of states had ratified, a constitutional amendment providing, in part, for the filling of a vice presidential vacancy. When Vice President Spiro Agnew resigned his office in October 1973, President Richard Nixon nominated Gerald Ford as vice president. Ford was confirmed by Congress and took his oath on December 6, 1973, in the House chamber. When Nixon resigned the presidency on August 9, 1974, Ford became president and subsequently nominated Nelson Rockefeller as his vice president.

At a few minutes after eight o'clock on the evening of December 19, the House, following earlier Senate action, voted to confirm Nelson Rockefeller. At 10 p.m., a House messenger arrived at the door of the Senate chamber to announce that action. With nearly every senator in his seat and with one hundred House members crowded at the rear of the chamber, Chief Justice Warren Burger, President Ford, and the vice president-designate entered the chamber. At 10:12 p.m., the chief justice administered the oath to the nation's forty-first vice president, amid a sweltering blaze of television lights. This event opened the door for regular televising of Senate proceedings, which began in 1986.

Nelson Rockefeller

1975
NOVEMBER 5

Senate Opens All Committee Meetings

On November 5, 1975, the U.S. Senate voted 86 to 0 to open its committee meetings to the public and the press. This action was a part of the general "sunshine" movement that followed in the wake of Watergate and concern over excessive secrecy in government.

The Senate began by rejecting—by a margin of 16 to 77—a Rules Committee proposal that would have allowed each committee to set its own rules for opening hearings. It then adopted a more sweeping proposal, offered by Senator Robert Byrd, to open all committee meetings, including markup sessions, unless they dealt with issues of national security or personal privacy.

As Senator Mark Hatfield said during the debate over the measure: "For too long the major decisions affecting the lives of millions of Americans have been made behind closed doors. The pictorial image of smoke-filled rooms, unfortunately, has not only been applied to political conventions, but to the Congress as well." Senator William Roth added, "I believe that when we rid the government of unnecessary secrecy, there will be greater respect for the times when confidentiality is necessary."

Senator Edmund Muskie pointed out that the Budget Committee had already begun holding its markup sessions in public and, while he had at first had some misgivings, he found that it was quite possible to reach accommodations and debate difficult issues in open sessions. "Open meetings have encouraged responsible decision making," he reported. "They have improved our access to public opinion, and they have broadened both the debate and public involvement where our tax dollars will be spent."

Today, the Senate continues to work quite well under the open-door rule that we adopted in 1975.

1976
JUNE 16

Senate Convenes in Old Senate Chamber

On June 16, 1976, senators proceeded two-by-two out of this chamber, across the beautiful Minton tiles, to the room forty paces down the hall that served as the Senate's home between 1810 and 1859. On that memorable occasion, the Senate convened in the glorious gold, red, and mahogany chamber to celebrate its stunning restoration. Sitting where Webster, Clay, and Calhoun once debated the crucial issues of an earlier era, the Senate officially dedicated the newly restored chamber.

This event, occurring less than three weeks before the bicentennial of the nation's independence, marked the culmination of an extended effort to return the old chamber to its original appearance. In the mid-1930s, at the end of the Supreme Court's seventy-five-year residence in that chamber, Senate leaders sought unsuccessfully to obtain funding for the restoration. During the following three decades, the room served as a glorified storeroom, used occasionally as a sleeping area during all-night filibusters and for luncheons and conference committee meetings.

Finally, in 1964, through the dedicated efforts of our colleague John Stennis, funds were appropriated to undertake the necessary research, and to prepare working drawings and specifications. Architectural historians, curators, archivists, and others cooperated in an extraordinary effort to consider all appropriate resources to achieve an accurate re-creation. Working under the supervision of the architect of the Capitol, scores of artisans, including cabinetmakers, metalworkers, and stonemasons, translated this wealth of detail into the finished chamber.

On June 16, Senators Mike Mansfield and Hugh Scott, chairman and vice chairman of the Senate Commission on Art and Antiquities, which oversaw the restoration, joined Vice President Nelson Rockefeller in dedicating the chamber "as a new shrine of American liberty."

1976
SEPTEMBER 17

Mike Mansfield Sets a Record

On September 17, 1976, Senate Majority Leader Mike Mansfield requested the Senate's permission to be absent for the few remaining days of the Ninety-fourth Congress. In taking his leave, Mike Mansfield concluded sixteen years as Senate majority leader—the longest tenure in that position in the Senate's history. Earlier that year, Senator Mansfield had announced he would not seek reelection, concluding: "There is a time to stay and a time to go. Thirty-four years is not a long time but it is time-enough."

Mike Mansfield was born in New York City on March 16, 1903. When his mother died, he was sent west to live with relatives. Growing up in Montana, young Mike suffered from wanderlust. Dropping out of school, he ran off to join the navy during the First World War. After the navy he joined the army, and after the army he joined the marines, seeing service in the North Atlantic, the Philippines, and China. He returned to Montana and with the aid of his wife, Maureen, he went back to school, eventually becoming a professor of Asian history at Montana State University.

In 1942, he was elected to the U.S. House of Representatives, and in 1952 to the U.S. Senate. Lean, lanky, and laconic, Mike Mansfield earned the trust and respect of his colleagues on both sides of the aisle. Perhaps his closest friendship in the Senate was with Vermont Republican Senator George Aiken, with whom he had breakfast every morning that the Senate was in session.

When Lyndon Johnson became vice president in 1961, Mike Mansfield was elected majority leader. He held that post through the Kennedy, Johnson, Nixon, and Ford administrations, through the avalanche of Great Society legislation, the turmoil of the Vietnam War, and the trauma of Watergate. Later, President Carter appointed him ambassador to Japan, and President Reagan kept him there as well, another measure of the bipartisan respect and admiration in which we hold him.

Mike Mansfield of Montana

Philip Hart

On December 26, 1976, the man we called the Conscience of the Senate died at the end of his third term in the Senate. Today, Philip Hart's name is memorialized on the third Senate office building. In his lifetime he was honored for his integrity, his high ethical standards, and his commitment to public service.

Outwardly, Senator Hart was a quiet, unpretentious, and seemingly unaggressive man. His political opponents sometimes mocked him as timid and weak, but they grossly underestimated him. That gentle exterior masked a tough interior. He seemed to thrive on tackling powerful committee chairmen, corporate executives, and special interest lobbies. No matter whether they agreed with him or not, his colleagues in the Senate had to admit that Phil Hart never shied from a tough question and never ducked a politically unpopular issue, whether it was school busing, gun control, or antitrust laws. It was characteristic of him that, although he represented the largest automobile-producing state in the nation, he battled the auto industry to improve safety measures.

During World War II, Phil Hart was wounded on D-Day—in fact, I first met him at the Percy Jones Veterans Hospital in Battle Creek, Michigan, where we were both recuperating. He had a veteran's love of his country and a belief in supporting his president in time of war. During the Vietnam War, that loyalty placed Phil Hart in conflict with members of his own family, as his children were active in the antiwar movement and his wife, Jane, was arrested at a demonstration at the Pentagon. Hart's own views on the war changed, too; in later years, when he served on the Senate special committee that investigated CIA and FBI activities during the Vietnam War, Senator Hart went home one night to tell his wife, "Well, Janey, your wildest ravings were the truth."

Philip Hart of Michigan

1978
JANUARY 13

Hubert Humphrey

On January 13, 1978, the Senate and the nation lost one of their most popular political figures. Although Hubert H. Humphrey never achieved his dream of becoming president, he won a special place in the hearts of his colleagues and his countrymen.

Hubert Humphrey was elected to the Senate in 1948, after having served as mayor of Minneapolis. He burst onto the national political scene at the Democratic convention, where he led a surprisingly successful platform fight in favor of civil rights. As a result, many southern Democrats walked out of the convention and ran their own candidate, Strom Thurmond, for president that year.

During Humphrey's early years in the Senate, his aggressive style provoked hostility from some of the body's senior members. Eventually, he was befriended by the freshman senator from Texas, Lyndon Johnson, who taught him about the art of compromise. When Johnson became majority leader, Humphrey became his chief liberal lieutenant, later serving as his party's whip. Humphrey's energy and his good nature won him popularity even among those who had at first shunned him, and he became an effective proponent for a multitude of issues, especially civil rights and nuclear arms control.

In 1964, Johnson chose Humphrey as his vice presidential running mate. Serving as vice president aided Humphrey in winning the Democratic nomination four years later but hampered him in the general election. Defeated for president, he returned to the Senate in 1971 and remained here until his death. Once again, he won national admiration and respect, as demonstrated by the enormous crowds that ringed the Capitol Rotunda when he lay in state.

Hubert H. Humphrey of
Minnesota

Henry "Scoop" Jackson of Washington

1983
SEPTEMBER 1

Henry M. Jackson

On September 1, 1983, Senator Henry M. Jackson of Washington died at the age of seventy-one. Born in Everett, Washington, the son of Norwegian immigrants, he got his nickname, "Scoop," as a newsboy who delivered 74,880 copies of the *Everett Daily Herald* without a single customer complaint. He took a law degree at the University of Washington in 1935 and began his political career as prosecutor of Snohomish County. He immediately set about driving liquor and pinball machines out of the county, which earned him the title, "Soda Pop Jackson."

Jackson, a Democrat, was elected to the House in 1940. In 1953 he moved to the Senate, where the length of his service—thirty years—was matched by his influence. He served as chairman of the Energy and Natural Resources Committee, the Governmental Affairs Committee's Permanent Subcommittee on Investigations, and, at the time of his death, he was the ranking Democrat on the Armed Services Committee and a member of the Select Committee on Intelligence.

Even this impressive list of committee assignments, however, hardly conveys the extent of Henry Jackson's influence. Through his mastery of the ways of the Senate and the issues that concerned him, he became one of the most powerful and respected personages on Capitol Hill, an acknowledged authority on defense, energy, the environment, and related issues. National security was the area on which Senator Jackson left his strongest imprint. He once said that he regarded the Soviet Union "as an opportunistic burglar who walks down the corridors trying all the door handles to see which door is open." It was a conviction from which he never wavered.

At the time of his death, Henry Jackson had come to personify strength in national defense, wariness in dealing with the Soviet Union, and pragmatic approaches to domestic problems. On November 19, 1987, many of Scoop's friends gathered in the Russell Office Building for the dedication of a bronze portrait bust—a gift to the Senate from Mrs. Jackson and the Henry M. Jackson Foundation.

1988
October 21

Robert C. Byrd

For my final bicentennial minute on the Senate floor, I wish to honor the conclusion of Senator Robert C. Byrd's remarkable twenty-two years as a Senate leader.

Those of us privileged to call him our colleague and our friend recognize that Robert Byrd is a special human being, with a keen sense of vision, and possessed of an extraordinary memory, which boggles the minds of most of us out here every day. His service to the Senate has been characterized by hard work, attention to detail, boundless energy—we were together last night until about midnight working on the drug bill—and intense loyalty. He is an unrivaled master of the Senate's rules and precedents. I am certain members on both sides of the aisle will be going to Senator Byrd next year to check up on the rules to see if the parliamentarian had it right. And long after we have passed from the stage of public life, Robert C. Byrd will be remembered by those who care about the Senate, because he truly treasured its history. Alone among all who have served during the first one hundred congresses, Robert Byrd has worked to make the remembered history of this institution accessible to the widest possible audience. A century ago the Senate sadly and inexplicably allowed its one-hundredth anniversary to pass virtually unobserved. Determined to avoid another such oversight on the occasion of the Senate's second centennial in 1989, Robert Byrd provided the inspiration that will bring us a rich program of conferences, publications, exhibits, and ceremonial events next year.

The truth is, there is a penalty for leadership. You have to give up a lot, and sometimes even your own colleagues get a little out of sorts. But Robert Byrd has demonstrated that, if you are willing to pay the price, you can demonstrate leadership on a daily basis. When I first became the majority leader in 1985, Senator Byrd and I had not really had a lot of one-on-one contact. So there may have been a bit of suspicion: as our new leader, how is this Bob Dole going to be out here on the floor? But I had already learned a lot from observing Senator Byrd, Senator Long, Senator Stennis and others. I probably made a few mistakes, but in the final analysis we became close friends. We trust each other. We never surprise each other on the floor.

So I say, Thank you, Senator Byrd, on behalf of all Republicans who have had the privilege of working with you in the past twenty-two years.

The final chapter in Robert Byrd's Senate career is not likely to be written for some time, yet it is safe to say that he has set a standard as a senator, as a legislative leader, and as a statesman that will stand among the best as long as there is a Senate.

Bob Dole and Robert Byrd

1989
APRIL 6

Senate Celebrates Its 200th Anniversary

On April 6, 1989, at 11 a.m., the Senate convened in the old Senate chamber to commemorate the two-hundredth anniversary of its first quorum. This gathering included the five majority leaders who have served since 1961 and more than twenty other former members. Following a prelude concert by an ensemble from the United States Marine Band, President Pro Tempore Robert C. Byrd called this special legislative session to order. For the first time in history, two former members addressed the Senate.

Former Senator Thomas Eagleton discussed the nature of legislative accommodation, from the Compromise of 1850 to modern times. He reminded us that our diverse nation has held together because Congress has traditionally accepted the fundamental need for compromise. "Without some accommodation and compromise," Senator Eagleton observed, "our government cannot function and we will not be able to preserve the values we hold in common and in trust for future generations."

Former Senator Howard Baker spoke from his unique perspective as the son of two members of Congress and the son-in-law of Senate Republican Leader Everett Dirksen, as a former majority leader, and as chief of staff to President Reagan. He underscored the Senate's role as a national board of directors and noted that the greatest threat to the nation "is not that the Senate will do too much, but that the Senate will do too little." He expressed his hope that, as the Senate examines the elements that have contributed to its institutional strength over the past two centuries, it will recognize the primacy of a relationship with the presidency that is built on "friendship and civility and understanding and partnership."

Following these addresses, the Senate recessed and proceeded to its current chamber. A twenty-five-member Marine band greeted the arriving members. Following a roll call of the states, the Senate heard addresses from several of its current members. Senator Byrd outlined the challenges that confronted the Senate when it met for the first time. Senator Wendell Ford described the institutional Senate of 1789, and Senator Mark Hatfield carried the story ahead a century to 1889. Senator Ted Stevens then chronicled the major historic events that have taken place in this chamber since the Senate occupied it in 1859. Finally, Senator George Mitchell and I attempted to look ahead to the Senate of the future. Senator Mitchell observed that the Senate, possessing "a responsiveness and depth unmatched elsewhere in government," has fulfilled its constitutional mandate of being "a guardian of tradition without becoming a barrier to change."

I predicted that, despite the uncertainty of the future, we can expect that the Senate will live on, rich in tradition and richer still in democracy. I expressed my belief that two centuries from now the people's business will come first, just as it does now. It is never easy, but we must always be true to our forefathers' dream that we judge issues not by whether they are popular, but by whether they are best for America. Daniel Webster gave heroic expression to this dream on March 7, 1850, when he proclaimed, "I wish to speak today, not as a Massachusetts man, nor as a northern man, but as an American, and a member of the Senate of the United States."

Special session in the old Senate chamber commemorating the 200th anniversary of the U.S. Senate's first quorum

Thomas Eagleton of Missouri

Howard Baker of Tennessee

Chronology of Events with Credits for Illustrations

Index